Routledge Revivals

The Scholar-Critic

First Published in 1972, *The Scholar-Critic* argues that it's a mistake to consider literary criticism and literary scholarship as each other 's antitheses. The two approaches to literature are, except at the most superficial level, complementary, both indispensable, both equally honourable aspects of a single discipline. The book deals with themes like the sense of fact; works of reference; the literary object; style and interpretation; textual criticism and literary history; and presentation. This is an interesting read for scholars and researchers of English literature.

The Scholar-Critic

An Introduction to Literary Research

F. W. Bateson

First published in 1972
by Routledge & Kegan Paul

This edition first published in 2024 by Routledge
4 Park Square, Milton Park, Abingdon, Oxon, OX14 4RN

and by Routledge
605 Third Avenue, New York, NY 10017

Routledge is an imprint of the Taylor & Francis Group, an informa business

Publisher's Note

The publisher has gone to great lengths to ensure the quality of this reprint but points out that some imperfections in the original copies may be apparent.

Disclaimer

The publisher has made every effort to trace copyright holders and welcomes correspondence from those they have been unable to contact.

A Library of Congress record exists under ISBN: 0710072147

ISBN: 978-1-032-64271-0 (hbk)
ISBN: 978-1-032-64275-8 (ebk)
ISBN: 978-1-032-64273-4 (pbk)

Book DOI 10.4324/9781032642758

THE SCHOLAR-CRITIC

THE SCHOLAR-CRITIC

An introduction to literary research

F. W. Bateson

Formerly Lecturer in English
University of Oxford

Routledge & Kegan Paul
London

First published 1972
by Routledge & Kegan Paul Ltd
Broadway House, 68–74 Carter Lane,
London EC4V 5EL
Printed in Great Britain by
The Camelot Press Ltd., London and Southampton

ISBN 0 7100 7214 7

CONTENTS

PREFACE

Literary criticism and literary scholarship are often considered each other's antitheses. This is, I believe, a mistake. The two approaches to literature are, except at the most superficial level, complementary, both indispensable, both equally honourable aspects of a single discipline. If this modest treatise has a moral it is the elementary one that the best modern criticism – that of F. R. Leavis, for example, or that of Northrop Frye – would be better if it was more aware of its theoretical implications, which are facts as basic to it as the data of bibliography or linguistics, deficient though these may be (but in an opposite sense) in an awareness of the literary implications of *their* discoveries. (Here I have in mind such contemporary figures as Fredson Bowers or Roger Fowler.) It is not only literature that is *esemplastic*, to adopt Coleridge's term; the study of literature must be so too – in all its specializations and sub-divisions. To exclude either critical considerations from literature's ancillary techniques or scholarly considerations from the appreciation of such matters as imagery, style and emotional response is in either case to invite expert refutation.

But this is not primarily an excursus in literary polemics. It began as a textbook on the study of English literature by the graduate student, and though it has outgrown its original limited purpose it remains at least a *quasi-textbook*. Its origins were in fact a series of lectures given in various forms at Oxford, Cornell, Berkeley and the Pennsylvania State University for the benefit of students beginning their graduate work. The Select Bibliography is an abbreviated version of Chapter XI of my *Guide to English Literature* (Doubleday, New York, and

Longmans, London – both 1965, rev. 1970), a chapter in which I was helped by my bibliographical friend Harrison T. Meserole.

One difference from similar primers is that I have supplied a large number of examples in the progress of the argument. As far as I conveniently could I have tried to use new examples – or at least to say something new about such hoary cruxes as 'Kubla Khan' or 'his Nose was as sharpe as a Pen, and a Table of greene fields'. Some of the examples are lifted from earlier books or articles of my own, though I have occasionally dissented from my younger self. They are almost all from English literature (a category in which I refuse to include that of the Anglo-Saxons); my experience has been that though the same critical principles apply in the other literatures I have some acquaintance with, their application by a foreigner is a very hazardous business. I have probably burnt my finger-nails even in some of my interpretations of passages from the English classics.

I am grateful to the Society of Authors as the literary representative of the Estate of Katherine Mansfield, and Alfred A. Knopf Inc. for permission to include an extract from 'The Fly', from *The Garden Party and Other Stories*.

F. W. B.

FORMS OF REFERENCE

The following technical conventions have been observed:

1 The *titles* of books, essays, short stories, articles, etc., have been modernized, normalized and sometimes abbreviated in accordance with W. W. Greg's recommendation quoted on p. 170 below.

2 The *publisher's date* is that following each title in round brackets; it reproduces that given in the first edition, whether it is strictly correct or not, roman figures being regularly converted into arabic.

3 A *date in square brackets* indicates the absence of a publisher's date; in the case of modern books it is normally that of the year of their acquisition by the British Museum.

4 The *place of publication* is not given for books published in London (a term including those of the Oxford and Cambridge University Presses, both now publishing mainly from London).

5 *Publishers' names* are regularly omitted unless a part of the title; their inclusion, justifiable in a bibliography or a textbook of librarianship, is no more appropriate in one devoted to literature than the name of the printer or whoever was responsible for the illustrations.

6 *Quotations* follow the wording of the original edition (unless an error is corrected in square brackets) with the following exceptions: long *s* is always modernized, as is also the 'Elizabethan' use of *i*, *j*, *u* and *v*. When there is a standard modern edition the reference in the footnote will normally be to it; for English or other classics available in several reliable editions

a more general reference (chapter, act, scene, 'Book', number or similar subdivision) is used, unless this is likely to be misleading. In quotations from a manuscript abbreviations are expanded to the full contemporary form.

7 In other respects the footnotes follow the latest recommendations of *The MLA Style Sheet* (New York, 1951, rev. 1970). The logic underlying the conventions is discussed in some detail in Chapter Eight below.

ABBREVIATIONS

CBEL	*Cambridge Bibliography of English Literature*
CHEL	*Cambridge History of English Literature*
DNB	*Dictionary of National Biography*
ELH	*Journal of English Literary History*
JEGP	*Journal of English and Germanic Philology*
MLA	*Modern Language Association of America*
MLN	*Modern Language Notes*
MP	*Modern Philology*
OED	*Oxford English Dictionary*
OHEL	*Oxford History of English Literature*
PMLA	*Publications of the Modern Language Association of America*
PQ	*Philological Quarterly*
RES	*Review of English Studies*
SP	*Studies in Philology*
TLS	*The Times Literary Supplement*

ONE

THE SENSE OF FACT

However enlightened the tutor, of the Schools he has to think. The real discipline in the craft of research comes later, if at all, and its first step is to unlearn undergraduate method.

Oliver Elton

Unscholarly journalism, uncritical scholarship

Literary research is not the peculiar prerogative of young men or women reading for a higher degree. Many of the great names in English scholarship – from Edmond Malone to E. K. Chambers – were self-taught amateurs, whose intensive studies were a spare-time avocation. With others, like Austin Dobson or Edmund Blunden, the corruption of a poet was the generation of a scholar. Today, however, literary research tends to begin – or all too often not to begin – when the undergraduate with some interest in literature becomes a postgraduate student struggling for a doctorate, or some similar degree requiring a thesis. Elton's prescription quoted above is a blunt statement of what the metamorphosis entails. As a child puts off childish things, a graduate student is expected to enter into a new state of being – one without the irresponsible intellectual luxuries of undergraduate life if also without the pressures of its irrational examination system.

The epigraph to this chapter summarizes the academic moral of this book. Elton himself, in addition to writing three excellent author-by-author *Surveys* of English literature from 1730 to 1880, was the professor of English Literature at the University of Liverpool from 1900 to 1925. He knew what he was talking about. As an undergraduate he had been at Oxford (where he obtained a 'first' in Classical Greats), and in disparaging undergraduate method it was of Oxford that he was probably thinking, though his comment would have been equally applicable to almost any other university, then and now, in the English-speaking world.[1]

Why must the young man or woman with research ambitions begin by learning undergraduate method? Elton's disconcerting advice was provoked by the examination system for the B.A. he found operating in the British universities, most of which had taken Oxford as their model. The 'Schools' of which the typical tutor must always think are the pseudo-Renaissance building at the bottom end of Oxford's High Street which is known as the Examination Schools. It is there that the Oxford undergraduate reluctantly undergoes the Final Examination which will determine what his class in the B.A. is to be. The pattern of such examinations is all too familiar. At Oxford as elsewhere it consists of a series of invigilated three-hour papers, two a day for a week, with only the Saturday afternoon and the Sunday intervening. This physical and mental endurance test – in which all of the undergraduate's studies of the preceding two or two and a half years are theoretically being scrutinized – is primarily, as Elton realized, not a test of his understanding or appreciation of literature, but of an agile brain, a good verbal memory and a ready pen.

Elton went on to describe the B.A. as he knew it and as, essentially, it still persists (at least in England)[2] – as 'not strictly a training for any occupation except journalism, where

[1] *Frederick York Powell: a Life and a Selection from his Letters and Occasional Writings* (1906), I, 17. The comment occurs in the account of York Powell's undergraduate period at Oxford, where he later became the Regius Professor of Modern History. Powell also secured a 'first', in the then combined Law and History Schools, an honour, Elton caustically adds, 'which doubtless gives more satisfaction to an educated English youth than any other thinkable'.

[2] The American system is superior in that the 'grades' for each term's or semester's courses are taken into account in the award of the final degree.

the conditions of the Schools are nightly more or less reproduced'.

The point is not likely to be disputed. A hurried reporter is not expected or encouraged to quote his authorities, or indeed any of his evidence, with minute accuracy. It is sufficient in Fleet Street – if the 'story', reported or concocted, is a good enough one – to be approximately correct; originality in investigation and profundity of analysis are qualities the journalist learns to avoid because they waste time. But the pressure of time responsible for the journalist's thinness of matter and the pressure of space that produces *journalese* are intensified in a Final Examination. The consultations of the proper authorities and texts, processes difficult for even an experienced scholar, are denied to the examinee – unless he surreptitiously smuggles in notes and pocket editions. The contradiction is here complete: what is 'cheating' in an examination, the sin of sins, is 'scholarship' in the adult world, to be applauded instead of being penalized.

What Elton omitted when dismissing 'undergraduate method' is that the proper time and place for the conventional examination is for the schoolboy (or girl) – as there is a proper time and separate educational place for both schools and (later) universities. And the fundamental case against the Final Examination is simply that it is testing adults by methods only appropriate for adolescents.

A conclusion similar to Elton's is reached by T. S. Eliot in the note that he appended to the first chapter of *The Use of Poetry and the Use of Criticism* headed 'On the Development of Taste in Poetry'. Eliot proposed four consecutive stages in the attitude of the youthful male to the reading of poetry. The earliest stage, for boys at any rate, is 'a liking for martial and sanguinary poetry' – things like Macaulay's *Lays of Ancient Rome*, Tennyson's 'Revenge' and some of the Border ballads. This stage was followed in Eliot's own case, which is certainly not exceptional in this respect, by a period from about twelve to about fourteen of 'no sort of interest in poetry at all'. The third stage, from about fourteen to about twenty-two, was one that Eliot describes as 'the almost overwhelming introduction to a new state of feeling'. It was only when he was in his twenty-second year or thereabouts that he reached a genuinely 'critical' or 'mature stage of enjoyment of poetry'. The composition of 'The Love-Song of Alfred J. Prufrock', written when he was twenty-two, may be taken as evidence that Eliot's diagnosis of his own case at any rate was correct. The adolescent poet *imitates*; in 'Prufrock' Eliot *used* Laforgue.

Eliot refused to commit himself on any parallel evolution in the growing girl, who presumably does often share the boys' enthusiasm for 'martial and sanguinary poetry'. And, though he does not say so, the exact age at which each of the four phases occurs will obviously vary from one boy or adolescent to another. It is, however, the quality and the duration of Eliot's third state which raise the widest questions. Is this 'new state of feeling' really, as he asserts, confined to 'a small minority'? And does it normally begin with the dramatic suddenness and intensity with which he himself apparently experienced it? The crucial retrospective passage is worth quoting:[1]

> I can recall clearly enough the moment when, at the age of fourteen or so, I happened to pick up a copy of FitzGerald's Omar which was lying about . . . It was like a sudden conversion; the world appeared anew, painted with bright, delicious and painful colours.

For the reader who is not one of Eliot's exceptional 'small minority' the process both of emotional intoxication – in a later passage in *The Use of Poetry* Eliot tells us that he was 'intoxicated by Shelley's poetry at the age of fifteen'[2] – and of a subsequent 'critical' disintoxication is likely to be more gradual. Some degree of emotional poetic excitement may be felt at the age of fourteen or fifteen, but there is surely no general dramatically 'sudden conversion' at that age. The emotional condition described by Eliot is more characteristic of a boy with literary interests in his later 'teens; and in most adolescents the 'critical' phase has certainly already begun, however inadequately, by the time he reaches the university.

[1] *The Use of Poetry and the Use of Criticism*, p. 33. Eliot makes the not unusual mistake of mis-spelling Edward FitzGerald's name 'Fitzgerald'; there is no reason why the error or slip should be perpetuated here. The use of '*sic*' should be restricted to corrections necessary to the argument.

[2] *Ibid.*, p. 96.

It may be agreed, though, that disintoxication is normally not complete, or even almost complete, until the undergraduate is twenty-one or twenty-two. (Until recently, twenty-one was the recognized year for 'coming of age', the achievement of maturity in ordinary civil affairs.) In the competent reader of great literature that condition is signalized, in Eliot's words, 'when we cease to identify ourselves with the poet we happen to be reading; when our critical faculties remain awake; when we are aware of what one poet can be expected to give and what he cannot'.[1] An *active* critical awareness has then at last been achieved.

Elton and Eliot used different terms. It would be surprising if the professor and the poet had not done so. But the phenomenon they are describing is essentially the same. Elton's undergraduate who was at best only a journalist in the making is the same age when he takes his Final Examination as Eliot's self-centred reader of poetry is in the last phase of intellectual adolescence. They are now both ripe for a more mature and a more objective attitude to the serious reading of great literature.

Unfortunately, such terms as 'research' and 'criticism' turn out to be extraordinarily difficult to pin down, especially when one is used in conjunction with the other. A researcher tends to be thought of as a futile antiquarian; and to be 'critical' is dismissed as to be merely critical, a niggling fault-finder, or at best a man who preens himself on his 'taste'.

The most eloquent attempt to unify the two concepts was that made by Matthew Arnold towards the end of 'The Function of Criticism at the Present Time'. The crucial passage is worth quoting here because it is often overlooked:[2]

> The English critic of literature . . . must dwell much on foreign thought, and with particular heed on any part of it, which, while significant and fruitful in itself, is for any reason specially likely to escape him. Again, judging is often spoken of as the critic's one business, and so in some sense it is; but the judgment which almost insensibly forms itself in a fair and clear mind, along with fresh knowledge, is the valuable one; and thus knowledge, and

[1] *Ibid.*, p. 34.
[2] *The Complete Prose Works of Matthew Arnold*, ed. R. H. Super (Ann Arbor, 1962), III 283.

> ever fresh knowledge, must be the critic's great concern for himself. And it is by communicating fresh knowledge, and letting his own judgment pass along with it – but insensibly, and in the second place, not the first, as a sort of companion and clue, not as an abstract lawgiver – that the critic will generally do most good to his readers. Sometimes, no doubt, for the sake of establishing an author's place in literature, and his relation to a central standard (and if this is not done, how are we to get at our *best in the world*) criticism may have to deal with a subject-matter so familiar that fresh knowledge is out of the question, and then it must be all judgment: an enunciation and detailed application of principles. Here the great safeguard is never to let oneself become abstract, always to retain an intimate and lively consciousness of the truth of what one is saying, and, the moment this fails us, to be sure that something is wrong. Still, under all circumstances, this mere judgment and application of principles is, in itself, not the most satisfactory work to the critic; like mathematics, it is tautological, and cannot well give us, like fresh learning, the sense of creative activity.

Arnold does not use the term *scholar-critic* in the passage, or I believe anywhere else.[1] But his order of priorities – fresh knowledge first, and judgment, in general, only in the second place – is significant and represents an important theoretical advance upon the tepid *disinterestedness* with which his master Sainte-Beuve identified criticism.[2] The two faculties must certainly collaborate, but the fresh *learning* can give a 'sense of creative activity' that is absent from the *judgment* of familiar material. Arnold did not illustrate his point in this essay. He no doubt counted on the reprinted articles and reviews that followed in *Essays in Criticism* (1865) to do this for him. The

[1] Although in general use today the compound word is not recorded in the *OED*.

[2] Arnold's definition earlier in the essay, of criticism as 'a disinterested endeavour to learn and propagate the best that is known and thought in the world' (ed. Super, p. 283), is too vague to be useful. Sainte-Beuve had suggested the formula in *Chateaubriand et son groupe* (conclusion of the 1849 Preface). See Super, III, 477.

essays on Maurice and Eugénie de Guérin, Heine, Marcus Aurelius and Joubert do seem to have a freshness that is lacking in the essays on Wordsworth and Byron, for example, in the posthumous Second Series of *Essays in Criticism*. Arnold, having known Wordsworth's and Byron's poetry intimately for so many years, can in the end only 'criticize' them, often substituting pretty metaphors of his own for any radical re-thinking.[1]

Eliot took up the problem of the relationship of the creative to the critical faculty in his own essay 'The Function of Criticism' (1923), which is to some extent directed against Arnold's. On the presence of a necessary critical activity in the creative process itself he is convincing:[2]

> The larger part of the labour of an author in composing his work is critical labour; the labour of sifting, combining, constructing, expunging, correcting, testing: this frightful toil is as much critical as creative.

But the complementary conclusion – 'If so large a part of creation is really criticism, is not a large part of what is called "critical writing" really creative?' – is denied. A work of art, we are told, is essentially 'autotelic', whereas criticism is always 'about something other than itself'. Eliot's autotelic assumption however, is very questionable and is indeed only a variation of the doctrine of Art for Art's sake, which he imbibed as a young man from Ezra Pound and the French Symbolists.

The definition of criticism which finally emerges from Eliot's essay is that 'a critic must have a very highly developed sense of fact'. Eliot adds that, 'The sense of fact is something very slow to develop, and its complete development means perhaps the very pinnacle of civilization.' Its absence is illustrated by the case of a member of a Browning Study Circle, to whom 'the discussion of poets may seem arid, technical and limited', but that is because 'practitioners have clarified and

[1] The same pretty metaphor has even to be used for both Wordsworth and Byron. 'It might seem that Nature not only gave him the matter for his poem, but wrote his poem for him. He has no style.' This is Wordsworth 'at his best'. As for Byron, 'Nature herself seems to take the pen from him as she took it from Wordsworth, and to write for him . . . with her own penetrating simplicity'.

[2] *Selected Essays* (1932), p. 30.

reduced to a state of fact all the feelings that the member can only enjoy in the most nebulous form'. The sense of fact reduces itself, then, to an awareness of literary technique (and what is implicit in it), and this is another important theoretical advance. But Eliot finds it hard to specify exactly how such technical awareness is criticism rather than, say, prosody or the tabulation of figures of speech. And when he tells us on the next page that 'any note in *Notes and Queries*, which produces a fact even of the lowest order' must be considered criticism, whereas Coleridge's discussion of *Hamlet* is not,[1] it is clear that the sense of fact, except in the very general sense of objective statement, is too imprecise to serve as a working criterion. I retain it as a slogan.[2]

Some tentative conclusions can nevertheless be drawn from this analysis. It is clear that what Elton called 'research' is essentially identical both with Arnold's 'knowledge' and with Eliot's 'sense of fact'. Realism, it appears, must permeate any serious or mature discussion of literature. What Arnold calls 'judgment' (the 'value' element in literary criticism), though it cannot be eliminated, is a secondary requirement – if only because a work of literature cannot be judged correctly until it has been understood correctly. A work's 'significance' presupposes a comprehension of its 'meaning'. Literature, or any aspect of literature, is therefore primarily 'an intellectual thing' (like Blake's tear) rather than an immediate emotional stimulus, though the comprehension of the scholar-critic will necessarily include an appreciation of the pleasure that he and others derive from it. It follows that the scholar-critic must be a scholar, a researcher, *before* he can become a really competent critic. There are, therefore, almost no reputable 'critic-scholars', even if the adolescent self-identification with the literary hero of the moment is a necessary prerequisite to what may seem to be pure scholarship. If this were not so, literary research could be left to the computers.

The enthusiasms of adolescence are genuine and intense, but

[1] *Selected Essays* (1932), p. 33.

[2] In assimilating his 'practitioners' with the writer of 'any note in *Notes and Queries*' Eliot is asserting an essential identity between the critic and the scholar. But in this essay the link remains tenuous - an extreme statement which does not approach demonstration.

they are liable to be intemperate and mistaken because the schoolboy or undergraduate *misreads* the immediate object of his enthusiasm, unaware of the wider contexts in which this favourite book or author must be read. Eliot's intoxication with Shelley when he was fifteen may be contrasted with the disenchanted references in his later writings. (In Eliot's case the extremity of the disintoxication was perhaps an adult revulsion from the adolescent's excessive enthusiasm.)

The two phases are often labelled respectively 'subjective' and 'objective'. Strictly speaking, however, they are two degrees of the 'intersubjective' – a useful philosophical term defined by the *OED* as the condition 'existing between two different conscious minds'. The experience that the young Eliot underwent when he first discovered FitzGerald's *Rubáiyát of Omar Khayyám* may have seemed a private revelation to him, but his ecstasies depended after all on a prior knowledge of the English language and of some at least of the conventions of poetry (such as metre, rhyme and metaphor). Its causes were certainly in part non-subjective. And a similar limitation applies *vice versa* to any literary fact. However conclusive the external evidence surrounding it may seem to be, a literary object can never have the strict objectivity of a physical phenomenon. (It is useless to read a poem to a stone.) What the study of literature provides us with is a *scale of intersubjectivity*. At the bottom end of this scale of common consensus is a child who is beginning to learn his parents' language and is liable to misunderstand even the nursery rhymes or simple hymns that they teach him. A sensitive scholar-critic's concern, on the other hand, is with an intersubjectivity that approaches a total comprehension potentially available to all the sane human beings living in a single society. In other words, we assume 'common sense', a consensus of opinion on the levels both of 'meaning' and of 'significance'. It is true, of course, that such a consensus is not always obtainable. Juries disagree and social, political and religious differences complicate our lives; but at least on literary issues a degree of consensus is usually to be reached if all the relevant evidence is assembled, examined and checked.

And for Arnold, as for all scholar-critics, the mere acquisition of such knowledge is *creative*; unlike 'judgment' (which is 'tautological') it gives 'the sense of creative activity'. George Savile, the great Marquess of Halifax, made much the same point much more vividly in one of his *Miscellaneous Thoughts and Reflections*: 'The Struggling for Knowledge hath a Pleasure in it like that of Wrestling with a fine Woman.'[1]

A few specific examples of the failure of a proper sense of fact in the study of English literature will usefully supplement these general considerations. They should demonstrate for one thing the way in which what one thinks of as 'fact' (a historical event accurately reported) tends in literary practice to be inseparable from 'taste' (which is only in a last analysis the agreed reactions of the human intersubjective sensibility). The critic who gets his facts wrong will be responding to a non-existent meaning, or at best to one that is his own creation, a mirror-image of some aspect of his own private internal life. And the minutest findings of scholarship, however trivial they may often seem to be, justify themselves at least as a 'control' by keeping the meanings assigned or assumed within the limits of human reality. For Leopold von Ranke, the great German historian of the Papacy, history reduced itself to *wie es eigentlich gewesen* (what really happened),[2] whether it was fully known to its actors or not. A parallel criterion applies to the 'meanings' of literature – which may or may not be *precisely* those either of the original author or of his earliest readers or auditors, though they are likely to be closely related to them. Except incidentally or occasionally, however, as in Chapter 9 of Aristotle's *Poetics*, or in parts of Lessing's *Laokoön*, or in passages in Coleridge, there has been no literary equivalent until recently to the 'philosophy of history'. But today the study of literature cannot be immune from the influence either of the new 'scientific' historians or of science itself. If the strict presentation of the facts, which Ranke called the supreme law of historiography has not achieved the same supremacy in literary scholarship, it is nevertheless our first premise. The discipline of 'what is really meant' is the one that the graduate student of literature often finds peculiarly hard to acquire.

[1] *The Complete Works of George Savile, First Marquess of Halifax*, ed. Walter Raleigh (1912), p. 249.

[2] The dictum will be found in the Preface to Ranke's *Geschichten der romanischen und germanischen Völker*.

Nevertheless it is the essential *sine qua non*. Without the basis in scholarship the young critic, however talented he may be, is unlikely to become more than a clever journalist or reviewer, at best a writer who is read once and then consigned to the waste-paper basket. Oliver Elton was right, though he should have added that the craft of research does not terminate, as is often thought, in the accumulation of single precisely accurate and historically verifiable facts. A literary critic is not a literary detective, though he will often use a detective's findings – on such things as order of composition, attribution of authorship, or more specialized linguistic or bibliographical problems – for his own essentially aesthetic purposes.

Three examples of criticism without scholarship

The literary critic who aspires to be something more than a journalist or a reviewer must be – at least within the area of his special interests – something of a scholar. That is our initial premise. What do the words on the page *really* mean? Until this question has been answered, however approximately, criticism proper cannot begin.

In this section three examples of such failure will be paraded before the reader. Two of the failures are in passages from familiar essays by Matthew Arnold and T. S. Eliot – the two best critics, in my opinion, of the last hundred years, at least of those who have written in English. But my first exhibit is anonymous – a doctoral candidate whose thesis I was once invited to read and which my fellow-examiner (of another university) and I felt compelled to reject. My object in introducing this victim of our scholarly scrupulosity is to show that exactly the same criteria of accurate and relevant detail apply at both the highest and the lowest levels of literary criticism.

I confine myself to the first sentence of the anonymous thesis. It has been selected not because it, or indeed the thesis generally, was grossly imperfect, but because of a general imprecision and diffused if minor inaccuracy that betrayed an ignorance of scholarly methods and standards. Since it was the first sentence in a long thesis on a literary topic it naturally did not commit itself to a critical judgment, but as the thesis proceeded the same factual imprecision and looseness of statement appeared in its literary comments. Throughout, a defective scholarship infected and contaminated the critical pronouncements.

The first sentence (of the first chapter) ran as follows:[1]

> In 1663, three years after the return of Charles to the throne, John Dryden published, as a tribute to his friend Dr. Charleton, an apostrophe to the Royal Society, of which Dryden was a new member.

At a first glance this sentence will seem innocuous enough. No one could object to it in an undergraduate essay or in an article in a popular journal. But to a scholar it has several self-evident faults, the index of inaccurate or imprecise thinking, and the more the information that it purports to convey is checked, the more errors, inconsistencies or improbabilities the sentence turns out to contain.

Loose or imprecise statements:

1 Strictly speaking Charles II did not 'return' to the throne of his father. His official coronation in Westminster Abbey did not take place until 23 April 1661. Three years after April 1661 is not 1663 but 1664.
2 The lines to Charleton were not 'published' by Dryden; they are, as the most cursory examination reveals, simply commendatory verses prefixed to his friend Charleton's book. (The 'bookseller', or publisher in the modern sense, was Henry Herringman.)
3 If Dryden's Christian name is given, why should Charleton's be suppressed? Dryden is much the more familiar figure of the two and the 'John' is really superfluous here.
4 The Royal Society was, and is, made up of Fellows; to describe Dryden as a 'member' understates the dignity of the honour.

[1] It has not seemed unfair to use this sentence from a thesis that I actually examined. The candidate published the chapter later as an article without correcting any of the numerous errors that were pointed out to him at the time.

Errors and improbabilities:

1 Dryden's poem cannot be divorced from Walter Charleton's *Chorea Gigantum*, a work intended to refute Inigo Jones's theory that Stonehenge was built by the Romans. (Charleton attributed it to the Danes.) Dryden's poem is largely devoted to this topic and to eulogizing Charleton's exposition of it. (The error here is one of omission.)

2 It cannot possibly be described as 'an apostrophe to the Royal Society'. Of the five English scientists mentioned in it, excluding Charleton himself, three had died before the Royal Society was founded, and there is not one reference in the poem to the Royal Society, even by implication.

3 *Chorea Gigantum* is dedicated to Charles II, the dedication being dated 27 April 1662. It received its *imprimatur* from the Censor on 11 September 1662 and was entered in the Register of the Stationer's Company on 18 September. Modern Dryden scholars who discuss the question are agreed in assigning the actual composition of the poem to the summer of 1662; it may even have preceded the date of Charleton's dedication.

4 Be that as it may, the date (1663) on the title-page of *Chorea Gigantum* cannot be taken at its face-value. John Nichols, who had been a printer himself, says that in the eighteenth century, 'The Rule in general observed among Printers is that when a Book happens to be ready for publication before November, the date of the ensuing year is used.'[1] The convention applied equally at the Restoration.

5 *Chorea Gigantum* was therefore probably published early in November 1662. It may have been already in type when submitted to the Censor and in any case would normally not have taken more than a fortnight to print. Dryden was not proposed for the Royal Society until 12 November and was not admitted as a Fellow until 26 November.

6 The interval between the Restoration (Charles arrived at Dover on 26 May 1660) and the appearance of Dryden's poem in print was therefore not three years but two-and-a-half years. Its date of composition, the one point of critical interest, was at most only some two years after Charles's arrival in London.

[1] *Literary Anecdotes of the Eighteenth Century* (1812), III, 249. Nichols was discussing a book printed in 1777.

7 It is unscholarly and misleading not to give, even in an abbreviated form, the actual title of Dryden's poem ('To My Honoured Friend Dr. Charleton, on his Learned and Useful Works; and more particularly this of Stonehenge, by him Restored to the True Founders').

Much of this fault-finding will no doubt seem unnecessary. But I have chosen this particular example not because of the grossness of its inaccuracies but because of the general inadequacy it exhibits to meet scholarly requirements. This was the first sentence of a thesis submitted for a doctoral degree in English literature; it is only thirty-five words long. Yet in those thirty-five words it manages to commit no less than eleven errors or near-errors. And it provides no evidence at all to substantiate any of its various statements. There is not one footnote or reference.

A more scholarly version of the sentence that I have been pillorying might have been:

> Dryden's commendatory verses originally prefixed to Walter Charleton's *Chorea Gigantum* (post-dated 1663 but almost certainly published early in November 1662)[1] begin with an eloquent summary of the progress of the physical sciences in England from Bacon to Boyle. Charleton had been one of the earliest Fellows of the Royal Society and proposed Dryden for it on 12 November 1662;[2] 'To my Honoured Friend Dr. Charleton' is generally taken to have been written in the summer of 1662,[3] almost exactly two years after the Restoration.

The number of words has increased in my version to about 190, but it would be difficult to abbreviate it without a serious loss in the precision with which the relevant evidence can be

[1] The dedication to Charles II is dated 27 April 1662. The book received the Censor's *imprimatur* on 11 September, and it was entered on the Stationers' Register on 18 September.

[2] See E. S. de Beer, 'The Earliest Fellows of the Royal Society', *Bulletin of the Institute of Historical Research*, 14 (1937), 85.

[3] See *Poetical Works of Dryden*, ed. G. R. Noyes (Boston 1909, rev. 1950), p. 17; *The Works of John Dryden*, ed. E. N. Hooker, H. T. Swedenberg and others (Berkeley and Los Angeles, 1956), I, 248; Charles E. Ward, *The life of John Dryden* (Chapel Hill, 1961), p. 32.

presented. About half the total of 190 words is in the footnotes. Footnotes, or their equivalents (such as a parenthesis in the text), are indispensable in scholarly writing because they make it possible for the reader to check for himself the facts, dates or quotations on which the argument depends. A series of statements unsupported by such references is unscholarly, if the research necessary to determine the truth or adequacy of the information has to be left to the unassisted reader. No doubt there are many facts which can be taken for granted except in certain special contexts. Charles II's Restoration in 1660, for example is a familiar fact that does not require elaborate demonstration. In the passage quoted from the doctoral thesis the year 1663 does not need to be related to Charles's movements; what is objectionable is the apparently superfluous information it provides. Since we know that the Restoration occurred in 1660, we do not need to be told that 1663 is three years later; the additional information about 'the return of Charles to the throne' was clearly meant to be a mere elegant variation on 'Restoration'. Unfortunately, in the particular context that is invoked, it happens to be untrue.

To the common reader such factual refinement will seem sheer pedantry. But it is useful to remember R. B. McKerrow's epigram. 'Pedant,' McKerrow once acidly remarked, 'is merely the name which one gives to anyone whose standard of accuracy happens to be a little higher than one's own.'[1]

My second example, by way of contrast, is from a familiar, almost dog-eared, classic of Victorian criticism. Matthew Arnold's niece Mary, the future author of *Robert Elsmere* (1888) and other novels that trembled on the edge of agnosticism, married Thomas Humphry Ward, a Fellow of Brasenose College, Oxford, who is still remembered for *The English Poets* (4 vols, 1880–1), to which most of the scholars and critics of the day, including Mary, contributed introductions or headnotes of some length.[2] Ward's guiding spirit in this influential venture was inevitably Arnold, who provided the introductions to Gray

[1] *Review of English Studies*, 16 (1940), 121.

[2] Ward enlisted Walter Pater, George Saintsbury and Swinburne in the enterprise as well as such minor figures as Austin Dobson, Edmund Gosse, W. E. Henley and Andrew Lang among others. His wife was given an Elizabethan quartet (Sidney, Greville, Dyer, Sir John Davies).

and Keats as well as 'most valuable advice'. But Arnold's most important contribution was the long 'General Introduction', now generally referred to as 'The Study of Poetry', the title given to it – perhaps by Lord Coleridge, the editor – when it was reprinted in *Essays in Criticism: Second Series* (1888) soon after Arnold's death.

Criticism has been almost exclusively confined to the theoretical parts of 'The Study of Poetry', as it is more convenient to call the essay. It will be remembered that they revolve round the three levels at which poetry tends to be studied. The first is what Arnold calls the 'historical estimate', by which he meant the Victorian habit of regarding a particular poem or poet as 'a stage in the development' of a national literature. This 'historic fallacy' – the tendency to overrate what is merely historically important – is matched by the 'personal fallacy', of which the young Eliot's series of adolescent enthusiasms from FitzGerald to Laforgue would presumably be examples. Avoiding the pitfalls of the false estimates that are either mere literary history or private preferences, Arnold's ideal student of poetry is advised to concentrate his attention on the 'real estimate', 'the class of the truly excellent'.

Arnold did not attempt to define what the reality was that distinguished a 'real estimate' of 'true excellence' from the fallacious estimates. Instead, it will be remembered, he provided ten short quotations from the *Iliad*, Dante, Shakespeare and Milton which he recommended as 'touchstones' that would help the student to discover 'what poetry belongs to the class of the truly excellent'. Eight of the ten passages are from epics and the one quality that they seem to share is what Arnold called High Seriousness (or the Grand Style), though Poetic Diction now seems a better term. Arnold did allow, however, that there is much excellent poetry which does not resemble the touchstones ('it may be very dissimilar'), an admission that makes their practical utility doubtful. In the absence of a theoretical definition a real estimate, one that is objectively valid, may seem to end up, in fact, in being the personal estimate disapproved by Matthew Arnold. Arnold's sense of fact deserved a better justification. Nevertheless, even as a practical critic, Arnold could sometimes be demonstrably wrong.

A line from Chaucer's *Prioress's Tale*, which is used later as a touchstone, along with two of the already accredited passages, in the discussion of Burns in 'The Study of Poetry' is worth looking at more closely than it is usual to do. The line is first quoted with acclamation in the passage discussing Chaucer:

O martyr souded in virginitee . . .

Here a note is also provided: 'souded' is 'The French *soudé*: soldered, fixed fast'.[1]

The passage conveniently combines two levels of factual error, the linguistic and stylistic. Although Arnold's interpretation of *souded* is an etymological possibility, the boldness of the metaphor that such a sense would introduce is wholly un-Chaucerian, suggesting instead such a poet as Donne or Hopkins. Chaucer, though sometimes daring in his similes, is almost always conventional and traditional in his metaphors. Modern editors therefore prefer the alternative sense of 'confirmed', literally 'enlisted as a solder'. The line's meaning is ultimately determined by its stylistic appropriateness to its context, and the dramatic and rhetorical context both impose some such sense.[2]

O martir, sowded to virginitee,
Now maystow syngen, folwynge evere in oon
The white Lamb celestial – quod she –
Of which the grete evaungelist, Seint John,
In Pathmos wroot, which seith that they that goon
Biforn this Lamb, and synge a song al newe,
That nevere, flesshly, wommen they ne knewe.

To introduce a plumber with his soldering-iron into this watered-down paraphrase of Revelation, Chapter xiv, would have been a grotesque breach of the decorum the Prioress set so much store by.

A more serious matter for the literary student is Arnold's

[1] *The English Poets*, Introduction, I, xxxvi.

[2] Text from F. N. Robinson's edition (2nd ed., Boston, 1933). Arnold's reading 'souded in' for 'sowded [or souded] to' is not found in any of the MSS. (see J. M. Manly and Edith Rickert, *The Text of the Canterbury Tales, Studied on the Basis of All Known Manuscripts*, Chicago, 1940) and is presumably a slip – another small failure of the sense of fact.

failure to recognize Chaucer's deliberate avoidance of 'high poetic quality' in the *Prioress's Tale.* In general, according to Arnold, Chaucer's poetry, though it has many minor virtues, is not that of 'one of the great classics' like Dante's because it lacks 'high seriousness'.[1] Presumably, then, the *Prioress's Tale* – the one work of Chaucer's that Arnold actually quotes (eleven lines of it in all) – *is* serious. But of course it isn't. The tale reflects more precisely than any of the other *Canterbury Tales* the comic character of its speaker as she is delineated in such brilliant detail in the *General Prologue.* (Note, for instance, the unusual 'quod she' in the stanza quoted above, which detaches Chaucer from any possibility of being identified with the Prioress at the same time that it emphasizes her specific implication as narrator.)

The clearest link with the Prioress's own sentimentality – it will be recalled that she wept if she saw a mouse caught in a trap – is a continuous emphasis in the *Tale* not only on the boy's age, which is reduced from ten or more in the sources to seven, but also on the diminutive stature of the Jews' victim. In the 203 lines of the *Prioress's Tale,* the word *litel* recurs no less than twelve times,[2] and it is difficult to see how Arnold could have missed the sub-comic flavour of

> This litel child, his litel book lernynge . . .

And the 'litel child' (a phrase that appears five times) is reinforced by 'this innocent' (three references), 'young and tendre of age' and other variants of the 'yong' motif. As in the *General Prologue* Chaucer is delicately criticizing the Prioress, though the satire is more oblique here and below the immediate narrative

[1] *The English Poets,* I, xxxiv.

[2] The word is used by Chaucer eighty times in the other *Canterbury Tales* (excluding the prose tales). This adds up to eighty occurrences in 16,753 lines, or once per 209 lines, as against once in the *Prioress's Prologue* and *Tale* together per twenty lines. The fact that *litel* is used ten times more often than Chaucer's norm *must* be significant. Florence H. Ridley's useful *The Prioress and the Critics* (Berkeley, 1965), which summarizes earlier criticism, points to Alois Brandl (in H. Paul's *Grundriss der germanischen Philologie,* Strasburg, 1889–93, II, i, 680) as the initiator of a satiric interpretation of the *Prioress's Tale,* but the identification of the *kind* of satire intended seems to have been missed.

sense. The general effect, however, is to deflate, if ever so slightly, the Prioress's various rhetorical apostrophes and hyperboles – and among them Arnold's favourite:

O martir, sowded to virginitee . . .

This line is not, in a final analysis, high seriousness but low seriousness: a conclusion that Arnold did not reach because of a deficiency on this occasion of that 'very highly developed sense of fact' which Eliot rightly demanded in a critic. Eliot's thesis was, it will be remembered, that the 'sense of fact', as he used the term, 'clarified and reduced to a state of fact all the feelings' that the common reader only enjoys in a vaguely emotional form. He had added that 'the dry technique implies, for those who have mastered it', all that such a reader thrills to but made into something precise, tractable, under control. And this is why, for Eliot, a 'practitioner's criticism' is likely to be especially valuable ('he is dealing with his facts and he can help us do the same').[1] Arnold was a 'practitioner', and one aspect of 'the dry technique' that he should have been able to reduce poetry to, according to Eliot's argument, is the precise definition of the genre or literary kind that a particular poem attempts. It is, for example, a question of 'fact' whether a poem is an eighteenth-century 'imitation' (in the special sense that the term had for Pope or Johnson), or whether one by Ezra Pound and his associates, such as Richard Aldington or 'H.D.', is or is not 'Imagist'. In the case of the *Prioress's Tale* Arnold is factually mistaken in the genre that he implicitly assigns the poem to. Unlike the *Second Nun's Tale* and the other pieces in rime royal in the *Canterbury Tales*, all of which are without any ironic intentions, the *Prioress's Tale* is a pastiche of a Saint's Legend (or, more specifically, a Miracle of the Virgin). It is presented to us by a mature Chaucer primarily as the kind of story that his Prioress might be expected to tell – as in *Hamlet* the Players' recitations from an old favourite in their repertoire are simply the kind of dramatization of the Fall of Troy that might be expected from Marlowe and his imitators *c.* 1590. These are not tragedies (in which the author invites his audience's emotional participation), or parodies (in which we are invited to laugh or to sneer), but a half-way condition

[1] 'The Function of Criticism', *Selected Essays*, pp. 31–2.

between genuine pathos and strict literary satire, in which the author's skill in fabricating what looks extraordinarily like a real article is displayed for our technical admiration. The pastiche is a literary form *sui generis*,[1] and the *Prioress's Tale* is one of its masterpieces in English; Arnold has missed an important critical point in failing to recognize what Chaucer's literary intention in it was.

Similar errors at various levels of literary fact are to be found in the following passage in Eliot's 'Notes on the Blank Verse of Christopher Marlowe':[2]

> The rapid long sentence, running line into line . . . marks the certain escape of blank verse from the rhymed couplet, and from the elegiac or rather pastoral note of Surrey, to which Tennyson returned. If you contrast these two soliloquies [from *Tamburlaine*] with the verse of Marlowe's greatest contemporary, Kyd – by no means a despicable versifier – you see the importance of the innovation:
>
> The one took sanctuary, and, being sent for out,
> Was murdered in Southwark as he passed
> To Greenwich, where the Lord Protector lay.
> Black Will was burned in Flushing on a stage;
> Green was hanged at Osbridge in Kent . . .
>
> which is not really inferior to:
>
> So these four abode
> Within one house together; and as years
> Went forward, Mary took another mate;
> But Dora lived unmarried till her death.
>
> (Tennyson, 'Dora')

[1] It has unfortunately been omitted from the comprehensive and generally reliable *Encyclopedia of Poetry and Poetics* by A. Preminger, F. J. Warnke and O. B. Hardison (Princeton, 1965).

[2] *The Sacred Wood* (1920), p. 83. The essay was reprinted in *Selected Essays* (1932) as 'Christopher Marlowe', but although the text has been revised none of the errors are corrected. 'So these four abode' should be 'So those four abode'. A line immediately precedes the *Arden* quotation which is needed for the sense:

As for the ruffians Shackbag and Black Will . . . .

The first quotation, though Eliot conceals the fact as if it was one of common knowledge, is from the epilogue to the anonymous *Arden of Feversham* (1592), which has been occasionally attributed – on the flimsiest of evidence – to Thomas Kyd. This, however, is an error of fact at the lowest level, like Arnold's misquotation of Chaucer and misinterpretation of *souded.* The comparison with Tennyson is more seriously misleading, because the 'fact' asserted here is a technical one and shows a misunderstanding of the respective genres or literary kinds being attempted. In the lines from 'Dora' Tennyson was being deliberately laconic in an effort to outdo the matter-of-fact conclusion of Wordsworth's 'Michael'. Arnold's verdict that 'Dora' merely achieves *simplesse,* an affected naïvety,[1] has been generally accepted. To say that this clever if hollow imitation is not really inferior to the metrical prose of *Arden* is about as helpful as saying that chalk is not really inferior to cheese. In fact, Tennyson's best blank verse, such as that in *Ulysses,* exploits the long sentence and the medial pause very much in the manner of Marlowe's plays, and it is difficult to see in what way it represents a 'return' to the end-stopped lines of Surrey's blank verse. Finally, to call the latter either elegiac or pastoral is more unexplained assertion.

What did Eliot mean?[2]

Did he mean anything at all?

1 'The real quality it [French criticism] calls *simplicité* the semblance *simplesse.* The one is natural simplicity, the other is artificial simplicity' (*The Complete Prose Works of Matthew Arnold,* ed. R. H. Super, (Ann Arbor, 1960) I, 206). Arnold cites the beginning and end of 'Michael' to illustrate *simplicité,* and for *simplesse* the beginning and end of 'Dora'. The sentence with which 'Dora' ends is identical with Eliot's quotation except that Eliot has *these* for *those.*

2 I made most of these points in a letter to *Scrutiny,* 4 (1935), 181–5. F. R. Leavis agreed in his reply that he had been 'in the habit of making certain critical comments on the passage that Mr. Bateson criticizes', but he added that 'Mr. Eliot might reply to Mr. Bateson's criticisms that, as they stand, they combine pedantry with inaccuracy'. The charge of pedantry invites a repetition of McKerrow's epigram quoted earlier in this chapter; the inaccuracies, if there are any, have not as yet been specified either by Leavis or by anybody else.

A scholar in critical error

The point that is being made in this chapter can be enforced and illustrated by a complementary example from the writings of Sir Walter Greg (better known as W. W. Greg). Greg was the dominant figure in the English scholarship of his period, a man whose influence as a scholar was as decisive within his own narrower area as Arnold's or Eliot's was in the field of criticism. But even Greg was not impeccable. One of his best papers (F. P. Wilson considered it his masterpiece) is 'The Function of Bibliography in Literary Criticism Illustrated in a Study of the Text of *King Lear*', which includes the following statement:[1]

> Bentley knew that when Milton wrote 'Hermione' he should have written 'Harmonia', and he therefore condemned the passage: what he did not know was that the error occurred in the authority on which Milton relied.

The passage as quoted here is in the final form in which it will be found in Greg's *Collected Papers* edited by J. C. Maxwell. A slightly different version appears in the World's Classics selection of *Shakespeare Criticism 1919-35* (1936), where the passage runs:[2]

> Even Milton has 'Hermione' where he should have had 'Harmonia', but no one now follows Bentley in therefore dismissing the passage as spurious.

A final 'Note' then adds: 'Dr. J. W. Mackail tells me that this instance of error in Milton . . . , which I lifted from his Warton Lecture, is a bad example. It appears that the mistake is found in the only authorities that were accessible when Milton wrote.'[3]

Two comments immediately suggest themselves:

1 Greg cannot have known much about Milton if he imagined that Milton of all people, in *Paradise Lost* of all poems, would be likely to make a blunder in classical mythology. Milton was, I suppose, incomparably the most learned and scholarly mythologist in the whole history of English poetry; Robert Graves is a gullible innocent compared with him.

[1] *Collected Papers*, ed. J. C. Maxwell (1966), p. 270.
[2] p. 81. [3] p. 108.

2 It was naïve of Greg to accept J. W. Mackail as an authority on such an issue. Mackail, the author of the official life of William Morris and a connection both of Burne-Jones, the Pre-Raphaelite painter, and of Rudyard Kipling, was a competent and agreeable popularizer of classical literature, but he was not a scholar in the strictest sense of the word. Greg has paid the penalty of being too limited a specialist; he has not checked the information that Mackail supplied.

The passage in Milton that Greg was referring to is, of course, *Paradise Lost*, ix, 504–6, where Satan in his serpentine disguise is described as:

> never since of serpent kind
> Lovelier, not those that in Illyria changed
> Hermione and Cadmus . . .

At the time, though Mackail apparently did not know it, there were two forms current for Cadmus' wife: Harmonia, the original Greek form, which Milton had himself used as a student at Cambridge in his second Prolusion, and Hermione (pronounced *Harmione* in English),[1] the more usual Renaissance form and the one adopted by Carolus Stephanus (Charles Estienne) in his standard *Dictionarium Historicum, Geographicum* of which Milton almost certainly had a copy.

Greg should have checked Bentley's censure ('The Ignorant [i.e. Milton's hypothetical secretary] mistakes Hermione, the daughter of Menelaus and Helena, for Harmonia, the daughter of Mars and Venus, wife of Cadmus') against the note in the excellent eighteenth-century edition of *Paradise Lost* (2 vols, 1749) by Bishop Thomas Newton. Newton's note on the passage runs as follows:

> Cadmus and his wife *Harmonia* or *Hermione*, for she is called by either name, and I presume Milton thought *Hermione and Cadmus* more musical in verse as it certainly is than *Harmonia and Cadmus*.

The question which form is 'more musical' is the crucial critical point. Greg has ignored altogether the question of

[1] The English pronunciation enabled Shakespeare to indicate the 'harmonizing' role of Hermione in *The Winter's Tale*. The name is deliberately contrasted with that of her 'leonine' husband Leontes.

euphony, one of importance in any poem and often decisive in determining a Milton reading, Harmonia is clearly an impossible emendation because its last two syllables would have introduced an intolerable jingle with the last two syllables of 'lovelier' and 'Illyria' in the preceding lines:

> LovelIER not those that in IllyRIA changed / HarmoNIA..·

A single error such as that which I have just described is a very small blot on Greg's scutcheon as a scrupulous scholar. But a moral may nevertheless be drawn from it: *it is just as limiting to be a pure scholar as it is to be a pure critic.* The criterion of euphony – the quality Arnold had in mind when applauding 'Chaucer's divine liquidness of diction, his divine fluidity of movement'[1] – is as much a literary 'fact' as the minute textual and bibliographical accuracy to which Greg devoted his intellectual life. What is needed is both in collaboration. If they constitute, as is sometimes suggested, two separate levels of truth, the two orders of fact are at least intimately interconnected. A critical judgment will not carry much weight if it has mistaken such details as the authorship of a work, its date, or its best text; but the specialist, who is merely interested in such things as these, is in danger not only of becoming a dry-as-dust only read by a few fellow-specialists but also of omitting essential elements in the precise determination of such scholarly matters as the attribution of authorship, the exact date of composition, or the correctness of a text.

Some further examples of both deficiencies will be found in the following pages. Fortunately both are to some extent corrigible. And if it is better to be a good scholar-critic than to be either a good scholar and nothing else, or a good critic and nothing else, it is the good critic who is probably the rarer bird. A. E. Housman, one of the greatest of modern Latin scholars as well as a good minor poet in English, had no doubt of the superior virtue of the critic:[2]

> Matthew Arnold went to his grave under the impression that the proper way to spell *lacrima* was to spell it with a *y*, and that the words ἀνδρὸς παιδοφόνοιο ποτὶ στόμα

[1] *The English Poets*, I, xxxii.

[2] 'Introductory Lecture (1892).' Reprinted in Housman's *Selected Prose* (1961), p. 15.

> χεῖρ' ὀρέγεσθαι meant 'to carry to my lips the hand of him that slew my son'. We pedants know better: we spell *lacrima* with an *i*, and we know that the verse of Homer really means 'to reach forth my hand to the chin of him that slew my son'. But when it comes to literary criticism, heap up in one scale all the literary criticism that the whole nation of professed scholars ever wrote, and drop into the other the thin green volume of Matthew Arnold's Lectures on Translating Homer . . . and the first scale, as Milton says, will straight fly up and kick the beam.

Housman may have overstated the critic's superiority; the spelling of *lacrima* does not really matter, but clearly if you are to lecture on Homeric translation it is desirable to be able to translate the *Iliad* correctly. Still, Housman's point was one well worth making. The scholar-critic, if he is to succeed in his profession, must generally speaking be more critic than scholar. If you cannot tell good literature from bad, or the better elements in a poem or a novel from the less good, your learning is likely to be wasted. To this extent, then, a continuity can be demanded between adolescent literary enthusiasm and the more responsible approach of the sensitive adult. They both share the conviction that great literature *matters*; but with the mature reader who has some literary sense the response is communicable, an experience that he can share with others, because its 'value' is also 'fact'. And it owes this greater objectivity, or more strictly intersubjectivity, primarily to some of the ancillary disciplines provided by scholarship. If the light that they throw on the literary object is a rather dry light (Bacon's *siccum lumen*), that is surely preferable to the will-'o-the-wisp of neurotic critical fantasy. 'Things are what they are,' as Bishop Joseph Butler put it (in a different context), 'their consequences will be what they will be. Why then should we deceive ourselves?'[1] Scholarship is above all an antiseptic against aesthetic self-deception. And mature criticism is not possible unless it has been preceded by a modicum of scholarly discipline.

[1] Butler's actual words were, 'Things and actions are what they are, and the consequences of them will be what they will be: why then should we desire to be deceived?' (*Fifteen Sermons*, No. 7, Section 16, 1726). I prefer the pithier version that is now current.

TWO

WORKS OF REFERENCE

The verification of literary evidence

On 29 November 1847 a young Oxford graduate called John William Burgon, who is still remembered for one line in his Newdigate Prize Poem,[1] found it necessary to consult the great Dr. Routh, who had already been President of Magdalen since 1791, on some point in the patristic learning which was Routh's special field. As he expected, Burgon soon obtained the information he required. Then, greatly daring, he ventured to ask the patriarchal President (who is reputed to have been the last man in England to wear a formal wig) if he would give him 'some one axiom or precept' to guide his future studies. Routh, who was then ninety-two years old, was not taken aback:[2]

> 'I think, sir, since you care for the advice of an old man, sir, you will find it a very good practice' – (here he looked me archly in the face), – *'always to verify your references, sir!'* . . . I can better recall the shrewdness of the speaker's manner than his exact words; but they were those, or very nearly those.

Why is it so desirable to verify your references? Because, I suppose, a young man or woman cannot, it seems, be taught to be a critic. *Criticus nascitur, non fit.* A scholar, on the other hand, will only acquire the virtues necessary to scholarship by a conscious submission to the discipline of literary verification.

[1] 'A rose-red city – half as old as Time' (*Petra*, 1845).
[2] *Lives of Twelve Good Men* (1888), I, 73. There are some minor differences in Burgon's account of the episode in *Quarterly Review*, 146 (1878), 29.

A certain predisposition to scepticism is no doubt useful. But, if you are not born with it, it can be learnt. Today the acreage of print calling for verification is so enormous that works of reference of one kind or another have had to be compiled on a comparable scale. The budding scholar cannot do without these books of reference, but an almost immediate discovery that he makes is that none of them can be trusted even at the lowest factual level. And with the discovery comes the beginning of mature scholarship.

The fallibility of reputable works of reference can be demonstrated by a single but typical example. What was the title of Mary Wollstonecraft's pioneering masterpiece of feminist propaganda published by Joseph Johnson in 1792? Is it the *Rights of Woman* or the *Rights of Women*? The works of reference cannot make up their minds. The *Dictionary of National Biography* (better known as the *DNB*) is at least consistent in preferring *Women* in the main entry (by Leslie Stephen), where there are two references, as well as in its *Concise* form, but *The Cambridge History of English Literature* (the *CHEL*) has *Women* in the Index volume and *Woman* in the three passages of text referred to there. That useful and authoritative handbook the Oxford *Annals of English Literature* (which gives the principal books published each year as well as miscellaneous items of historical or biographical information on the margin of each page) has the same discrepancy: *Women* in the index, *Woman* in the text. (The second edition of the *Annals*, which claims to have been drastically revised, repeats the contradiction.) *A Literary History of England*, edited by Albert C. Baugh, the best of the American one-volume histories, has *Women* in both text and index.[1] And *CBEL* (*The Cambridge Bibliography of English Literature*), though it has *Woman* in the main entry, has *Women* in two of the subsidiary references.

Which is right, the singular or the plural? The problem is easily solved. The first edition of Mary Wollstonecraft's book reads on its titlepage: *A Vindication of the Rights of Woman: with Strictures on Political and Moral Subjects*. There are no bibliographical complications of cancelled title-pages, half-titles with a different wording from the title-page, or changes

[1] The error is repeated in the revised second edition (1967).

of title in American or later editions, to befog the issue; *Rights of Woman* is correct, *Rights of Women* is wrong. Almost every major library will possess a copy of this first edition (which could be bought in the original binding and with the pages completely uncut for only £40 a few years ago), and the early reprints, which can still be bought at a very modest price, all have the correct title.

Yet works of such eminence, usefulness and general reliability as the *DNB*, the *CHEL*, *Annals of English Literature* (which was supervised by R. W. Chapman of the Oxford University Press, one of the most scholarly of modern editors), the Baugh *History*, and even *CBEL*, all commit this elementary error.

For the error *is* elementary. Mary Wollstonecraft's title derives directly from one of the best known books in the English language – Paine's *Rights of Man*, the first part of which had been published the preceding year (1791) by the same London publisher (Joseph Johnson). Nobody gets Paine's title wrong; why should they blunder over Mary Wollstonecraft's title? It is not even necessary to know – though presumably Leslie Stephen, R. W. Chapman and the others must have known it – that Paine and Mary Wollstonecraft both belonged to the same group of radical intellectuals (which also included Godwin, who later married Mary,[1] Blake and even, briefly, Wordsworth) which then revolved round the kindly Johnson.

But, if works of reference should always be viewed with a certain suspicion (especially the indexes or synopses), it is equally fatal to ignore or by-pass these *biblia abiblia*. A preliminary precaution, as we have seen, is simply to check the statements of one work of reference by those in another work of reference. An error may of course slip through them, when one work blindly copies another, but discrepancies between works of reference in one minor detail or another are at least as common, and such discrepancies will serve to alert the reader to the need for further investigation. If, to take a common example, two titles both prove to be incorrect, the difference may be due to an unnoticed revision or issue. Many books have passed as first editions that afterwards turn out to be later

[1] She died shortly after the birth of Mary Godwin, who was to be Shelley's second wife.

reprints[1] – or even, as the ingeniously criminal activities of Thomas J. Wise have illustrated,[2] later forgeries of non-existent first editions.

Nevertheless the standard works of reference are the point of departure for the literary investigator. Their value lies in the time that they save in the general fact-finding process and not primarily in any facts of which they may claim to be the definitive depository. A scholar will ultimately check every relevant item or statement that he can, but he will naturally begin with the information that his predecessors have already assembled, even if it proves in the end to be mistaken. The more usual situation, however, is to find the traditional information or evaluation partly true: relevant but incomplete. Existing references should therefore be taken as signposts to what may still remain to be said or recovered. As Routh may even have intended as a corollary to his dictum, the verification of one or more old references has its incidental utility in providing new clues or new points of view that will lead to the discovery of more 'facts' – documents, links in the chain of evidence, critical reappraisals – that are the special reward of literary scholarship.

The particular work of reference with which a scholar-critic begins his fact-finding will naturally depend on the nature and the chronological extent of the problem he is investigating. The error that Greg attributed to Milton in preferring the form *Hermione* to *Harmonia* was not, as we have seen, an error at all. Greg was wrong, not Milton. The facts of this particular case are set out in two modern works of reference – Douglas Bush's excellent *Mythology and the Renaissance Tradition in English Poetry* (Minneapolis, 1932), which is much more than a work of reference, and *Classical Myth and Legend in Renaissance Dictionaries* (Chapel Hill, 1955) by Dewitt T. Starnes and Ernest

[1] The first edition of *The School for Scandal* was long thought to be an undated pirated edition claiming to have been published at Dublin by 'J. Ewling'. There was in fact no Dublin bookseller of this name at any time in the eighteenth century and the text can be shown to derive from much earlier Dublin piracies.

[2] Wise's forgeries were of private 'trial' editions supposed to precede the actual first editions. They were exposed by John Carter and Graham Pollard in *An Enquiry into the Nature of Certain Nineteenth-Century Pamphlets* (1934).

William Talbert, a more mechanical compilation. Bush has a note referring to an article by Charles G. Osgood in the *American Journal of Philology*, 41 (1920), 76 ff., which confirms the reputability of *Hermione.*[1]

Of such specialized works of reference there are, fortunately for us, no end today. They were rarer and much less comprehensive when Burgon paid his call on Dr. Routh, though the same scepticism must still be observed to all of them. Some of the standard works will now be described, with an indication in each case of what the beginner may expect to find in them. At their best however they are not the 'facts' of literature so much as guides to 'facts' that are ultimately only obtainable by personal inspection and response.

The scholar-critic of English literature will probably begin by consulting some such work as *The Cambridge Bibliography of English Literature* (*CBEL*),[2] even if this is essentially only an elaborate finding-list. It provides bibliographies, however, of virtually all the authors or anonymous works that we think of as constituting English literature as well as much sub-literature too. Newspapers and magazines, for example, are listed in full with indications of each extant issue's date and number, and 'representative specimens of the enormous mass of ephemeral literature – political and controversial pamphlets, anonymous and pseudonymous squibs, mock-biographies, *et hoc genus omne*' (Preface) are also listed. Other genres, listed either more or less completely, are 'Book Production and Distribution', books on education, diaries, autobiographies, memoirs and collections of letters, the literature of sport, travel and science (including pseudo-science), and translations of foreign literature.

CBEL begins with the earliest writings in Old English and attempts to record all the more important writings by English-

[1] One of the best of Lully's operas is *Cadmus et Hermione* (1674).

[2] As originally planned *CBEL* was to be a reprint of the bibliographies in *The Cambridge History of English Literature* (*CHEL*), 14 vols, 1907–16 (general index 1927), in which each chapter has its own bibliography. When I took over the editorship of *CBEL* in 1930 I persuaded the Cambridge University Press that the work must be self-sufficient, although some of the old bibliographies were in fact worked in and merely brought up to date.

men (or residents in the United Kingdom) in Latin as well as in the vernacular. Its *terminus ante quem* is *approximately* 1900, the approximation enabling its first edition (4 vols, 1940) to include Anglo-Irish and Anglo-Indian literature as well as the literatures of Canada, Australia, New Zealand and South Africa when written in English. No attempt was made, however, to trespass on the literature of the United States, even doubtful cases like Henry James being excluded. But 1900 is only the terminus for primary works; *secondary* works, such as biographies or critical studies of particular 'schools' or authors, terminate *c.* 1935, though a *Supplement* (1957), edited by George Watson, has brought them down to *c.* 1955. The *Supplement* does not attempt to include either *addenda* or *corrigenda* to the lists of primary writings and a complete revision of the whole work is now in progress under George Watson's editorial supervision, its Volume III having appeared in 1969 (see below). A separate *Supplement* for the first half of the twentieth century is also expected shortly.

CBEL is confined to lists of separate publications. (Of the many thousand authors included only Dr Johnson and Goldsmith have been permitted complete lists of all their writings, including the articles, prefaces, etc.) What is normally recorded is the title and the sub-title of each book or pamphlet, though both are sometimes abbreviated without the dots now conventional. The first few words of the original title are, however, always given and the date – in square brackets unless it is on the title-page (or its verso) or in the colophon (the printer's note at the end of early printed books) – and the place of publication, unless it is London (as it usually is). Dates are always translated from roman figures into arabic, the date of the first edition being followed by those of reprints for the next fifty years and of the more important modern editions. The formula is naturally somewhat different for Old English and Middle English manuscripts and the attempt to list all reprints for the first fifty years and to distinguish reissues with a cancelled title-page from complete re-settings has generally been abandoned after *c.* 1850, when new printing methods have made such information increasingly meaningless.

The guiding principle in *CBEL* has been chronological order. A number of preliminary general sections are followed by 'The

Anglo-Saxon Period (to 1100)', 'Middle English Literature' (both with separate sections on 'Writings in Latin'), and 'The Renaissance to the Restoration (1500–1660)'. These constitute the first volume. Volume II is devoted to 'The Restoration to the Romantic Revival, 1660–1800' and Volume III to '1800–1900' (which includes those twentieth-century writers who might be considered 'established' by 1900). Some two-thirds of each volume are devoted to the poetry, drama, prose fiction and 'Miscellaneous Prose' of literary interest, and these general sections are subdivided chronologically into periods of about fifty years. The quantity of secondary matter – again confined to the titles of the relevant books and articles – naturally depends upon the degree of importance of the particular author. The remainder of the volume is occupied by such topics, to cite some from the 1660–1800 volume, as 'Bibliographies, Literary Histories and Special Studies', 'Literary Theory', 'Literary Relations with the Continent', 'Medieval Influences', 'Book Production and Distribution', 'Education', 'The Social Background', 'The Political Background', as well as such specialist genres as 'Periodical Publications', 'Books of Travel', 'Translations into English', 'Religious Prose', 'Historians, Biographers and Antiquaries', and 'Classical and Oriental Scholars'.

The New Cambridge Bibliography of English Literature (edited by George Watson, vol. III, 1969) is really a second edition of *CBEL*. Owing to the multiplication of secondary matter recently, though the terminal dates are the same (the 'New' Vol. III, is still 1800–1900), most of the marginally literary sections, including the literatures of the Commonwealth, have had to be sacrificed. But Henry James is now included.[1]

[1] The 'New' *CBEL* is dedicated to me, but its failure to do more than up-date and occasionally correct the original work was a great personal disappointment to me. Recent secondary material is after all recorded in greater detail in many other lists (for some see pp. 188–9 in the *Select Bibliography* below). Opportunities missed include such things as information on the contents of an author's standard bibliographies and collected editions, finer bibliographical distinctions, dates of publication in terms of months as well as the year, authorial revisions, translations, American titles, surviving prompt-copy texts, authors' contributions to periodicals and collaborative works, and (except erratically) the more important contemporary reviews. See also my letter in *TLS*, 25 December 1969.

CBEL, old and 'New', can only be described here in general terms; the young scholar will be well advised to explore it carefully for himself and, as usual, not to depend too much on the index (which constitutes Vol. IV). It is a collaborative work and like all such compilations some of its sections are more valuable than others. The shrewdest and fairest evaluations of it are still the long reviews it provoked on its original publications in 1940 (1941 in the U.S.A.): *TLS* (21 and 28 December 1940); *PQ*, 21 (1942), 251–6; *MP*, 39 (1941/2), 303–12; *MLN*, 57 (1942), 285–8; *RES*, 17 (1941), 490–4; *The Library*, 4th ser., 22 (1942), 250–5. The 'New' edition is eliminating most of the errors in the major writers as well as bringing the lists of secondary works up to date. A more difficult matter, considering that there are at least some three hundred separate compilers, continues to be to impose an appropriate adjustment of the scale of each entry to the importance of the topic. Thus the first edition has been criticized, to take a single example, because the Spenser section occupies only five columns as against Shakespeare's 136. This is said to be 'hardly a fair measure of the two poets' respective importance' (on which one may or may not agree); 'neither is it a measure of the work done on Spenser'.[1] But it must not be forgotten that *CBEL* was compiled in the 1930s; some of its sections are even older, though later biography and criticism have usually been added. George Watson's *Supplement* (1957), which covers such secondary matter as was published between 1934 and 1954, adds nine columns on Spenser and sixty-five on Shakespeare. The decreasing disparity these figures indicate between scholarly interest in Spenser and Shakespeare may, however, merely be a reflection of a momentary trend in modern criticism. *The Faerie Queene* is a gold-mine for symbol-seekers, allusion-hunters and iconographic interpreters; its relative importance in comparison with Shakespeare's plays is another matter altogether and one difficult to measure by columns in a bibliography. In any case the dissatisfied modern Spenserian can turn to Frederic L. Carpenter's *Reference Guide to Spenser* (Chicago, 1923), with its own supplements first by Dorothy F. Atkinson

[1] Richard D. Altick and Andrew Wright, *Selective Bibliography for the Study of English and American Literature* (2nd ed. New York, 1963), p. 9.

(Baltimore, 1937) and secondly by Waldo F. McNeir and Foster Provost (Pittsburgh, 1962).

CBEL is necessarily and intentionally selective. In addition to satisfying the casual searcher for information, the collector, or second-hand bookseller, its object is to provide a point of departure for further research by summarizing what is already known or conjectured. Its principal defect is that its titles of primary books, or secondary books and articles, are not sufficiently self-explanatory. Some notes are provided, but they are few and far between. The experienced scholar will generally know how to read between its lines, but the beginner may often find himself puzzled. George Watson's *Concise Cambridge Bibliography of English Literature* (1958) may be more immediately useful because it is less alarmingly detailed. Only some four hundred writers have been included in it and the less important of their works – and of the biography and criticism on them – have been omitted. A useful feature is a section on eighty writers between 1900 and 1950 which anticipates the volume of the parent work that is still in preparation.

When I was editing *CBEL* (it took me ten years in all) I was very conscious of the need for a shorter work which would give the young scholar more assistance in finding his way about the thousands of authors and commentators who constitute English literature. Within the limits I had to set myself my *Guide to English Literature* (New York, 1965, revised 1967 and 1970) is intended to do just this. The reader is told in so many words that So-and-So's edition of Such-and-Such is the best so far published and that it has, or has not, got explanatory notes. In addition to lists of this kind I inserted four 'Inter-Chapters' headed 'The Approach to Medieval Literature', 'The Approach to Renaissance Literature', 'The Approach to Augustan Literature' and 'The Approach to Romanticism' (which has a section on 'The Retreat from Romanticism' which sketches an introduction to modern English Literature). These 'Inter-Chapters' are in continuous prose and are intended to provide general guidance on the different ways in which the several periods invite critical attention. Two final chapters are devoted to 'Literary Criticism in English' and 'Literary Scholarship: an Introduction to Research in English Literature'.

If *CBEL* and its like are usually the first general works of reference to consult, there is a second level of catalogues and bibliographies to supplement them and often, within limited or special areas, to supersede them. The Select Bibliography (pp. 184–96 below) is a selected list of such works. The degree of their usefulness to the researcher will naturally depend upon the nature and range of the problem with which the particular researcher is momentarily concerned. One group of the subsidiary works of reference is, however, of special importance. I refer to the annual lists of the previous year's publications in the various periods of English literature, which are sometimes accompanied by summaries or critical comments. For the secondary works or scholarly editions that have appeared since the *CBEL* Supplement (which only comes down to *c.* 1955) they are indispensable and for recent years, because they are fuller than *CBEL*, they often add minor contributions – a note in *Notes and Queries* or a letter to *TLS* – that add details of great value and interest. Unfortunately they only begin with the list of publications in the English Renaissance period for 1916 that was published in *Studies in Philology* (*SP*) in 1917. Details about the other periods, some of which shift bewilderingly from journal to journal will be found in the Select Bibliography below. A general rule for the books, articles and editions recorded in these annual lists is to begin with the most recent items and work backwards. In this way the errors and omissions of earlier scholars are avoided and the secondary material on which you are building is less likely to be vitiated by the slips or fantasies of your predecessors.

The Select Bibliography also includes a representative list of such other assemblages of secondary material, principally limited to the titles of books and articles, as author-bibliographies, library catalogues, lists by period or by genre, etc.

Some non-literary works of reference

A bibliography like *CBEL* provides only the first step to those references that the scholar will need to verify. The second step will of course be to acquire or peruse a copy of any book or article that looks promising and relevant – if necessary in Xerox, photostat or microfilm form. Nowadays this second stage raises few technical problems except in the case of unique copies of manuscripts still in private hands. The trend towards what might be called the nationalization of research matter has become almost irresistible and the competition at auctions for the acquisition of rarities is less and less between one millionaire and another and more between one university library and another. Occasionally the enquirer finds himself baffled by eccentric clauses in a will – as in the notorious case of the Tennyson manuscripts at Trinity College, Cambridge[1] – but it is usually only when publication is contemplated that copyright difficulties or testamentary prohibitions arise.[2]

The third stage is reached when the reader finds himself face to face with an original document that he cannot understand, even if it is manifestly in English, or an edition whose status and make-up puzzle him. Problems of palaeography and analytical bibliography will have to be skirted here, but for English words that he does not understand (or whose range of shades of meaning has changed through the centuries) there is fortunately a work of reference of exceptional authority to which recourse can always be made. This is of course *The Oxford English Dictionary* (13 vols, 1933) which is usually abbreviated to *O.E.D.* (or *OED*), the alternative abbreviation *N.E.D.* being a relic of the first edition *A New English Dictionary on Historical Principles*, which was issued in 124 parts or sections (January 1884–April 1928) to form ten over-bulky volumes. The *OED* is a corrected re-issue of the *N.E.D.* to which a thirteenth volume has been added consisting of a Supplement for words or senses added to the language more recently; it also includes a bibliography of the books and periodicals combed by the army of compilers. Another Supplement is now approaching completion which will continue the up-dating of usages in the United Kingdom. What is in effect yet another supplement was edited by W. A. Craigie, one of the *N.E.D.*'s four general editors, in *A Dictionary of American English on Historical Principles* (4 vols, 1938–44). And there is also, underpinning

[1] Until recently, when a more generous policy was initiated, the Tennyson manuscripts might be consulted but not copied or reproduced. This restriction was withdrawn in 1969.

[2] A useful summary of the legal complexities will be found in Norman Holmes Pearson, 'Problems of Literary Executorship', *Studies in Bibliography*, 5 (1952–3), 14ff.

Craigie, the formidable Noah Webster, whose *American Dictionary of the English Language* (2 vols, 1828) reached its apotheosis in *Webster's Third New International Dictionary of the English Language* (1961).

Those of us who cannot afford the *OED* content ourselves with *The Shorter Oxford English Dictionary on Historical Principles* (2 vols, 1933), which has approximately the same relation to the parent work that the *Concise CBEL* has to the *CBEL* proper. English literature, whatever the exact definition may be that is preferred for it, is incontestably written in the English language, and the precise meaning of each word in whatever English author you happen to be studying is a scholar-critic's proper concern. He must therefore be prepared at any moment of the day or the night to consult the best authority on these basic linguistic facts. And for almost every word in English, especially in literary English, the best authority – apart from a few special studies – is still the *OED*. No fault is more common or more inexcusable in a doctoral thesis than the failure at some vital point of interpretation to consult the *OED*. *The Shorter Oxford English Dictionary* is much better than nothing, but under each sense of each word there are so many fewer exemplifying quotations that it is very much a second-best. *The Concise Oxford Dictionary* gives no examples at all and is more useful for the writer than the reader of modern English. One of its authors was H. W. Fowler, the author of the incomparable *Dictionary of Modern English Usage* (1926), which can be succinctly described as the best guide to lucid and pithy English ever compiled.

The special utility of the *OED*, the area where it is unsurpassed and indispensable, is in the quotations, each of which is dated and in the original spelling (normally that of the first edition). According to the Preface of the 1933 reissue, some 1,800,000 quotations are included,[1] and each quotation is long enough to ensure the immediate intelligibility of the sense that it illustrates. Because the context is given as well as the word

[1] Five-and-a-half million slips (instances of each word) were actually collected; the surplus have been given to the University of Michigan where they have been used as the basis of a *Middle English Dictionary*, (ed. H. Kurath and S. H. Kuhn (1952–) and an *Early Modern English Dictionary* (now in progress).

that is being defined, the reader is able to check one against the other, an essential scholarly precaution, and by their fullness the entries also serve as an encyclopedia – a much more extensive encyclopedia incidentally than most works describing themselves as such. Another subsidiary use that the *OED* has for the literary scholar is as a dictionary of quotations. If the quotation is not in a work for which a concordance exists, and so far they only exist for the Authorized Version of the Bible, the poetry and prose of Chaucer, Shakespeare and William Blake, and the poems of some thirty or so others from Wyatt to Yeats, or reference to any of the one-volume dictionaries of quotations (the latest Bartlett, Stevenson or Oxford *Dictionary of Quotations*) has failed to locate the passage, much the best chance of finding it is under one or other of its constituent words in the *OED*.

By the highest lexicographical standards the *OED* must be admitted to be tainted by a certain amateurishness. The segregation of a word's different senses and the transitions from one sense to another are not always strictly consistent. At times the order followed is merely chronological, and when logic intervenes to substitute a more rational order the reasoning is often mere rule-of-thumb. But a lexicographical amateur is at least a lover of literature. The readers who filled out the original slips out of which the *OED* was constructed were unpaid, and the four editors and their various predecessors and assistants were all grossly underpaid. A feeling of dedication provided them with a more effective incentive than German or American professionalism could have supplied.

In so far as there was a guiding spirit or ghostly influence in the *OED* it was that of Coleridge. Its first editor, who died when he was only thirty-one years old, was in fact Herbert Coleridge, the son of the poet's daughter Sara and his nephew Henry Nelson Coleridge (whose notes of his uncle's conversation survive as the *Table-Talk*). The amusing and informative 'Historical Introduction' prefixed to the 1933 reissue also records that Coleridge's younger son Derwent read a paper to the Philological Society, the society responsible for initiating the Dictionary, on 10 May 1860, with the title 'Observations on the plan of the Society's proposed new English Dictionary'. Coleridge himself had realized more profoundly than any other

Englishman the cultural role of language. 'There are cases,' as he put it in *Aids to Reflection* (which was edited by Henry Nelson Coleridge in 1839),[1] 'in which more knowledge of more value may be conveyed by the history of a word, than by the history of a campaign.' The aphorism might serve as an epigraph to the *OED*. It was because its compilers set to work in this spirit that so much English literature – as distinct from the mechanics of linguistics – is preserved in its pages. In effect, it is the most elaborate anthology of English literature ever assembled.

Even so, as the reduction of the 5,500,000 quotations assembled to the 1,800,000 used will have suggested, certain restrictions had to be imposed. One that is not often remembered is the Hundred Years' Rule – 'about one [quotation] for each century, though various considerations often render a larger number necessary'.[2] It is unfortunately not always clear whether intervening quotations have been deliberately omitted in obedience to the Hundred Years' Rule or whether no instances have been found. An example of such an uncertainty is the word *recover* in the sense used in the first line of one of the best of A. E. Housman's poems (*A Shropshire Lad*, No. XVI):

> It nods and curtseys and recovers
>   When the wind blows above,
> The nettle on the graves of lovers
>   That hanged themselves for love . . .

The *OED* cites this under *recover* 21c, 'To rise again after bowing or curtseying'. The only other example of this sense given is from *The Spectator*, No. 240 – a letter probably by Steele himself but professing to be from a country gentleman complaining about the arrival of 'a Courtier, or Town-Gentleman', who on entering a room 'made a profound Bow and fell back, then recovered with a soft Air and made a Bow to the next, and so to one or two more'. But between this *Spectator* (5 December 1711) and Housman's poem (1896) almost two centuries had elapsed. Had the usage persisted? In the absence

[1] p. 6.

[2] 'General Explanations', I, xxxii. One quotation, that is, for each meaning or sub-meaning of the word.

of intervening quotations it is difficult not to suspect a confusion of senses – perhaps with the more familiar *recover* 16a 'To regain one's natural position or balance', examples of which are provided for 1706, 1715, 1856 and 1895. Some of Housman's critics have adopted the meaning ascribed to the line by the *OED*, though his point can hardly have been that a nettle completes its curtsey by a reversion to a normal posture, since this is what all curtseying entails. It is surely the nettle's *resilience* in spite of the wind that is contrasted here with the lover's static suicide ('The man he does not move'), and in that case *recover* 18c ('To regain health after a wound or sickness; to get well, or become healthy again') is also not implausible.

The *OED* does not do your thinking for you; it is fallible, and is incomplete. An area in which its incompleteness has recently become particularly obvious is that of critical terms. When was 'Augustan' first applied to English literature by analogy with the classic period of Latin style? The best the *OED* can do is to give under its Sense 2 ('the period of highest purity and refinement of any national literature') a quotation from 1819: 'The period of queen Anne is often called the Augustan age of England.' As the 'often' implies this sense was by 1819 already a cliché; in the form 'Augustean' it had been used by Francis Atterbury as early as 1690.[1] Other critical terms on which the *OED* is sadly inadequate are: *classic, comedy of manners, common reader, correctness, delicacy, ease, gothic, grand style, intense, metaphysical, picturesque, poetic diction, pure poetry, reading public, romantic, sentimental, simplicity* (metrical), *softness* and *sweetness, strong lines, wit.* With some of these terms, however, special studies are now efficiently filling the gaps.[2]

The information provided by a bibliography such as *CBEL* is external and preliminary. Here is a list of the other books associated in one way or another with the book you happen to be interested in at the moment – for example, the titles and dates of publication of the other books by the same writer and whatever has been written about them, the writings in the

[1] Preface to *The Second Part of Mr. Waller's Poems.* The Preface is not signed, but the ascription to Atterbury has not been disputed.
[2] Details will be found in the Select Bibliography, pp. 194–6 below.

same genre or of the same period, and those describing the various contexts – critical, social, religious, philosophical – within which your book falls. With the *OED* the reader passes from external to internal information. A dictionary in providing the various contemporary meanings of the vocabulary employed in this or that work of literature is contributing to our comprehension of the meaning of the work as a whole. It is true that considerations of word-order and aesthetic significance are also involved, and some works of reference exist in these areas too. But such works – which pass from syntax into rhetoric ('the best words in the best order') – are discussed in Chapter Four below.

Histories of literature and collections of literary lives may, however, be discussed here. *The Cambridge History of English Literature* (edited by A. W. Ward and A. R. Waller, 15 vols, 1907–27) has already been mentioned. The most obvious and important difference between *CHEL* and its Oxford rival *OHEL* (*The Oxford History of English Literature*, edited by F. P. Wilson and B. Dobrée, 12 vols in fourteen parts, of which ten had been published 1945–69) is that the Cambridge history has a different author, often a distinguished scholar or critic, for each chapter whereas each volume or part of *OHEL* is by one man. Inevitably the one man cannot cope equally successfully with all the various subdivisions of his period and the range tends to be narrower as modern times are approached. On the other hand, *OHEL* is more up-to-date. The *CHEL* formula enabled it to make use of some first-rate scholars (e.g. W. P. Ker and H. J. C. Grierson) and some first-rate literary critics (e.g. George Saintsbury and Arthur Symons), whereas only one volume of *OHEL* is comparably successful – C. S. Lewis's brilliant if perverse *tour de force* on *The Sixteenth Century (excluding Drama)*. But the scholar-critic will consult both series. *OHEL* is not yet complete and the volume on the Victorian period by Geoffrey and Kathleen Tillotson may well prove to be its *chef d'œuvre*. As it is, the best modern literary histories, those combining scholarship with criticism, have been independent works outside either *CHEL* or *OHEL*. Some recent examples are M. H. Abrams's, *The Mirror and the Lamp* (literary criticism of the Romantic period) and René Wellek's *A History of Modern Criticism: 1750–1950*, which sets English literary theory authoritatively within its general European and American context (4 vols, 1955–65, with the final vol. still to come). A brilliant survey at the other end of English literature's time-scale is Rosemary Woolf's *The Medieval Religious Lyric* (1968).

A work of reference on a heroic scale that is comparable with both the *OED* and the *CBEL* is the *Dictionary of National Biography*, edited by Leslie Stephen from the first volume (1885) to the twenty-first (1890), from Volume XXII (1890) jointly by Stephen and Sidney Lee (who had been the assistant editor from the beginning) to XXVI (1891), and from XXVII to LVIII (1900) by Lee alone. Supplements followed: *First Supplement*, made up of accidental omissions and recent deceases, 3 vols, 1901; an *Errata* volume 1904; *Second Supplement* (1912) – all three edited by Lee. The 1912–1921 Supplement (1927) was edited by H. W. C. Davis and J. R. H. Weaver (1927), 1922–1930 by Weaver alone (1937), 1931–1940 by L. G. Wickham Legg (1949), 1941–1950 by Legg and E. T. Williams (1959). The most recent addition to the series is *Corrections and Additions to the Dictionary of National Biography* (1966), which was issued by the Institute of Historical Research in whose *Bulletin* corrigenda and addenda had been appearing from 1923 to 1963. The most convenient edition of the *DNB* itself is the reprint in 22 volumes (1922–50) which embodies the earlier Supplements.

As the names of its more recent editors will suggest, the *DNB* is primarily a work of reference by historians for historians. But its architect and original editor, the man who determined the *DNB*'s general structure and contents, was essentially a literary critic. (We probably get nearest the essential Leslie Stephen in his collected essays called *Hours in a Library* and *Studies of a Biographer* which at their best are comparable with Matthew Arnold's *Essays in Criticism* or the *Lundis* of Arnold's master Sainte-Beuve.) It is no accident either that Stephen's first wife was Thackeray's daughter or that his own daughter, by his second wife, was Virginia Woolf. There was therefore a certain literary bias in the original *DNB*, many of the biographies of English writers being the actual work of Stephen himself. (Shakespeare unfortunately fell to his efficient but heavy-handed assistant and successor Sidney Lee.)

The *D.N.B.* (to adopt its own abbreviation; *DNB* is the form more generally preferred today) is primarily a biographical dictionary. Thus the first entry is Jacques (or James) Abbadie (1654?–1727); Abbadie is followed by Charles Abbot (d. 1817), and so on down to William Nassau de Zuylestein or Zulestein, second Earl of Rochford (1681–1710). As these names will immediately suggest, the net thrown is a very wide one; the number of separate entries to 1911, i.e. including the first two Supplements, is 30,378 and there are also 3,474 cross references. Each article is a miniature biography in continuous prose, to which are added lists of the subjects' publications and the compiler's own authorities. The original contributors included, in addition to the two editors, most of the professional historians of the period, and Stephen's tactful sub-editing has eliminated the copious exuberance of Victorian prose. An instructive critical exercise is to compare the style of the various compilers – keys to the initials are supplied in each volume – in and outside the *DNB*.

The emphasis is naturally on *events*, i.e. public achievements or failures, in the careers of those selected for inclusion. The characters of the eminent men and women are not analysed, the comments of their contemporaries are heavily pruned, their letters are only quoted for the light thrown on the dates and places of the actions in which they were engaged, and in the case of writers a book's title is likely to get more attention than its literary value, genre or style. The bibliographies of writers normally attempt completeness, but errors of omission and commission are frequent, and 'ghosts' (books that never existed at all) sometimes complicate a later investigator's labours.

In spite of Stephen, literary figures, especially the poets, receive less than their due of attention and a useful supplementary volume might well be devoted to those unjustly omitted. A poetess who certainly deserved a place in the *DNB* is Frances MacCartney or Macartney (d. 1789). Her 'Prayer for Indifference' is one of the best poems so far written by an Englishwoman; three stanzas from it are in *The Oxford Book of English Verse*, where they are attributed to Fanny Greville (her married name). George Saintsbury has three pages in *The Peace of the Augustans* (1916) on 'the singular throb which pulses through' the poem's 'polished and conventional phrase and versification', though the handsomest compliment paid to Mrs Greville's wit and intelligence is in Sheridan's elaborate dedication to her of *The Critic* (1781). (She was also Fanny Burney's godmother, who was called after her.) Nevertheless she is not in the *DNB*, though her father George MacCartney is, although all he is remembered for is that he was the second to the infamous Lord Mohun in the duel with the Duke of Hamilton on which Thackeray based a familiar episode in *Esmond*.[1]

On the *DNB*'s original publication its biographies were, with extraordinarily few exceptions, the most detailed and reliable short accounts of their subjects then available. They completely superseded even those in the *Encyclopaedia Britannica* (1768–71, 9th edition, 1875–89), whose biographical contributors included Matthew Arnold, Mark Pattison and Macaulay. But for the more eminent figures the *DNB* has itself generally been superseded by later research. Sidney Lee's Shakespeare entry – and the book that he based on it (*A Life of William Shakespeare*, 1898, rev. 1915) – is not in the same class as E. K. Chambers's *William Shakespeare: the Facts and the Problems* (2 vols, 1930), and a similar verdict applies to Leslie Stephen's Milton in comparison with such a modern life as W. R. Parker's *Milton: a Biography* (2 vols, 1968). But the faults are primarily of omission and for the scholar in need of a single date or sequence of events the *DNB* is still extraordinarily useful, however exalted your man is, and for the lesser figures – in spite of the thousands of modern biographical theses, or theses dressed up as books – it is literally indispensable. Unless you are very unlucky you will find in its articles a solid basis for further and more elaborate research. And for the scholar in a hurry its epitome *The Concise Dictionary* – first issued down to 1900 only – is a *sine qua non*.[2] A copy

[1] Thackeray made 'captain Macartnay' Mohun's second in the duel with *Esmond*'s Lord Castlewood, which was supposed to happen twelve years before the historical duel.

[2] The *Concise DNB* has a *Part II, 1901–1950* (1961), which includes some corrections to the five twentieth-century Supplements and a subject Index. The number of the Supplement determining an inclusion depends upon the date of death; if you do not happen to know when a contemporary died you should turn first of all to Part II.

bought, begged or borrowed (as mine was from the Cambridge University Press thirty years ago – and still unreturned) is indispensable. Here, in potted form and in one stout volume, are all the original entries, all 30,378 of them at least, and the density of the information retained is remarkable. Here is one of Pope's 'dunces' as a specimen:

> OLDMIXON, JOHN (1673–1742), Whig historian and pamphleteer; published poems, 1696; produced at Drury Lane, London, his opera, 'The Grove, or Love's Paradise', and at Lincoln's Inn Fields, London, his tragedy, 'The Governor of Cyprus', 1703; published 'The British Empire in America', 1708, 'History of Addresses', 1709–10; contributed to 'The Medley', 1711; answered Swift's 'Conduct of the Allies', in 'The Dutch Barrier Ours', 1712; published 'Secret History of Europe' (in parts, 1712, 1713, 1715) and other works against the Stuarts; collector of Bridgewater, 1716; attacked Clarendon's 'History of the Rebellion' in his 'Critical History', 1724—6; placed in the 'Dunciad' and the 'Art of Sinking in Poetry' by Pope, in retaliation for reflections upon him; made unwarranted attacks upon Clarendon's editors in his 'History of England during the Reigns of the Royal House of Stuart', 1729; published as a second volume, 'History of England during the reigns of William III, Anne and George I', 1735 (third volume dealing with Tudor period, 1739); his 'Memoirs of the Press, 1710–40', issued posthumously, 1742; perhaps author of 'History and Life of Robert Blake'.

A single breath-taking sentence! And if it does not tell the whole truth about him (Oldmixon's intelligent literary criticism, for example, has got left out), it does him greater justice than either Pope's note in the 'Variorum' *Dunciad* of 1729 (ii, 199) or the comments on it of James Sutherland in the Twickenham edition (1943) of Pope's poem.

An example of the literary uses to which the *DNB* can be put – and also of its limitations – is Steele's list of minor contributors to *The Spectator* in No. 555. Of the eight named only Pope and Thomas Tickell have attracted a modern biography, though John Hughes, Thomas Parnell and Laurence

Eusden are well-known minor Augustans. But who were Henry Martyn, 'Mr. *Carey* of *New College* in *Oxford*' and 'Mr. *Ince* of *Grey's-Inn*'? Henry Martin or Martyn (d. 1721) *is* in the *DNB*, as is Henry Carey (d. 1743), the author of 'Sally in the Alley' – though Donald F. Bond, the latest editor of *The Spectator*, has shown that Walter Carey (1685–1757), who is not in, is a more likely candidate. And there is no plausible Ince in it. In all, then, for four of the eight minor contributors identified by Steele – Hughes, Parnell, Eusden and Henry Martyn – the *DNB* still provides the best summary of the relevant facts and dates.

Leslie Stephen was not a stylist, but he wrote and exacted from his contributors a straightforward masculine English prose. It is reassuring to find in a mere work of reference a comment such as the following – by Stephen himself, as it turns out – in the article on Aaron Hill: 'His self-importance and pomposity would now be rather amusing if less terribly long-winded.' Unfortunately few standard works of reference provide such stylistic consolations.

Finally, though entirely without such consolation, there is the British Museum's *General Catalogue of Printed Books to 1955* (1964), of which a 'Compact Edition' was published in 1967 in 27 volumes. Although naturally not confined to English literature this is incomparably the fullest list of English books ever published. And it has astonishingly few errors. The 'Compact Edition', which packs some ten volumes of the original into each of its volumes, has reduced the size of the type proportionately, but – *mirabile dictu* – it is still easily if not comfortably legible. For prolonged use a magnifying glass is, however, recommended.

Other standard works of reference are listed in the Select Bibliography (pp. 184–94 below). Useful guides to this rapidly growing area are the *Selective Bibliography for the Study of English and American Literature* (New York, 1960, rev. 1963) by Richard D. Altick and Andrew Wright, *A Reference Guide to English Studies* (Chicago, 1962) by Donald F. Bond, and Chapter XI of my own *Guide to English Literature* (1965, rev. 1970).[1]

[1] This particular chapter in my *Guide* is largely the work of Harrison T. Meserole.

Critical uses of works of reference

The critical uses of a work of reference – as distinct from the labours that it can save us in fact-finding – may not be immediately obvious. Here, however, are two examples to whet the young researcher's appetite.

The first comes from T. S. Eliot's early essay 'Shakespeare and the Stoicism of Seneca', which includes the following sentence:[1]

> Whether Mr. Strachey, or Mr. Murry, or Mr. Lewis, is any nearer to the truth of Shakespeare than Rymer, or Morgann, or Webster, or Johnson, is uncertain; they are all certainly more sympathetic in this year 1927 than Coleridge, or Swinburne, or Dowden.

The names in this roll-call are those of some of the most celebrated critics of Shakespeare in their several periods – with one disconcerting exception. We recognize Lytton Strachey, Middleton Murry and Wyndham Lewis (who presumably are to be taken as the representatives of twentieth-century Shakespeare criticism, though it is odd that A. C. Bradley should have been left out); Coleridge, Swinburne and Dowden represent the nineteenth century, and Thomas Rymer (of *A Short View of Tragedy*, 1693), Maurice Morgann (of *The Character of Falstaff*, 1777), and Dr Johnson stand for the Restoration and the eighteenth century. But who is Webster? As one of the eighteenth century critics who are more sympathetic to the twentieth century – at any rate to 'this year 1927', when Eliot originally read the essay to a meeting of the Shakespeare Association in London – this Webster might be expected to be a reasonably familiar figure, a name at least as well known to the academic common reader as that of Rymer or Morgann. But you will not find a Webster in any of the anthologies of Shakespeare criticism. Indeed, no one of this name seems to have even mentioned Shakespeare in print between John Webster the dramatist (who has a patronizing sentence on Shakespeare, Dekker and Heywood in 'To the Reader' prefixed to *The White Devil*, 1612) and Noah Webster, the American lexicographer. Eliot had evidently got the name wrong; and the critic he was really referring to can be identified

[1] *Selected Essays* (1932), p. 126.

immediately by consulting *CBEL*'s Shakespeare section which has a special sub-division 'The Principal Critics to 1800'. As *CBEL* uses a chronological order wherever practicable, the eye has only to skim down some two columns before it reaches: 'Whiter, W. Specimen of a Commentary on Shakespeare. 1794'.

Although Eliot did not correct the error when he included 'Shakespeare and the Stoicism of Seneca' either in his *Selected Essays* (1932) or his *Elizabethan Essays* (1934), it is a virtual certainty that by '*Webster*' he must have meant Walter Whiter (1758–1832), whose discovery of Shakespeare's most striking 'image-clusters' has recently revived some interest in his book.[1] Eliot's error is of course no more than a curiosity of literary history. I have used it simply to show how a work of reference can be used to identify and correct a slip of this kind in a matter of minutes.

A second example of the potential critical uses of a work of reference is the remarkable Blake concordance recently completed by David V. Erdman (Ithaca, 1967). Blake's poetry has a peculiar fascination for the reckless guesser and the wild-eyed interpreter; a cold douche of tabulated detail such as is provided in this concordance's Appendix A ('Index words in order of verse frequency') can do nothing but good. (Since this is a concordance of the entire Blake corpus – including the marginalia, the letters and the titles whenever they are ascribable to Blake himself of his paintings, engravings and drawings – the Appendix differentiates between the verse and prose uses of the same word.) The difference in numerical frequency is often surprising; thus *howl, howls, howling* and *howlings* occur 166 times altogether in the verse and only five times in the prose (which includes several pieces of poetic prose). This Appendix therefore enables the student to identify Blake's poetic diction with a new precision. A more refined exercise is to use the proportion of poetic to non-poetic diction as a guide to the period of the poem's composition. Applied to the much-vexed problem of the two versions of the seventh Night of *The Four Zoas*, the test strongly suggests the precedence of what is known as Night VIIb, and this conclusion seems to be confirmed by changes in Blake's spelling (also recorded in the concordance).

[1] It has now been edited by Alan Over and Mary Bell (1967).

All concordances have to omit a few very common words, such as the definite and indefinite articles, which might easily occupy as many pages as the more important words put together. But the necessary omissions vary from writer to writer. Blake uses *I* 3,651 times, and *me* and *my* 1,017 and 2,159 times respectively. These three words have accordingly been excluded from the concordance. Matthew Arnold on the the other hand, uses the three words comparatively rarely and each occurrence can be given in the Arnold concordance (Ithaca, 1959). The implications of the differences are clearly critically significant. Blake's special egocentricity also appears in the frequency with which Los (who was Blake's mythological superego) makes his appearance. If the possessive *Los's* is added to *Los* Blake's prophetic name is only exceeded in the verse-frequency tables recorded in the concordance by *all*. By the side of his 556 mentions of Los, Los's wife Enitharmon's 258 seem ungallantly few.

The only scholar to have realized hitherto the mine of critical material that lies buried in concordances is Josephine Miles, whose *Major Adjectives in English Poetry* (Berkeley, 1946) was something of a landmark in the new alliance between scholarship and criticism. One example will have to suffice. That Wordsworth's two favourite adjectives are *good* and *old* and Shelley's *sweet* and *deep* is at least a suggestive fact. The possibility that for Wordsworth whatever is old is likely to be good may prove a useful critical clue. Perhaps his conservatism goes deeper than one had realized – to the point indeed of primitivism. And that Shelley should find what is deep peculiarly sweet seems to confirm his curious tendency to what may be called the Dream of a Dream of a Dream. A simple example of the conceit occurs in 'Ginevra' (1821):

> Like one within a dream who dreams
> That he is dreaming.

(A depth of three stages from actuality.) In 'Prince Athanase' (1817) Shelley reaches a depth of five levels:

> the shadow of a dream
> Which the veiled eye of Memory never saw.

But even this is exceeded by *Prometheus Unbound*, IV, 244–5:

> unimaginable shapes
> Such as ghosts dream dwell in the lampless deep.

Here there is deep upon deep: the 'shapes' cannot be imagined except by ghosts when dreaming and what the ghosts see in their dreams are shapes in the ocean depths where there is no source of light at all!

With the arrival of the computer more and more concordances are being compiled; they are also more complete and more reliable than their hand-made predecessors (the Pope and the Tennyson were particularly imperfect). It is a pity greater critical use is not made of them. Concordances of the range and degree of detail made available in Erdman's Blake can be made to unlock many primarily aesthetic problems.

A caveat has, however, to be added to the deduction reached from concordances. A concordance, because it includes every example of each major word in an author's verse, is almost certain to be too inclusive. Shelley, for one, wrote bad poems as well as good ones, and for the critic, however minute his researches may be, it makes all the difference if a particular example comes from the juvenilia or the mature works. (In Wordsworth's case of course the opposite is true: the words used in his later poems, or in a later stratum superimposed upon an early poem, can generally be ignored.)

A similar caveat must be extended to all works of reference. They save the investigator much time and trouble, but they can never be a substitute for a re-reading of the original work or document – partly because the possibility of error in the transcription can never be excluded but primarily because the compiler of a work of reference is not as such a scholar-critic. It is not his business to see the literary object as in itself it really is. Works of reference are guides, crutches, points of departure, but what they refer us to is matter different in kind from what they are themselves. In Chapter Three an attempt will be made to analyse the central concern of all literary studies. What do we mean by 'literature'?

THREE

THE LITERARY OBJECT

> Many objections have been made to a proposition which, in some remarks of mine on translating Homer, I ventured to put forth; a proposition about criticism, and its importance at the present day. I said: 'Of the literature of France and Germany, as of the intellect of Europe in general, the main effort, for now many years, has been a critical effort; the endeavour, in all branches of knowledge, theology, philosophy, history, art, science, to see the object as in itself it really is.' I added, that owing to the operation in English literature of certain causes, 'almost the last thing for which one would come to English literature is just that very thing which now Europe most desires, – criticism'; and that the power and value of English literature was thereby impaired.
>
> Matthew Arnold[1]

In search of a definition

The sentences in the epigraph to this chapter, magnificent both in their confidence and their courtesy, come at the beginning of 'The Function of Criticism at the Present Time' which introduces Arnold's first series of *Essays* in Criticism (1865). And no doubt our criticism *has* improved in the last hundred years, even if our creative literature has deteriorated (*Dramatis Personae*, 1864; *Our Mutual Friend*, May 1864–

[1] *The Prose Works*, ed., R. H. Super (Ann Arbor, 1962), III, 258. Arnold is referring to *On Translating Homer* (1861), ed. Super, (1960), I, 140.

Nov. 1865; *Atalanta in Calydon*, 1865, *Poems and Ballads*, 1866; *Middlemarch*, 1871–2). Much of the critical credit too is certainly due to Arnold. But the literary object 'as in itself it really is' remains obstinately obscure and undefined. Arnold himself, according to Eliot, was not so much a critic as 'a propagandist for criticism';[1] as Leavis has demonstrated more recently in his own person, it is not impossible to be both at the same time. But on the all-important issue of what it is that the critic criticizes Eliot, in spite of his philosophical training at Harvard, the Sorbonne and Oxford, can only contribute occasional *aperçus*. Indeed, his colleague I. A. Richards in *Principles of Literary Criticism* (1924) is refreshingly contemptuous of all earlier criticism (including Arnold's) – and perhaps even Eliot's:[2]

> A few conjectures, a supply of admonitions, many acute isolated observations, some brilliant guesses, much oratory and applied poetry, inexhaustible confusion . . . But . . . no explanations. The central question, What is the value of the arts, why are they worth the devotion of the keenest hours of the best minds, and what is their place in the system of human endeavours? is left almost untouched, although without some clear view it would seem that even the most judicious critic must often lose his sense of position.

Brave words, but unfortunately most of Richards's own explanations have turned out to be equally self-contradictory or irrelevant; the *Principles* is stimulating but disorganized, and Richards's principal influence has been through the practice of his pupil William Empson.

The most informative theoretical definition of the literary object is probably the central chapter in *Theory of Literature* by René Wellek and Austin Warren. The chapter is called 'The Analysis of the Literary Work of Art' in the first edition (New York, 1949) and, more pretentiously but more accurately, 'The Mode of Existence of a Literary Work of Art' in the second edition (1956). In both editions it is the structural hinge on which *Theory of Literature* turns, being preceded by

[1] *The Sacred Wood*, p. 1.
[2] pp. 6–7 (1960 ed.).

five chapters with the general heading 'The Extrinsic Approach to the Study of Literature' (biography, psychology, society, ideas, other arts) and succeeded by six chapters on 'The Intrinsic Study of Literature' (prosody, style, metaphor, 'narrative fiction', genres, evaluation). Austin Warren, Wellek's junior partner in the enterprise, was a member of the 'New Criticism' group in America, and his formalist predilections may be largely responsible for the emphasis throughout on the 'intrinsic' rather than the 'extrinsic' approach. Wellek, on the other hand, was a Czech, but he had been sympathetic as a young man to the Russian Formalists who flourished *c.* 1910, if he is now primarily an erudite *Philolog* of the old Continental school permanently in exile in America (first at Iowa, then at Yale). The central theoretical chapter, however, is by Wellek (who is in fact responsible for thirteen of the nineteen chapters which make up the book), and this no doubt explains a certain clumsiness of expression in the presentation of the often acute arguments.

Wellek opens the key chapter by asking 'an extremely difficult epistemological question, that of the "mode of existence" or the "ontological situs" of a literary work of art'. Although he does not actually suggest a parallel with painting, his problem is essentially that of a painting in a public gallery *after closing hours*. The *real* 'Primavera' only exists as an object of aesthetic contemplation when the Uffizi Gallery is open to the public; a spectator can then be in direct communication, as it were, with Botticelli. After dark a painting must be presumed to continue to exist physically, as certain pigments applied in a certain manner on canvas or wood within a frame, but it is then only potentially a work of art. If the Uffizi should be burnt down and all its masterpieces destroyed, they would only survive in the memories of those who had seen them, or in imperfect photographic reproductions; every night the *real* 'Primavera' is temporarily 'extinct'. Its aesthetic survival depends upon the hazards of a daily resurrection.

Literature's case is not quite the same. Since hundreds of thousands of copies must exist, say, of *Hamlet*, the condition of its survival is not so obviously a physical matter – the paper, print or ink of extant editions or manuscripts – but of the existence of readers capable of reading and responding to

Elizabethan English and the Elizabethan drama. Shakespeare is no doubt at one end of the line of communication, but an interested reader or auditor is also needed at the other end. The survival of the 'real' *Hamlet* depends upon the persistence of such intercommunication. And what is true of *Hamlet* is true of all the arts.

Wellek did not develop the ontological argument as far as I have done, but he was at least aware of a necessary intersubjective premise. His final definition of the literary work of art deserves quotation, even if certain qualifications must be made to it:[1]

> The work of art, then, appears as an object of knowledge *sui generis* which has a special ontological status. It is neither real (like a statue) nor mental (like the experience of light or pain) nor ideal (like a triangle). It is a system of *norms* of ideal concepts which are intersubjective. They must be assumed to exist in collective ideology, changing with it, accessible only through individual mental experiences, based on the sound-structure of its sentences.

The *sui generis* is irrelevant. A fire at the Uffizi would destroy such artifacts as the gallery's brushes and brooms as well as Botticelli's paintings, and they might also have a similar imperfect survival. In what way the reality of a statue differs from that of other works of art is also not clear. And the difference between being ideal like a triangle and the 'ideal concepts' of the following sentence is not clear. But it is the intersubjective norms in the collective ideology that create the real difficulties, though they also raise the most stimulating problems, in Wellek's definition.[2] A norm is a standard, a pattern, or type. Who or what imposes Wellek's norms on the

[1] *Theory of Literature* (New York, 1956), p. 144.

[2] I. A. Richards has 'norms' in *Principles of Literary Criticism*, p. 198 (1960 ed.), but they are introduced to clarify his concept of psychological waste. 'The mind which is, so far as can be seen, least wasteful, we take as a norm or standard, and, if possible, we develop in our degree similar experiences. The taking of the norm is for the most part done unconsciously by mere preference, by the shock of delight which follows the release of stifled impulse into organized freedom.'

writer? Unless the norms are derived from the 'collective ideology' (society), can they have any force or authority? But if they are the products or reflections of society, as I am inclined to think they must be, then the definition is seriously incomplete and the consequent emphasis throughout the book should be at least as much on the 'extrinsic' as on the 'intrinsic'. An individualist bias is natural in an anti-Communist living in America, but the arguments of the Marxists must be met and not merely evaded.

Unconscious creation, conscious criticism

An English student will probably find it more useful to turn to Coleridge, fragmentary though his theory of literature was, and to use Wellek and Warren as an encyclopedia rather than as a guide-book. *Theory of Literature* is indispensable because of its range of reference, but it is not a book that every graduate student needs to read right through. Coleridge, on the other hand, even if his ultimate sources often prove to be German, is the central figure in all English theorizings about literature, and his influence, as first felt by Mill and Pater, and more recently elaborated by Richards (in *Coleridge on Imagination*, 1934, rev. 1950), continues to dominate the more abstract critical thinking on literature.

We may agree, however, with Wellek that a work of literature is an object of knowledge, and the proper subject as such of academic study rather than as a source of entertainment or emotional excitement. (These other aspects, as will be seen later, are incidental or at most consequential.) As an object of knowledge it presupposes in its readers a reaction in them that is as far as possible continuously conscious. The scholar-critic differentiates himself from the creative writer principally by this greater degree of conscious attention to every aspect or detail of the object studied. This is essentially what Eliot meant by the 'sense of fact'. On the other hand, the creative writer tends to a remarkable extent not to be fully conscious of what he is writing, especially in the first flush of original composition. Heminge and Condell's tribute to Shakespeare in the 1623 Folio is well known: 'His mind and hand went together: and what he thought, he uttered with that easiness, that wee have scarse received from him a blot in his papers.'

The three pages by Hand D (who is now generally agreed to have been Shakespeare) in the manuscript play (now in the British Museum) *Sir Thomas More* confirm what Heminge and Condell say: in what is clearly a first draft there are only minor and occasional corrections. The paradoxical evolution of such characters as Shylock and Prince Hal may also be held to confirm a tendency to quasi-unconscious composition. On the other hand, Ben Jonson's gruff comment in *Discoveries* ('Would he had blotted a thousand'[1]) was that of a man who was a natural critic; it may be compared with Eliot's complaint about the pains of composition quoted above.[2] The case of 'Kubla Khan' is therefore exceptionally interesting as being the completely unconscious product of our greatest literary theorist. According to Coleridge's own first account – now in the British Museum and written on paper with the same watermark as a letter of 1796 – 'Kubla Khan' was the product of 'a sort of Reverie brought on by two grains of Opium, taken to check a dysentery',[3] the process of creative composition being almost wholly unconscious or subconscious.[4] But that Coleridge was normally a critic and not a poet is suggested by his later dismissing 'Kubla Khan' as 'a psychological curiosity', not worth publishing 'on the ground of any supposed *poetic* merits'.[5]

The more normal condition in the creative writer, even in one who is not also a critic, is of a conscious awareness of the indispensable contribution of his unconscious mind. Keats's

[1] Ben Jonson, ed. C. H. Herford and Percy and Evelyn Simpson (11 vols, 1925–52), viii, 583.

[2] See p. 7.

[3] Headnote to Crewe MS. (printed by Alice D. Snyder, *TLS*, 2 August 1934). When Coleridge printed the poem in 1816 the medical detail was reduced to 'a slight indisposition' and 'an anodyne'.

[4] Miss E. W. Schneider has argued at great length in *Coleridge, Opium and Kubla Khan* (Chicago, 1953) that Coleridge's account of the poem's origin was a fabrication. She was apparently unaware that Wordsworth was convinced that 'it was actually composed in a dream, certainly Coleridge believes so' (account of conversation with Wordsworth, 19 December 1830, recorded in Henry Alford's diary and published in *Life of Henry Alford*, 1871, p. 62).

[5] Headnote to *Christabel; Kubla Khan: a Vision; The Pains of Sleep* (1816), p. 52.

friend Richard Woodhouse has reported in detail a conversation that he had with Keats in or about July 1820.[1] Woodhouse had been puzzled by the phrase 'the magic hand of chance' in Keats's sonnet that begins, 'When I have fears that I may cease to be', and asked Keats what exactly he had meant by it. The preceding lines in the sonnet are:

> When I behold, upon the night's starr'd face,
> Huge cloudy symbols of a high romance,
> And think that I may never live to trace
> Their shadows, with the magic hand of chance . . .

A prose paraphrase of the lines might be that Keats was afraid he might die and so not be able to translate the symbolic message of the night sky into a poem. 'Magic' is often used in this sense in Romantic poetry,[2] and Keats elaborated the point to Woodhouse, giving as an example some lines from *Hyperion*, iii 79–82:

> Apollo then,
> With scrutiny and gloomless eyes,
> Thus answer'd, while his white melodious throat
> Throbb'd with the syllables.

> He has said, that he has often not been aware of the beauty of some of his thought or expression until after he has composed and written it down – it has then struck him with astonishment – and seemed rather the production of another person than his own. He has wondered how he came to hit upon it. This was the case with the description of Apollo . . . it seemed to come by chance or magic – to be as it were something given him.[3]

Keats summed up on the same occasion the whole process of original composition – and at the same time the case against

[1] *The Keats Circle*, ed. Hyder E. Rollins (Cambridge, Mass., 1948), I, 128–30.

[2] Some examples will be found in my *English Poetry: a Critical Introduction* (1950), p. 33 of 1966 ed.

[3] Coleridge had used the same expression in the headnote to 'Kubla Khan' (1816): '. . . the Author has frequently purposed to finish for himself what had been originally, as it were, given to him.'

later revision – in three memorable sentences which Woodhouse recorded verbatim:

> My judgment, he says, is as active while I am actually writing as my imagination. In fact, all my faculties are strongly excited and in their full play. And shall I afterwards, when my imagination is idle and the heat in which I wrote has cooled off, sit down coldly to criticize when in possession of only one faculty what I have written when almost inspired?

By the 'imagination' Keats no doubt meant what we would now call the unconscious or subconscious mind; his 'judgment', on the other hand, was essentially our conscious mind. The two terms were in fact survivals from neo-classic critical theory. What is original in Keat's reformulation is the inclusion of *all* the faculties, sensual as well as intellectual. Coleridge only extended the concept in Chapter XIV of *Biographia Literaria* in his definition of the Imagination as a 'synthetic and magical power' which 'reveals itself in the balance or reconcilement of opposite or discordant qualities'. The 'magic' was essential to the synthesis.

Three stages in the critical process

The Romantic poets, while insisting on what I once called the Principle of the Semantic Gap as a criterion of great literature,[1] did not make it clear how wide the gap could be or how the poet could bridge the gap if it was a wide one. The literary object is insipid if the opposites balanced or the discordancies reconciled are commonplace or self-evident (there is no surprise); and if the opposites are too extreme and the discordancies too discordant, neither a balance nor a reconciliation can be achieved. This is an issue that is crucial to any critical theory; its solution in particular intelligible and convincingly inter-subjective terms is the challenge that a literary object offers even the most mature student.

Coleridge's most coherent statement of his general theory of literature will be found in the same chapter of *Biographia Literaria*. Although primarily concerned with poetry, which he

[1] See *English Poetry*, p. 39 of 1966 ed.

ascribes to the individual poet's creative imagination, a passage in it describes such wholly conscious activities as those of literary scholarship. Starting from a favourite premise that 'distinction is not division' Coleridge proposes three stages in any serious intellectual process. We begin with 'any truth' (some traditional proposition or personal experience). If we are to obtain 'adequate notions' of this intersubjective 'truth', the conscious attention will have to be directed towards it so that we can 'intellectually separate its distinguishable parts'. In other words, a strict analysis is required – whatever the area under investigation may be. Literary scholarship is primarily devoted to the establishment of distinctions in or around a particular literary object that is being consciously interpreted. This second stage, according to Coleridge, should be followed by a third stage. Having established the relevant distinctions 'we must restore them in our conceptions to the unity in which they actually co-exist'. Such a restoration is the critic's function in the partnership with the scholar. A scholar distinguishes the meanings and contexts of the literary object; he is the analyst. The critic, on the other hand, consciously synthesizes the various distinctions that have been provided for him by the scholar, the synthesis being always within 'the unity, in which they actually co-exist'.

Arnold's use of Chaucer's line can be used to illustrate the process defined by Coleridge:

O martyr souded to virginitee!

The naïve first stage might be exemplified by our first uncritical reading of the *Prioress's Tale* (and perhaps the *Prologue* immediately preceding it). The common reader's reaction will probably be a sentimental one. (Or if he is not moved to a tear he will be moved to a yawn.) Chaucer's own comment on the Pilgrim's reception of the *Prioress's Tale* was that it *sobered* them:

Whan seyd was al this miracle, every man
As sobre was that wonder was to se.

And the host then rashly invited Chaucer himself to contribute 'a tale of myrthe' to dissipate the general solemnity. What Chaucer provided was, of course, the *Tale of Thopas*, an essay in literary sophistication similar in some respects to the *Prioress's Tale.* (Neither is what it proclaims itself to be.)

Coleridge's second stage is analytic. The common reader's naïve initial response is felt to be inadequate and scholarship is imported to supplement the superficial interpretation. The Prioress's character as presented at length in the *General Prologue* is clearly relevant to the 'meaning' of the Tale. So is the high proportion of diminutives. The apostrophes (as in the line selected by Arnold for special commendation), which tend to interrupt the direct progress of the narrative, are noted and perhaps tabulated. So too might be the use of a stanzaic form (rime royal) and its relationship to the probable date of the Tale's composition. A 'magic and synthetic' (unconscious and conscious) unity in Coleridge's third stage, as the conflation of the various aspects reveals the particular literary object's unity, as it 'actually' exists. The 'meaning' of Chaucer's tale, it turns out, is very different from the impression conveyed at a first reading. Essentially the Tale is an illustration of the Prioress's character in action, one condemning her prejudices and limitations out of her own mouth. And the literary form Chaucer has chosen to use for this purpose is *pastiche.*

The choice of a 'form' or genre – as of the linguistic medium (Gower selected French for his long *Le Mirrour de l'Homme,* Latin for his shorter *Vox Clamantis,* and English for the *Confessio Amantis*) – is a necessary part of any literary object's 'meaning', but it is no guarantee in itself that the object is *literary.* To be literature the 'meaning' must have 'significance'; it is impossible, and fatal, to exclude a criterion of 'value' from the definition. A poem, to adopt Coleridge's 'homely' formula, offers itself as 'the *best* words in the best order',[1] and its interpretation, however casual it may be, cannot avoid the introduction or implication of such adjectives as *good, beautiful, intense, sublime, successful,* etc. In *Biographia Literaria* the criterion that keeps recurring is *unity.* The imagination is the 'esemplastic power' which unifies opposite and discordant qualities. What is implied, however, in the famous formula is a successful unification, and the two terms tend to overlap: if *unified,* more or less *good* (aesthetically); if not unified, more or less *bad.*

[1] *Specimens from the Table-Talk,* I, 84.

But what is an aesthetic unit? The problem is one that Coleridge and his modern followers tend to evade. The concept of an 'organic' unity is a convenient escape-route, but as a work of literature is not really an animal or a vegetable the organic metaphor cannot be taken very seriously. Instead it is better to accept as a potential literary unit whatever Coleridge's synthesis is applicable to – from the single-sentence poem to a novel or an epic. (The smallest unit, the line or two recorded in a dictionary of quotations, is often the most useful for critical analysis.)

The English language has no single all-embracing word for all such units of literature. In its absence we have generally to make do with one of the various genres – a poem, a play, a novel, an essay, etc. For the purposes of straightforward description such labels are no doubt usually sufficient, but for a strict definition of the nature of the objects that confront the scholar-critic what is needed is not terms that differentiate one genre from another but a single term that will include within itself the category or quality that is equally applicable to *all* the genres. *Faute de mieux* I shall use the term *literary artifact*. An *artifact* is a word in general use among archaeologists, who apply it to any object turned up in their excavations that appears to be man-made, whatever its original domestic or social function may ultimately prove to have been. But etymology inevitably adds a further connotation: the object discovered, however unconscious its human maker was of it, is to some degree a *work of art*. An aesthetic criterion is irresistibly invoked in epithets like 'imperfect', 'fine' or 'magnificent' which have a way of insinuating themselves into the prosaic reports of an archaeological excavation. The special advantage of the term *artifact* in a literary application is that it enables a distinction to be made between the unit as it left the writer and what have proved to be the portions which can be discarded. Anthologists will often leave out one or more stanzas from the poems that they include in their selection, and in this their instinct is certainly sound. The epitaph by William Browne that most of us think of as beginning 'Sydney's sister, Pembroke's Mother' originally had two inferior lines[1] preceding it. And in

[1] Underneath this sable Herse
Lyes the subject of all verse:

the same way a literary artifact may be longer than the unit that is preserved in one writer's works. Donne's lyric 'The Bait' (in the *Songs and Sonnets*) is incomplete without Marlowe's 'Come live with me and be my love', on which it is a variation. A writer's complete works, with the omission perhaps of the juvenilia, the 'dotages' and those written in a foreign language, form another level of the aesthetic unit. 'Shakespeare', for example, is short-hand for the complete works, more or less, of William Shakespeare. The literary unit can even be extended under certain circumstances to a whole 'movement' or 'school' of writers. Thus the sonnets of Daniel, Drayton, Barnabe Barnes, Henry Constable, and even those of the Scotch laird William Drummond, are best considered as extensions of Sidney's *Astrophil and Stella,* forming with it a single literary artifact – the Elizabethan Petrarchan love sonnet-sequence. Such subtractions and additions need to be handled with tact, but there can be no doubt of their theoretical justification. It will be prudent, however, to begin a definition of the literary unit in simpler terms.

Literature, would-be literature, sub-literature, non-literature

A point of departure will be to distinguish between literature proper and three related verbal areas: (1) would-be literature, (2) sub-literature, (3) non-literature (such as official forms). Whatever literature is, it is not the poem or novel that is unreadable because of its total incompetence (would-be literature). Nor is it the pot-boiling journalism, whoever the author was, that is only potentially more than mere entertainment (sub-literature). Nor finally is it the use of language, in print or in speech, that is wholly trivial ('Good morning, Mrs Brown') or strictly utilitarian (non-literature). Each of the four types presents superficially a continuous verbal series, approximately the currently correct words in their currently correct order, but would-be literature, sub-literature and non-literature almost immediately lose anything but a historical interest. They are artifacts without being works of art, the products of human beings, each performing one or more recognized social services, but these subordinate verbal artifacts differ *toto caelo* from the *literary artifact* (in its various forms), if only because great literature represents by general agreement one of the pinnacles of human civilization. It was Arnold's most daring and provocative contribution to literary theory to say outright, in so many words, that under modern conditions literature – or, as he calls it, poetry – now performs the cultural function previously monopolized by religion and philosophy:

> More and more mankind will discover that we have to turn to poetry to interpret life for us, to console us, to sustain us. Without poetry, our science will appear incomplete; and most of what now passes with us for religion and philosophy will be replaced by poetry.

The passage comes in the second paragraph of 'The Study of Poetry' in the posthumous collection entitled *Essays in Criticism: Second Series.* Arnold's simplifying tone in it was presumably determined by the essay's original function as 'General Introduction' to T. H. Ward's *The English Poets.* It is only necessary to thumb through Ward's collection to see that its selections are intended for a literary beginner. Nothing has been included in this anthology to bring a momentary puzzle or blush of embarrassment to the silliest Victorian virgin. And the first paragraph, a revised version of Arnold's introduction to the poetry volume in a popular collection called *The Hundred Greatest Men* (1879), is equally simplified:

> Our religion has materialized itself in the fact, in the supposed fact; it has attached its emotion to the fact, and now the fact is failing it. But for poetry the idea is everything; the rest is a world of illusion, of divine illusion. Poetry attaches its emotion to the idea; the idea *is* the fact. The strongest part of our religion today is its unconscious poetry.

Arnold was capable of statements a good deal more sophisticated than this. Nevertheless, and with the appropriate reservations, a crucial point is made in these two paragraphs. It is not only that literary artifacts can be objects of immense 'value', but that the nature and degree of their present value have been determined by the recent evolution of our society – and in particular by the modern dissociation in religion of idea-as-fact from idea-as-illusion (or in philosophy idea-as-hypostatization).

The three other varieties of verbal artifact have a more limited interest for the scholar-critic. Would-be literature is the tribute that literary snobbery pays to the real thing – and except as social curiosities such things as eighteenth-century tragedy, for example, can be ignored. Sub-literature, on the other hand, even if of little value in itself, may be the prelude to some new mutation in the combination of meaning and significance that constitutes literature proper. An example of such a mutation is Sir Thomas Wyatt's transformation of the medieval love-song into lyrics not depending on musical accompaniment;[1] in Wyatt the refrain, instead of being a more or less meaningless chorus, acquires a dramatic role that will sometimes change from stanza to stanza.[2] By releasing the songs of the Tudor Court from their dependence on music Wyatt made possible the sequence of lyrical masterpieces that culminates in Donne's *Songs and Sonnets*. It is true that many of Wyatt's 'ballets' are themselves literature rather than sub-literature, though many are not, but even his best poems presuppose an earlier separation of the words of a love-song from the music, whether the innovator was Wyatt himself or some unknown and wholly sub-literary predecessor or contemporary.

The crucial moments in the history of a literature occur at such points of transformation of a sub-literature into literature. Elizabethan tragedy, for example, grew out of the melodrama of the English Senecans, and was reinforced by the 'emotional acting' developed in the public theatres. Defoe's novels are based on the sub-literature of the lives of pirates, highwaymen and other criminals, as *Pamela* is Richardson's development of such model letters as his own *Letters Written to and for particular Friends, Directing the Requisite Style and Forms to be Observed in writing Familiar Letters* (1741). Burns used folk-songs as the basis of his own lyrics, and the roots of Romantic poetry are

[1] The subject is discussed in detail in John Stevens's *Music and Poetry in the Early Tudor Court* (1961).
[2] Kenneth Muir's edition (1949), Nos 103, 107, 111, 143, 166, 167, etc.

unquestionably to be found, as Wordsworth recognized in his 'Essay Supplementary to the Preface' (1815), in the traditional popular ballads. Similarly the crude summaries of the *Monthly Review* are the beginnings of the nineteenth-century occasional critical essay as practised by Jeffrey, Hazlitt, Macaulay, Carlyle, Mill and Arnold.

The examples need not be multiplied here. In each case, however, the emergence of the new 'kind' or 'movement' is critically meaningless, a mere chronicle of specimens and dates, unless some explanation is available of why the particular mutation of sub-literature into literature occurred when it did occur, neither earlier nor later. Some change in society, or at least in the reading public, has to be posited. Without such a social analysis, however perfunctory or hypothetical, the progress out of sub-literature into a 'classical period' and a subsequent one of decadence easily degenerate either into mere source-hunting or the affixing of superficial labels. It is true that the exact historical connections are often hard to establish, but a social context must always be presumed. Literature does not compose itself, and once it is composed, either sooner or later, a mode of communication must be established between the author and an audience.[1] Without some such communication – because the text seems to have been lost, or an interested audience is unavailable – the particular artifact cannot function as literature.

A sub-literature prepares the way for a literature and determines the form which that literature will take. It must therefore precede the literary artifact, though it will often accompany and succeed it as well. Would-be literature, on the other hand, presupposes a literary model already existent that it will do its feeble best to imitate. Finally, non-literature, because its constituent parts are ordinary words and sentences, will normally precede, accompany and succeed the particular literary artifact. Even so literature and non-literature can only be in parallel, as it were, because of the presence in one and the absence in the other of 'value'. The process by which their common linguistic constituents become the best words in the best order of literature repeats on a smaller scale that in

[1] *Sir Gawain and the Green Knight* (written *c.* 1390) survives in only one manuscript.

which sub-literature develops into literature. There is a necessary relationship between language and style (which will be considered in more detail in Chapter Four) as there is a relationship between the literary artifact and its sub-literary origins (which will be discussed more fully in Chapter Five), but both connections are subordinate to general considerations of 'value' – which in their turn reflect a civilized human society. Unless the future scholar-critic can discriminate between what is good and what is less good in ordinary human behaviour, he will not know whether what he is reading is or is not of literary value. And it is only as he acquires some literary taste that it becomes useful to ask him either to distinguish between language and style or to identify the relevant historical source of a work of literature.

With one or two lonely exceptions like Arnold, who was more critic than scholar, the nineteenth and early twentieth centuries tended, especially in their academic representatives, to reverse the proper procedure of enquiry. Instead of asking, as a first premise, 'What constitutes a Good Society?' and secondly, 'What is the Good Literature and the Good Style which express and reflect such a society?', the questions asked were primarily historical. And so, when English literature was added to university syllabuses, the evolutionary approach dominated graduate studies. Ferdinand Brunetière's *L'Evolution des genres dans l'histoire de la littérature* (Paris, 1890) was only the extreme example of a general trend for which Henri Taine provided the slogan. But of his three components – *race, milieu, moment* – it was *milieu* that receives Taine's emphasis.

The historicism of the nineteenth century culminated in the specialized studies that have become parasitic on the study of English literature: paleography, bibliography, the attribution of authorship, source-hunting, the history of the language (especially in its earlier phases), textual criticism, prosody, book-production, bibliopegy (the study of bindings), *et hoc genus omne*.

The specialized techniques have their limited uses, as will become clear in later chapters of this book, but the scholar-critic must not exaggerate their literary importance. It is especially significant that they allow themselves to be applied to non-literature, or at best would-be literature, at least as often as to literature proper. An expert in bibliography (in any of its modern senses), or even in textual criticism, the most reputable of the specializations, makes a good Literary Detective rather than a good critic or scholar. Leslie Hotson, whose fascinating discoveries in the Public Record Office, such as the documents surrounding Marlowe's melodramatic death, or a new Shakespeare signature, and similar *trouvailles*, have caught our imaginations, has almost no literary sense, as his *Shakespeare's Sonnets Dated* demonstrated. But it is not impossible to combine the two professions – provided the priority of literary considerations is never lost sight of. A detective detects; it is usually a non-detective who must be introduced to expound the wider implications of such findings as Hotson's. The healthy development from the multiplication of the ancillary disciplines has been the recognition that the literary artifact is primarily an object of knowledge. It can be studied in the home, the school or the university in a way comparable with a science – even if the facts of literature, being human in origin, are different in kind from the facts of science. And, more important still, the point at which specialization is liable to become antiquarianism depends upon the scholar's continuous consciousness of the aesthetic centre from which such enquiries radiate. In spite of McKerrow's epigram, pedantry is not necessarily a higher factual standard than the next man's: it may also be a greater degree of literary irrelevance.

The initial question when the student is faced with a literary artifact must always be 'What does this mean?' – not privately to me but to all its other readers. The final question is its significance ('How good is it, and in what ways?'). Until I. A. Richards's *Practical Criticism* (1929) it had always been assumed that the answer to both these questions would be self-evident and could be taken for granted. *Of course* an educated Englishman would understand the words and sentences of an English work of literature, unless it was written hundreds of years ago. *Of course,* with the same reservation, all educated Englishmen would agree with only minor differences of emphasis about the artifact's worth or worthlessness as literature. Richards discovered that in fact we differ enormously on both counts. The serious study of English literature may be said to begin with Richards's disconcerting discovery of the average reader's unpredictable subjectivism, both its kind and its degree.

Richards's method, it will be remembered, was to distribute to his students at Cambridge and Harvard duplicated copies of thirteen poems of different periods and literary value. The first and the most sensational part of *Practical Criticism* was devoted to an analysis of these students' written comments on the poems, some of which exhibited misreadings at the lowest semantic level (e.g. elementary mistakes in the grammar ascribed to the poems). He added in an appendix the order of merit that the students had assigned to the thirteen poems. Their four favourites turned out to be pieces of little or no literary merit by conventional standards, the order of preference being J. D. C. Pellew, one of the most minor of the Georgians, Edna St Vincent Millay, Wilfred Gordon Childe and a certain 'Woodbine Willie' (the Rev. Studdert Kennedy). On the other hand the four poems most generally disliked were those of Donne, Hopkins, D. H. Lawrence and Longfellow. Today there would probably be general agreement that the best of the thirteen poems is Donne's Holy Sonnet 'At the round earth's imagined corners blow . . .', which Richards's students put tenth in the order of merit; the worst is almost certainly 'Woodbine Willie's' sentimental imitation of A. E. Housman, which they put third.

Richards obtained his sensational results by suppressing both the author's names and the poems' titles. The experiment was therefore a little artificial, a laboratory exercise. Moreover the poetry of Donne, Hopkins and D. H. Lawrence was much less familiar to university students than it is today. But the experiment was not essentially unfair: its demands upon the reader of poetry are not dissimilar from those made by an unfamiliar folk-song or traditional ballad. And the information that Richards suppressed enabled him to make his point with a maximum effect. Clearly something was seriously wrong with the permissive methods of reading that the English and American universities had inherited from Romanticism. But if Richards demonstrated what the deficiency was, the positive programme of reform was mainly left to William Empson in *Seven Types of Ambiguity*, and to a lesser extent to F. R.

Leavis and L. C. Knights in collections of essays most of which had originally appeared in their Cambridge journal *Scrutiny*. The American 'New Critics' followed, notably in the brilliant anthology *Understanding Poetry* edited by Cleanth Brooks and Robert Penn Warren. The doctrine that they preached, and of which F. R. Leavis and Cleanth Brooks have since been the principal prophets, became known as 'close reading' or 'the eye on the page'. A closer and more careful reading would certainly have saved Richards's students from the errors and silliness that are clinically investigated in *Practical Criticism.*

The classical theoretical statement of the New Criticism is 'The Intentional Fallacy' by W. K. Wimsatt (with Monroe Beardsley collaborating), which was originally published in *The Sewanee Review*, 54 (Summer 1946), though the seeds of the doctrine are much older. To commit the fallacy was to ask what the author's intentions were when writing. Instead of peering into dead men's minds criticism's proper concern, according to the anti-intentionalists, is with what the literary artifact *says*, not with what its author may have meant.

Literary history and its companion art of literary biography fell as a consequence into disgrace. *The Explicator*, a useful by-product of the critical dictatorship of Eliot, I. A. Richards and their associates, carries in each issue the following caveat:

> The editors are glad to receive any contributions relevant to *explication de texte* in prose or poetry. Material concerned with genesis, parallelism, or biography cannot, however, be accepted unless it has a direct bearing upon the interpretation of the text.

The original editors have told us that the notice was criticized, not because of these exclusions, but 'because the magazine admits the possibility of biography affecting the interpretation of the work'. The poem, according to these objectors, 'exists as a public performance, and concern with its author is at best irrelevant and at worst misleading'.[1] *The Explicator* was less dogmatic on literary history than on literary biography, but its distinction between a 'then-meaning' (the meaning at the time of the poem's composition) and a 'now-meaning', with its

[1] George Arms and Joseph M. Kuntz, *Poetry Explication* (New York, 1950), p. 21.

corollary 'if you had to discard one meaning or the other, the now-meaning is what should be retained', comes to much the same thing.[1]

The expulsion of the author from literature was a reaction against the biographical extremism which was one critical legacy of Romanticism. The principal innovation that the nineteenth century had introduced was to centre the critical process in the private life, conscious or unconscious, of the individual writer. To a greater or less extent in the best poems of Wordsworth, Coleridge, Shelley and Byron the poetry *was* autobiography, and the process continued in the best novels and short stories of Dickens, the Brontës, George Eliot, Kipling and D. H. Lawrence. Even Tennyson and Matthew Arnold have proved to be secret autobiographers.[2] But the biographical formula is obviously inadequate even as a key to much Romantic literature, and when applied to Chaucer, Shakespeare or Dryden it is almost useless. What is needed is a definition that will include both intentionalism and anti-intentionalism.

The scholar-critic's questions to the literary object

The first question that the scholar-critic will put to what is *prima facie* a literary artifact is whether on a preliminary inspection or first reading it seems to be literature or merely sub-literature or would-be literature. Errors are always possible at this stage; a work that finally proves to have great literary interest will often introduce itself as mere catch-penny journalism (consider the case of Swift), and contrariwise most modern 'epics' and 'tragedies' are not genuinely epical or tragic. But such traps can almost always be avoided if the first inspection is reasonably careful. The point of departure, then, for a study in depth is the conviction that the student is in

[1] *Ibid.*, p. 22.

[2] That *Maud* is largely based on Tennyson's abortive love affair with Rosa Baring – of the wealthy banking family – has been demonstrated by R. W. Rader (*Tennyson's 'Maud'*, Berkeley, 1964). Arnold's 'Marguerite episode' (1848–9) is obscure, but that there was a love affair with an unidentified French girl in Switzerland seems certain.

direct or indirect contact with what he believes to be literature – *considered as an object of knowledge.*

The qualification may seem to deny to the literary student the emotional satisfaction that Longinus' treatise on the Sublime, or Wordsworth's Preface to the second edition of *Lyrical Ballads*, to cite two familiar critical classics, lay such stress on. But this is to miss an essential point. A time-interval must necessarily intervene between the reader's comprehension of the text's meaning – with all its human implications and complexities – and the response or emotional reaction to this meaning. Whatever the speed that one can be trained to acquire in one's reading, applause or disgust *follows* the elaborate psychological process which begins with the translation of visual symbols on the page into words and sentences and is not complete until the sentences have become, by the various devices of literary illusion, human situations with 'real' characters, plausible social settings, natural background, etc. It will be remembered that Aristotle's definition of tragedy *terminates* in what he called the 'catharsis' of the emotions of pity and fear. The emotional confirmation is no doubt one that must not be absent. Unless the process of reading does terminate in a positive emotional reaction, the specimen being studied is not likely to be a literary artifact. A corollary is that negative emotional responses, such as the conscientious reader's total lack of interest in a book, are also a fact of criticism. The right not to be unnecessarily bored is one of the most important of our literary rights as scholar-critics.

The possibility that the article or thesis which the scholar-critic is about to write has been anticipated by a mature scholar must, of course, also be faced. A brief check on what is already in print – or even lurking in an unprinted thesis from some distant part of the English-speaking world[1] – is a necessary precaution, but you should not be unduly discouraged if your topic seems to have been exhaustively examined already. The intersubjective premise that the 'poem', the literary artifact, combines what is individual with what is collective carries with it the probability that its meaning and significance are continually capable of being extended and re-defined. One individual differs from another individual and one society

[1] For these see under the Select Bibliography, p. 189 below.

from another; in the process of differentiation new aspects of the original work manifest themselves. The history of the criticism of Shakespeare's plays – from Ben Jonson to Dryden and then to Pope, Dr Johnson, Coleridge, A. C. Bradley, G. Wilson Knight and Jan Kot – is a simple example of a universal law that has been repeated in the case of each play. (*Measure for Measure, King Lear, Antony and Cleopatra* and *The Winter's Tale* have proved especially sensitive to changes in the social climate.)

The second question the scholar-critic must ask arises directly from the first. If a preliminary inspection of the literary artifact has proved promising, problems of authorship, dates of composition, the audiences envisaged and the original contemporary reception, immediately arise. An interrelationship between the individual – either as author or reader – and his immediate society is the point at which the literary artifact comes into being. The concept is a critical commonplace whether we think in terms of Wellek's 'norms' or the Grimms' account of ballad origins (*das Volk dichtet*). Eliot sometimes puts the emphasis on the author: 'The great poet, in writing himself, writes his time' ('Shakespeare and the Stoicism of Seneca'[1]), and sometimes on the writer's society – 'If he is sincere, he must express with individual differences the general state of mind – not as a *duty*, but simply because he cannot help participating in it' ('Baudelaire'[2]). Variations on the notion are to be found in *The Use of Poetry and the Use of Criticism*, the most elaborate being in the 'Introduction':[3]

> The people which ceases to care for its literary inheritance becomes barbaric; the people which ceases to produce literature ceases to move in thought and sensibility. The poetry of a people takes its life from the people's speech and in turn gives life to it; and represents its highest point of consciousness, its greatest power and its most delicate sensibility.

[1] *Selected Essays*, p. 137.
[2] *Ibid.*, p. 386.
[3] p. 15. Eliot makes a somewhat different if related point on p. 75: 'Any radical change in poetic form is likely to be the symptom of some very much deeper change in society and in the individual.'

The problem that Eliot and similar theorists leave us with is what precise methods can be adopted to relate such generalizations to a particular artifact or group of artifacts. Wellek has a masterly chapter in *Theory of Literature* on 'Literature and Society' which surveys the various attempts that have been made by literary historians, sociologists and economists to explain literature in terms of its social origins and its society as reflected in its literature. But since his own bias is towards 'pure poetry', i.e. literature as self-explanatory and self-justifying, his conclusion is certainly too sceptical. The impression one carries away is that patrons, audiences and reading publics have a minor and marginal influence in determining the creation of literature. And his own 'norms' remain up in the air, fairy godmothers who never assume their responsibilities at the actual christening. The chapter is useful, however, because it provides detailed and accurate examples of what earlier theorists – mainly German and Russian – have proposed. A typical passage is the account of Shakespeare:[1]

> Many Marxists – and not Marxists only – attempt far too crude short cuts from economics to literature. For example, John Maynard Keynes, not an unliterary person, has ascribed the existence of Shakespeare to the fact that 'we were just in a financial position to afford Shakespeare at the moment when he presented himself. Great writers flourish in the atmosphere of buoyancy, exhilaration, and the freedom of economic cares felt by the governing class, which is engendered by profit inflations'.[2] But profit inflations did not elicit great poets elsewhere – for instance, during the boom of the twenties in the United States – nor is this view of the optimistic Shakespeare quite beyond dispute. No more helpful is the opposite formula, devised by a Russian Marxist: 'Shakespeare's tragic outlook on the world was consequential upon his being the dramatic expression of the feudal aristocracy, which in Elizabeth's day had lost their former dominant position.'[3] Such contradictory

[1] p. 95 (1956 ed.).
[2] *A Treatise on Money* (1930), II, 154.
[3] A. V. Lunacharsky quoted from the *Listener*, 27 December 1934.

> judgments, attached to vague categories like optimism and pessimism, fail to deal concretely with either the ascertainable social content of Shakespeare's plays, his professed opinions on political questions (obvious from the chronicle plays), or his social status as writer.

The point that Wellek seems to miss is that such contradictions are a proper and inevitable response to literature. Shakespeare was both an optimist and a pessimist. The 'ascertainable social content' of the plays varies from play to play and even from scene to scene. And its historical sources are complex and sometimes contradictory. But such disagreements as those cited by Wellek are *confirmations* of Shakespeare's greatness. The ability 'to balance or reconcile opposite or discordant qualities' extends beyond an author's creative imagination. May it not be that the literary artifact considered as an object of knowledge *requires* contradictions for its reader to synthesize? Johnson made what is essentially this point when discussing similes: 'A simile may be compared to lines converging at a point, and is more excellent as the lines approach from greater distance'.[1] But Coleridge and Johnson omitted to add that the reader must be persuaded somehow or other to accept the synthesis of the dissimilarities that constitute literature. In a scientific investigation or a mathematical calculation the requisite termination is rational assent; its aesthetic equivalent is surprise followed by assent. The methods that a writer uses to convert surprise into assent are best deferred to the next chapter, but the central problem that literature poses as an object of knowledge may be illustrated briefly by the case of a modern artifact that I happen to think overrated.

A specimen object cross-examined

Johnson's dictum about similes has the advantage – which I presume to have been unintentional – of illustrating itself: the nature of a simile, an artistic device of style, is exemplified by a surprising simile from the alien science of geometry.

[1] Life of Addison in *Lives of the Poets* (1781). Johnson was discussing the once much-admired simile of the storm in *The Campaign*.

Why, then, did Johnson deplore Donne's 'comparison of a man that travels and his wife that stays at home with a pair of compasses' (a simile in which 'it may be doubted whether absurdity or ingenuity has the better claim') in the life of Cowley? The explanation that he gives there is that such conceits are 'a voluntary deviation from nature'; and with the word 'nature' (human realities) he introduces an essential limitation on Coleridge's opposite and discordant qualities. The discordance must be wide but not too wide; the distance from which the lines converge should be great but it must not be intolerably prolonged. It is in the reconciliation of the two ideals that criticism finds its most immediately useful function, and because critical judgments are useful a measure of disagreement can be tolerated in their application. One reader is not identical with another, in spite of the intersubjective links that connect them, and 'collective ideologies' change to some extent from continent to continent and from century to century. If we now find nothing objectionable in the 'compasses' in Donne's 'Valediction forbidding Mourning', it is perhaps because a more democratic society has modified our concept of literary decorum.

The modern poem which I think overrated is A. E. Housman's 'Epitaph on an Army of Mercenaries':[1]

These, in the day when heaven was falling,
  The hour when earth's foundations fled,
Followed their mercenary calling,
  And took their wages and are dead.

Their shoulders held the sky suspended;
  They stood, and earth's foundation stay;
What God abandoned, these defended,
  And saved the sum of things for pay.

In Johnson's terminology the lines of this simile certainly converge from two distant points in Housman's poem. A semantic gap cannot be denied. Between Kaiser Wilhelm II's perhaps legendary dismissal of the British Expeditionary Force of 1914 as contemptible mercenaries and the cosmic powers of salvation attributed to them by Housman the gap could hardly

[1] Printed in *The Times*, 31 October 1917, under a leading article headed 'The Anniversary of Ypres'. The exact date of the composition of Housman's poem is not known.

be wider. But unfortunately one side of the gap is distressingly literary. Did the sky fall on 4 August 1914? And is not the 'hour' of l.2 simply an elegant variation on the 'day' of l.1? The Professor of Latin at Cambridge is also much too prominent in the second verse. It was, we remember, Atlas who first 'held the sky suspended', and l.7 had been put better in a famous line by Lucan (whom Housman later edited):

> Victrix causa deis placuit, sed victa Catoni.

Finally, the 'sum of things' clearly derives from Lucretius' *summa rerum* (for whom, however, it had a more prosaic meaning).

The objection, then, to the Shelleyan poetic diction of the first verse and the classical references in the second is not so much that they are literary as that they are *literary commonplaces*, second-hand and tawdry. Their function in fact turns out to be merely to provide a framework for the one good line in the poem:

> Followed their mercenary calling . . .

But to me – and surely to others too – it is the Human Context that is particularly distressing, reducing Housman's discordant qualities here to empty rhetoric. This 'Epitaph' is presumably intended to recall the most famous of all epitaphs – that by Simonides on the Spartans at Thermopylae, of which the most successful English translation is the anonymous eighteenth-century version:

> Go, tell the Spartans, thou who passest by,
> That here, obedient to their laws, we lie.

But Leonidas and his heroic three hundred were killed to a man in the attempt to halt the whole Persian army at the pass of Thermopylae; the B.E.F. suffered severe casualties, but a large proportion survived to make merry after the War as the Old Contemptibles. And the claims that Housman makes for their superhuman gallantry at Mons, the Marne and the Aisne are simply not true. The French played a far more important part in 1914 in halting the German invasion. Housman's jingoistic exclusion of the German soldiers as well as the French – both after all human beings – compares unfavourably with the 'laconic' dignity of Simonides, who only alludes implicitly to the conquering Persians. Housman is indulging here in what used to be called 'Home Front' patriotism, a feature of World War I that those on leave from the trenches found particularly nauseating. It can be documented from the poems of Siegfried Sassoon, which are often clumsy but at least escape the rhetorical dishonesty of Housman.

FOUR

STYLE

> In general, the essence of poetry as an art is not so much that it is rhythmical (which all elevated language is), or that it is metrical (which not all poetry is, except by a considerable extension of the meaning of the word), as that it is patterned language. This is its specific quality as a 'fine art'. The essence of 'pattern' (in its technical use, as applied to the arts) as distinct from 'composition' generally, is that it is composition which has what is technically called a 'repeat'; and it is the 'repeat' which technically differentiates poetry from non-poetry, both being (as arts) composition. The 'repeat' may be obvious as in the case of rhymed lines of equal length, or it may be more implicit, to any degree of subtlety; but if it does not exist, there is technically no poetry. The artistic power of the pattern-designer is shown in the way he deals with the problems of 'repeat'; and this is true of poetry likewise, and is probably the key (so far as one exists) to any technical definition or discussion of the art.
>
> J. W. Mackail[1]

Good English

Style is not confined to poetry, but except in metaphorical extensions of the word it *is* confined to literature. And even when applied metaphorically – as to a stylish stroke in tennis or to a stylish batsman in cricket – the word is restricted to the

[1] *OED* under 'Poetry'. The definition was specially 'communicated' in 1906 by Mackail, who was the Professor of Poetry at Oxford from 1906 to 1911.

almost aesthetic excellence of an economy of means to ends, a maximum effect from an apparently minimal expenditure of energy. Significantly, the derivation is from the Latin *stilus*, the sharp-pointed implement of metal or bone then used for incising letters on a wax tablet – a use, in other words, by writers rather than speakers. Literature too, being ultimately derived from the Latin word for *letter* (*littera*), carries with it the same original physical connotation of the written or printed word. The 'repeat', whether it is in prose or verse, is therefore normally seen on the page before it is heard (even by the 'inner ear'). In a Victorian or earlier poem in which a line ending *wind* precedes a line ending *kind* the modern reader does not need to go back and start all over again with a long vowel in *wind*; a sight-rhyme, simply because it is visual, permits *wind* a notional existence that is not strictly either long or short (unless other words in either line by introducing assonance insist on sound superseding sight).

A conclusion follows: literature does not need to be recited or read aloud. A corollary is that the more closely literature approaches the spoken language – the more, that is, that it invites oral recitation – the less likely it is, at least in literate cultures, to achieve style. The criterion applies even to the drama; the good play must read well, even if it also acts well. (In the end the former is the decisive criterion.)

Language is often said – especially by linguists – to be the medium of literature. In a sense clearly it is; but equally clearly literature transcends its primitive linguistic origins (as *homo sapiens* transcends the ape). It is the area of transcendence that is the primary concern of the scholar-critic.

Otto Jespersen, the Danish philologist, has distinguished three levels of language.[1] The lowest is *intelligible speech.* A foreigner stumbling through a conversation in a language he is unfamiliar with is one example of more or less intelligible speech; another might be an Englishman trying with the help of a dictionary to read Dante in the original Italian. A superior level is *correct speech.* Correctness is the passive condition of observing the linguistic rules of the society into which one happens to be born, or which one is hoping to acquire (for a dead

[1] *Mankind, Nation and Individual from a Linguistic Point of View* (1946), pp. 132–3.

or foreign language). It is the verbal parallel to driving a vehicle on the public road either on the left-hand side of the road (in England) or on the right-hand side of the road elsewhere. The individual is not asked if he has any preference for one side or the other – or one pronunciation or other linguistic usage rather than any other. Jespersen himself, though a Dane, wrote correct English, and most non-literature or sub-literature that achieves the dignity of print may be assumed to be in more or less correct English. But, as Jespersen proceeds to show, there is a higher linguistic level, that of *good English*. Here Jespersen admits that he is 'straying into the science of Style, which is properly outside my province'.[1] However, he allows himself to play with the formula (attributed to a certain Tegnér) 'easiliest uttered is easiliest received', which certainly summarizes an important element in the oral evolution of language. The test is then applied to the fifth line in *The Ring and the Book*:

> Spark-like 'mid unearthed slope-side figtree-roots,

This Jespersen calls ugly because it is 'hardly pronounceable'. But is the reader's 'inner ear' expected to pronounce it? The condition that psychologists call 'inner speech' is an obscure one, but the effect in it of Browning's line may simply be to slow down the unspoken speed of the blank verse – as Swinburne's anapaests accelerate a line. In any case, however, such considerations are only marginally relevant to the real question Jespersen raised. What is it that makes good English good rather than merely intelligible or correct?

Two simple examples will illustrate the linguistic nature of goodness of style. (They are both nonce-words.) The first is Blake's 'Nobodaddy'. This portmanteau-word is found only four times in Blake's complete works, all of them in manuscript fragments and impromptus written *c.* 1792 or 1793. It is not 'correct' English, though it is immediately 'intelligible' as a gesture of contemptuous atheism against the orthodox Protestantism of the time. In its original satiric context the coinage is certainly successful; it is unquestionably 'good' English.

My second example is from the *Philosophical Papers* (1961) of the Oxford philosopher J. L. Austin. A paper with the stylistic-

[1] p. 133.

ally provocative title 'Ifs and Cans' begins with a question:[1]

> Are *cans* constitutionally iffy? Whenever, that is, we say that we can do something, or could do something, or could have done something, is there an if in the offing – suppressed, it may be, but due nevertheless to appear when we set out our sentence in full or when we give an explanation of its meaning?

The word 'iffy' is not recorded in any English dictionary. It is not 'correct', though it is certainly 'good' English, as well as being 'intelligible' English, in its own context. What Austin has in fact done in this passage is to translate the good English of his first sentence into the correct English of his second sentence. Having aroused our interest with the amusing suggestion of a philosophical nursery rhyme, he proceeds to the technical logical problem which is his real concern.

Non-literature becomes literature

The cases of *Nobodaddy* and *iffy* are extreme examples of 'style' that is not, in the normal sense of the word, 'language'. Being single words in sentences that are otherwise 'correct' they call attention to their difference from the words surrounding them. Two examples of neutral or merely ordinary English that a poet has succeeded in transforming into good English may be more useful in proceeding to the crucial distinction between language and style. The first is a familiar one. It will be remembered that in Coleridge's final account of the origins of 'Kubla Khan',[2]

> he fell asleep in his chair at the moment he was reading the following sentence, or words of the same substance, in 'Purchas's Pilgrimage': 'Here the Khan Kubla commanded a palace to be built, and a stately garden thereunto. And this ten miles of fertile ground were inclosed with a wall.'

The actual words in *Purchas his Pilgrimage* differ in several significant details from the 'substance' Coleridge remembered. Purchas wrote:[3]

[1] p. 135.
[2] *Christabel: Kubla Khan, a Vision; the Pains of Sleep* (1816).
[3] p. 418. Purchas was apparently reporting information received from an unidentified traveller.

> In Xamdu did Cublai Can build a stately Palace, encompassing sixteene miles of plaine ground with a wall, wherein are fertile Meddowes, pleasant Springs, delightful Streames, and all sorts of beasts of chase and game, and in the middest thereof a sumptuous house of pleasure, *which may be removed from place to place.*

Coleridge's summary of the passage he asserts he had been reading when he fell asleep may be ignored. Some twenty years had intervened between its composition and the experience it recorded. What it does do, however, is to make it possible to identify with precision the source in Purchas and the stages in which he retained a degree of consciousness of Purchas's words as he fell deeper and deeper asleep. (I have italicized the clause which he cannot have reached since it contradicts the account of the 'pleasure-dome' given in the poem.) The first two lines exemplify two stages in the departure from Purchas:

> In Xanadu did Kubla Khan
> (In Xamdu did Cubla Can *Purchas*)
> A stately pleasure-dome decree
> (build a stately Palace . . . house of pleasure *Purchas*)

Up to the word 'dome' there is nothing in Coleridge that is not in Purchas, though Coleridge was presumably mistaken in identifying the Khan's 'Palace' with the light and movable 'house of pleasure', the two words (*palace/pleasure*) becoming confused as he lost consciousness. The most obvious sign of a progress from common speech here is the introduction of metre. In l.1 Coleridge has changed 'Xamdu' to 'Xanadu' and 'Cublai' to 'Kubla', so turning five words of prose into an iambic tetrameter; the change into verse accentuates the stressed syllables and in the process creates internal rhymes (*Xan/Khan, -du/Ku-*). The second stage, one of greater independence from Purchas, is only reached at the dome, a favourite in Romantic poetic diction.[1] There is now, the reader discovers, repeated emphatic short-interval alliteration added at the end of both lines (*Kubla Khan, dome decree*) as well as lesser half-rhymes and internal alliteration. In sum, the prose has acquired pattern. Although the paraphrasable content of both passages is almost

[1] See G. Wilson Knight, *The Sacred Dome* (1941).

identical, the total verbal effect has been completely transformed by this imposition of what Mackail called 'repeats'.

A second example of the transformation of prose into poetry is the first two lines of T. S. Eliot's 'Gerontion';

> Here I am, an old man in a dry month,
> Being read to by a boy, waiting for rain.

Eliot admitted publicly in 1938 that the lines were 'lifted bodily from a life of Edward Fitzgerald' in the English Men of Letters series.[1] In *Edward FitzGerald* (1905) in this series, A. C. Benson had summarized a letter from FitzGerald (p. 142) as follows:

> Here he sits, in a dry month, old and blind, being read to by a country boy, longing for rain.

In this case as in 'Kubla Khan' the first change is from prose to verse (decasyllabic blank verse), but the third person has also become the first person, the words 'blind' and 'country' have been omitted and 'longing' has become 'waiting'. Two internal rhymes derive from these changes (*I/dry, wai-/rai-*), and in the second line the latent alliteration both with *-ing* and with *b* is accentuated.

The change from commonplace prose into verse of great distinction introduces a more fundamental level of change – that of genre. Detached from its context in Purchas, Kubla's project in landscape-gardening was potential ballad material. Compare 'In Scarlet town where I was born' (*Barbara Allen*), or the following openings of ballads in Percy's *Reliques of Ancient Poetry* (1765), with some at least of which Coleridge was familiar:

> In Ireland, ferr over the sea . . . (*Sir Cauline*)
>
> The king sits in Dumferling toune . . . (*Sir Patrick Spence*)
>
> On yonder hill a castle standes . . . (*The Child of Elle*)
>
> In Carleile dwelt king Arthur . . . (*The Boy and the Mantle*)

A ballad has a habit of localizing itself by beginning 'In' or 'On', and Coleridge was already a ballad-connoisseur when he began

[1] See Eliot's article in *Purpose*, 10 (1938), 93. The mis-spelling 'Fitzgerald' has again been corrected.

reading Purchas. ('The Ancient Mariner' followed only a month or two after 'Kubla Khan'.) It was natural therefore for Purchas's words 'In Xamdu did Cubla Can . . .' to suggest to the drowsy reader that he was back in a favourite genre, the 'In' being confirmed by the 'did', an 'expletive', as Pope called it, that had been banished from polite poetry. The first five lines of 'Kubla Khan' are also metrically a ballad stanza. It is true that other genres intrude later, including an echo of *Paradise Lost* in 'Mount Abora' ('Amora' corrected to 'Amara' in the Crewe MS.); Milton has 'Mount Amara' (*Paradise Lost*, iv, 281). But the poem begins as ballad because this is the genre that the source had suggested and the style is continually reverting to the ballad, 'For he on honey-dew hath fed' actually anticipating 'The other was a softer voice, / As soft as honey-dew' of 'The Ancient Mariner' (ll. 406–7).

The virtual identity of the first two lines of 'Gerontion' and the passage in A. C. Benson's book on FitzGerald raises similar questions of genre. Benson's book is competent and inoffensive, but it is at best superior non-literature. (The prickly problem of FitzGerald's homosexuality is evaded altogether.) But the change from Benson's prose to Eliot's blank verse, and from Benson's third person to Eliot's first person, takes us into a different world, a world that is unquestionably literature. The words become more emphatic, more semi-audible – and also, from their detachment by Eliot from the preceding sentences in A. C. Benson's book, more unexpected. Why should a boy be reading to him? Who is the boy and why is there no reference to him later in the poem? Why above all is the old man waiting for rain? No climatic or agricultural explanation is suggested. The reader finds himself introduced into a dramatic situation that invites symbolic explanation but does not receive it; the reader must do his best to explain it unaided by the author.

The genre of 'Gerontion', as of several of Eliot's earlier poems, is the dramatic monologue. The models in the later part of the poem are clearly the soliloquies of Shakespeare and of such Jacobean successors as Webster, Tourneur and Middleton; but 'Gerontion' begins under the influence of Browning. In a dramatic monologue the author's own personality is intentionally concealed behind a mask or 'persona' (the Latin word for mask), and, though the first person singular has to be used, a distinction between the poet's 'I' (generally unspoken if inevitably implied) and the persona's 'I' must be made as soon as possible in the poem and as completely as possible. Many of Browning's most successful poems make such a distinction both in their titles and in their opening lines. For example:

> That's my last Duchess, painted on the wall . . . (*My Last Duchess*)
>
> My first thought was, he lied in every word . . . (*Childe Roland to the Dark Tower came*)
>
> I am a Goddess of the ambrosial courts . . . (*Artemis Prologizes*)
>
> I am poor brother Lippo, by your leave . . . (*Fra Lippo Lippi*)

Though it is difficult to be certain why the one sentence from A. C. Benson's book adhered like sticking-plaster, almost word for word, in Eliot's memory, its suggestiveness as the opening lines of a dramatic monologue of the Browning type is clear. There is an 'I' in the first line, but as 'Gerontion' was written in 1919, when Eliot would have been thirty or thirty-one, he was not *autobiographically* 'an old man', and as he was living in London at the time 'a dry month' cannot be taken quite literally. The monologuist's character can be allowed to develop in a medley of cultural references without the possible relevance of any of the details to Eliot himself[1] occurring to the reader. That the speaker was a dramatic figure not to be identified with the author is evident from among other passages, the third line in which the 'little old man' (the literal meaning of the Greek γερόντιον)[2] admits that he had not been 'at the hot gates' (the

[1] *The Waste Land*, on the other hand, is cryptically though irregularly autobiographical. See John Peter, *Essays in Criticism*, 2 (1952), 242 ff. Eliot had proposed at one point prefixing 'Gerontion' to *The Waste Land* as its first section but was dissuaded by Ezra Pound (*Letters*, 1907–41, ed. D. D. Paige, 1951, pp. 236–7).

[2] Eliot's knowledge of Greek, like that of his mentor Ezra Pound, was very superficial. The word is relatively rare in classical Greek and may have been lifted from Aristophanes (*Acharnians*, l. 993).

literal meaning of Thermopylae). The 'cutlass' of l. 5[1] has the same effect of adding to a chronological and geographical phantasmagoria, and the combination of realism with fantasy suggests a monologue that is more French than English. (Gérard de Nerval's 'El Desdichado' provided l. 429 of *The Waste Land.*)

Delusion and illusion

The preceding analysis has revolved around two dominant concepts: style as 'good English', and style as the superimposition by 'repeats' in one or more literary 'genres' upon verbal material that is not literary at all. The *tertium quid* of subject-matter, content as opposed to form, has been held in reserve. But if we now turn to it the stylized subject-matter will also be found to have changed from what it was in the source. Purchas's account of Cublai's summer palace and gardens has ceased to be historical fact, the sort of event we may encounter in a newspaper, and from the reader's point of view it has entered into another form of reality. Kubla, the pleasure-dome and the gardens acquire for us the reality of an ideal world, the reality of, for example, figures like Agamemnon, Don Quixote or Sherlock Holmes, which is parallel to but not identical with the reality of, say, Pericles and Winston Churchill. What is the technical process by which this secondary or aesthetic reality is created for us?

Coleridge evaded the metaphysical difficulties of the problem in the convenient psychological formula that he used to distinguish Wordsworth's contributions to *Lyrical Ballads* from his own. All that he claimed for 'The Ancient Mariner', much the most important poem in the volume, was 'a semblance of truth sufficient to procure for these shadows of imagination that willing suspension of disbelief for the moment, which constitutes poetic faith'.[2] The concept of a 'willing suspension of disbelief' had its apologetic uses for a man as theologically committed as Coleridge was, but it has the serious disadvantage of describing a positive condition in negative terms. The reader of great literature does not momentarily or voluntarily suspend a dis-

[1] To us today a *cutlass* is primarily a sword used by an eighteenth-century pirate (see *OED*).

[2] *Biographia Literaria*, Ch. 14.

belief. He goes to the classics of literature because they have something positive of value to tell him. The fictions of literature are not just 'a semblance of truth' but a symbolic mode of statement that communicates intersubjective truths not otherwise publicly available.

Some such symbolic assumption underlies language in all its uses. Metaphor, however, is the clearest case of the 'suspension of disbelief' if that condition is considered positively. When we speak of the 'arm' or the 'leg' of a chair we are not committing ourselves to a temporary mis-statement; we are *using* the resemblance of these parts of a chair to the human arm or leg as an economical way of describing an aspect of physical reality for which the language cannot supply other words. Literature is metaphoric in a similar sense: it facilitates a commentary on human behaviour which is more effective, more concentrated, more 'intense', than common speech can provide. Moreover, whereas the more or less dead metaphors that speech uses generally refer back when decoded to some aspect of *physical* reality – such as the parts of a chair – literature prefers to use the more complex metaphors which refer back to the human condition or to an aspect of human society.

A metaphor is not strictly 'true' (chairs do not have knees or calves or toes). The literary equivalent of such pragmatic validity is the condition conventionally, and conveniently, known as 'illusion'. Coleridge does not use the term in this technical sense in *Biographia Literaria,* but he has a useful passage in the 'Notes on *The Tempest*' on the distinction between delusion and illusion:[1]

> I find two extremes of critical decision; the French, which evidently presupposes that a perfect delusion is to be aimed at, – an opinion which needs no fresh confutation; and the exact opposite to it, brought forward by Dr. Johnson, who supposes the auditors throughout in the full reflective knowledge of the contrary. In evincing the impossibility of delusion, he makes no sufficient allowance for an intermediate state, which I have before distinguished by the term, illusion, and have attempted to illustrate its

[1] *Coleridge's Shakespearean Criticism,* ed. T. M. Raysor (Cambridge, Mass.), 128–9.

> quality and character by reference to our mental state, when dreaming. In both cases we simply do not judge the imagery to be unreal; there is a negative reality, and no more. Whatever, therefore, tends to prevent the mind from placing itself, or being placed, gradually in the state in which the images have such negative reality for the auditor, destroys the illusion, and is dramatically improbable.

The 'French' delusion had been derived by their seventeenth-century critics from Castelvetro, the Italian prophet of the Three Unities in his edition of Aristotle's *Poetics* (Basle, 1576) as well as to some extent from the elder Scaliger, another Italian, whose own *Poetices Libri Septem* (Lyons, 1561) is the most elaborate exposition of general neo-classic critical theory. Coleridge's reference to Johnson here is to the preface of his edition of Shakespeare (1765), which had effectively disposed of the theoretical necessity of the Three Unities, though it ignored their entirely proper thematic uses.[1] The 'intermediate state' of 'illusion' Coleridge had borrowed, with so much of his other theoretical baggage, from the Germans. As early as 1766, before Coleridge had even been born, Lessing had made most of the essential points in the *Laokoön*. A typical passage in Robert Phillimore's Victorian translation (1874) runs as follows:

> The poet wishes not only to be intelligible, . . . the poet desires to make the ideas which he awakens in us so vivid, that from the rapidity with which they arise we believe ourselves to be really as conscious of his subjects as if they were actually presented to our senses; and in this moment of illusion we cease to be conscious of the means – that is, of the words – which he employs for this purpose.
>
> (Chapter xvii)

Repetition the means to illusion

What neither Lessing nor Coleridge attempted to explain was the technical basis of illusion, though a hint of it is suggested by

[1] Thus Barrie's *Admirable Crichton* depends on the change of place from Mayfair to the Pacific Island; Arnold Bennett's *Milestones* – a collaboration with E. Knoblock – hinges on changes of time for three generations exhibited in sequence.

Lessing's term 'rapidity' in the passage just quoted. How is it that the theatrical spectator, or even the mere reader, is persuaded to lose consciousness of the poet's words and believe himself to be actually seeing and hearing the objects that the words denote? How have the words become things – not as in a hallucination but as in a dream? In the note prefixed to 'Kubla Khan' Coleridge informs us that 'all the images rose up before him as things, with a parallel production of the correspondent expressions, without any sensation or consciousness of effort'; for the reader of literature in a state of illusion the words also rise up as images without any consciousness of effort. But how is this effected?

No doubt something similar occurs whenever speech is interchanged. A passing motorist asks where the nearest garage is. And an image of the nearest garage presents itself internally to his informant without any conscious effort and with the appropriate words following. But in literature, as Lessing pointed out, there must be an addition of the quality that he called vividness, though memorability might seem a better term. Why does literature differ from common speech in this crucial additional quality? It is at this point that style enters the argument. Vividness or memorability is the result of a conglomeration of devices of style within the literary text. The two examples analysed in some detail earlier in this chapter – from 'Kubla Khan' and 'Gerontion' – are typical of the process. In them the closeness of the non-literary sources to the final texts makes it possible to point to the synthetic effect of some comparatively trivial changes. The various metrical and stylistic effects rub against each other, as it were, and so ensure Lessing's 'vividness'.

If the ultimate function of style is to induce the symbolic condition in which words seem to assume the property of human things, 'significant' human situations or problems, its method is to use language so that the constituents of each word, phrase, sentence or larger unit are repeated as often as is compatible with intelligibility and the avoidance of monotony. Mackail's 'repeats', in the epigraph to this chapter, will be remembered. Metre is perhaps the simplest example of the phenomenon. In a poem stanza follows stanza, each with the same rhyme-scheme and the same number of syllables within the line. (In addition to syllabic regularity, and often overriding it in the best English poetry, the line may no doubt sacrifice its pattern of stresses to a recurrence of total stress-weight.)[1] Single words may often be repeated almost to excess:

> Alone, alone and all alone,
> Alone on the wide, wide sea.

Phrases or phrase-patterns may also be repeated or reversed in much the same way, especially in poetry:

> though fall'n on evil dayes,
> On evil dayes though fall'n, and evil tongues
> (*Paradise Lost*, vii, 25–6)

With metaphor, allegory, irony and ambiguity we are at the heart of the figures of speech, and every statement, however brief or extended, will now have a double or triple sense. Literature cannot exist without such an extra dimension of meaning whereas most non-literature prefers meaning that is direct and unambiguous. (Lawyers make a living out of the common man's verbal uncertainties.) Further stylistic complexities are provided by conscious or unconscious imitation, formal quotations or the 'topos' (conventional literary subject-matter, such as the medieval May morning or the neo-classic description of night).

'Movement' and genre

This is not the place for a catalogue of the various devices of style. (The Renaissance rhetorics listed over a hundred 'colours', or figures, of speech alone.) Their critical interest depends upon the adherence to or breach of the particular 'kind' or genre used and the attitude to the subject-matter in the literary object

[1] Modern prosodists prefer to scan by four degrees of stress instead of the conventional two degrees of stress, with the iamb consisting (in English) of an unstressed syllable followed by a stressed syllable. See E. L. Epstein and Terence Hawkes, *Linguistics and English Prosody* (Buffalo, 1959). It will be found that one line in a couplet only balances the other if the total number of quarter-stresses is the same in each, a full stress counting for purposes of scansion as four stresses. For an example from Keats's 'Ode to a Nightingale' see p. 120 below.

under investigation. A further complication is the particular 'school' or 'movement' to which the work and its author happen to belong and the exact time of its composition. The three factors interlock to determine the nature of the style. Thus the drowning of Edward King, a Fellow of Christ's College, Cambridge, and the son of an Anglo-Irish grandee, 'provoked' the writing of 'Lycidas' in 1637. In the pathetic circumstances a pastoral elegy was the appropriate genre, models of which were available to Milton in Vergil, Spenser and others. But the indignant and egocentric intrusions in the poem, which are principally responsible for its memorability, can only be explained in the light of Milton's reaction to more general trends in English poetry and in the politics of the time. The classical and Renaissance concept of 'decorum' – which Milton himself described in *Of Education* as 'the grand master peece to observe' in literature[1] – made subject-matter the basis of genre, with genre then determining the medium (a choice of verse or prose, for example, each with its appropriate subdivisions of metre, diction, structure, etc.). But the formula was one that could not be applied mechanically because of the special circumstances relevant in each case. Milton was right not to be exclusively concerned with Edward King; his case raised that of 'our corrupted clergy then in their height'.

The advice that Walsh gave the young Pope was to make neo-classic regularity his constant 'study and aim' ('for though we had several great poets, we never had any one great poet that was correct').[2] What neither Walsh (whose intelligent Preface to his own *Letters and Poems*, 1692, also emphasizes decorum or 'propriety' as the poetic golden rule) nor Pope fully realized was that this criterion was necessarily flexible, varying to some extent from generation to generation and to a lesser degree from one poet to another.

[1] *Complete Prose Works* (New Haven, 1959), II, 405.

[2] Conversation with Pope in 1742; reported by Joseph Spence in his *Observations, Anecdotes and Characters of Books and Men* (ed. J. M. Osborn, 2 vols, 1966), I, 32. R. M. Schmitz (*Pope's Windsor Forest, 1712*, St Louis, 1952, p. 65) concludes after a careful analysis that Pope found it impossible to revise 'with one single view at a time'. But that this was the neo-classic impossible ideal remains true.

Pope's own practice, at least as he explained it to an admirer, was painfully conscientious:[1]

> After writing a poem one should correct it all over with one single view at a time. Thus for language, if an elegy: 'these lines are very good, but are not they of too heroical a strain?' and so vice versa . . .

Except in the shortest of poems, or in brief aphoristic prose, Pope's method might seem to ensure a guarantee of insipidity, and except in the early *Pastorals* he did not in fact adhere to the strict neo-classic law. What the doctrine of decorum really requires is a dominant level of style which will be primarily determined by genre (in the sense of attitude to subject-matter), but with the dominant style always capable of admitting other attitudes and stylistic levels. And this was in fact Pope's later practice. Without such infusions there will be no opposites to balance or discordancies to reconcile.

A comment by Yeats on the function of metre will be worth quoting here because of its wider implications:[2]

> The purpose of rhythm, it has always seemed to me, is to prolong the moment of contemplation, the moment when we are both asleep and awake, which is the one moment of creation, by hushing us with an alluring monotony, while it holds us waking by variety, to keep us in that state of perhaps real trance, in which the mind liberated from the pressure of the will is unfolded in symbols. If certain sensitive persons listen persistently to the ticking of a watch, or gaze persistently on the monotonous flashing of a light, they fall into the hypnotic trance; and rhythm is but the ticking of a watch made softer, that one must needs listen, and various, that one may not be swept beyond memory or grow weary of listening.

Yeats's psychological speculations, though no doubt mistaken (the essay was written in 1900), at least connect plausibly with the basic function of repetition not only in metre but in literature generally. According to Yeats, the use of rhythm is to combine 'an alluring monotony' (which sends us half to sleep) and a

[1] Joseph Spence, *Observations, Anecdotes and Characters of Books and Men*, I, 171.

[2] *Essays* (1924), pp. 195–6.

compensating 'variety' which will 'hold us waking'. Much the same would be true of all literature, though particularly of poetry, where an excess of repetition, as in much of Swinburne, has an almost hypnotic effect, though even Swinburne provides sufficient variety – by perversity or blasphemy – to ensure that the reader will go on reading. And whatever Yeats may or may not have meant by 'the moment of contemplation' and 'perhaps real trance', it is clear that the 'repeat' and the avoidance of repetition are each other's opposite which are yet somehow to be balanced.

Prose style

Hitherto the examples cited have all been from poetry. Good prose is less prone to flowers of speech, though examples are in fact available. Lord Acton's dictum about power – 'Power tends to corrupt and absolute power corrupts absolutely' (*Letter to Bishop Mandell Creighton*, 1887) – may be compared with Milton's 'though fall'n on evil dayes, / On evil dayes though fall'n'. Such inverted repetitions were called by the rhetoricians an *antimetabole*, which was itself a variant on the *chiasmus* in which the same words are not inverted but only the same parts of speech, as in the last line of 'Lycidas' (*chiasmus* in italics):

> Tomorrow to *fresh Woods*, and *Pastures new*.

(Here adjective plus noun is followed by noun plus adjective.)

One of the surprises in George Orwell's essay 'Why I Write' is that this master of prosaic prose – with Shaw perhaps the best English writer of pure prose of the first half of the twentieth century – underwent a similar 'conversion' to poetry 'about sixteen' that Eliot had had 'at the age of fourteen or so' from the accidental discovery of FitzGerald's *Omar*.[1] Orwell describes his own metamorphosis as due to a discovery of 'the joy of mere words, *i.e.* the sounds and associations of words'.[2] The example he gives of the kind of mere words that 'sent shivers down my backbone' is, as it happens, another *antimetabole* from *Paradise Lost*. As quoted by Orwell the lines (*PL*, ii, 1031–2) run:

[1] See p. 4 above.

[2] *Collected Essays* (1961), p. 421. The essay was written in 1947 and published in book form in *Shooting an Elephant* (1950).

So hee with difficulty and labour hard
Moved on: with difficulty and labour hee.

Orwell comments that 'the spelling "hee" for "he" was an added pleasure'. The quotation is correct except that all the early editions (and the modern reprints from them) only spell the second *he* with a double *e.*[1] They also have 'mov'd' for Orwell's 'moved' and a comma for his colon. It is apparent that Orwell was quoting from an affectionately retentive memory – in spite of the dismissive 'which do not now seem to me so very wonderful' that follows in his essay. The adult Orwell was probably wrong. Milton's fondness for *antimetabole, chiasmus* and similar figures (such as the noun immediately preceded by one adjective and then immediately followed by another, e.g. 'human face divine', *PL*, iii, 44) reflects a basic but harmonious dualism both in the *man* (a Puritan Humanist) and in his attitudes to his *dramatis personae.* The Lady *balances* Comus, Satan *balances* God, Eve *balances* Adam. (It is true the intersubjective dualism in English society was less harmonious, though by modern standards the Civil War was an oddly good-tempered family quarrel.)[2] In any case the gap between Milton's verse and Orwell's prose can easily be exaggerated. The climax in *Animal Farm* is the discovery by the rebellious animals that their Seven Commandments have been whittled down to 'All animals are equal but some animals are more equal than others', a paradox which might well be called a figure of speech. It has the incisive memorability of poetry adjusted to modern political conditions.

The novel is the genre most remote from 'style', in the sense of the best words in the best order. Coleridge's definition of prose

[1] The first edition known to me with the spelling 'hee' in l. 1021 is that by Helen Darbishire (1952). Her emendation was made on the assumption that the word is stressed and that Milton had intended every stressed *me, he, we,* and *ye* (but not, significantly, *she*) to be spelled with a double *e*. The evidence she assembles is inconclusive, and Orwell is unlikely to have known of Miss Darbishire's views before the publication of her edition. He died in 1950.

[2] According to John Aubrey, George Wither, a Parliamentarian poet, was once taken prisoner by the Royalists 'and was in danger of his life'. Sir John Denham saved him on the plea that while Wither lived 'he should not be the worst poet in England' (*Brief Lives*, ed. Anthony Powell, 1949, p. 83).

as 'words in the best order'[1] seems to reduce the difference from poetry to one of vocabulary and so to ignore completely the importance of the novelist's *le mot juste*. In a later elaboration of the distinction Coleridge is more explicit:[2]

> The words in prose ought to express the intended meaning, and no more; if they attract attention to themselves, it is, in general, a fault. In the very best styles, as Southey's, you read page after page, understanding the author perfectly, without once taking notice of the medium of communication; it is as if he had been speaking to you all the while.

Here Coleridge's analogy with speech invites the obvious objection that conversation is not monologue but dialogue. Coleridge has therefore to add that the 'unity' which limits the degree to which the words of poetry can call attention to themselves is equally necessary in prose. In the case of a book like Southey's *Life of Nelson* the unity is imposed by the subject-matter, but a novel is not a pseudo-biography. Coleridge was a great novel-reader, Jane Austen being one of his favourites, but his definition of prose does not quite cover the case of the novel. Strictly speaking, it does not even cover the general category of prose. The crux of the problem is that repetition or duplication, a heading that seems to include all of poetry's devices of style, appears to be resisted by all non-poetic prose and in particular by the novel. Whereas a poem welcomes the 'repeat' – Blake's 'The Tyger', in addition to metre and the initial 'Tyger, tyger, burning bright', has a series of thirteen rhetorical questions beginning 'What' – prose evades it as far as possible. (For a writer of prose 'Queen Victoria' tends to become successively 'she', 'The Queen', 'the monarch', etc.) Roget's *Synonym* is a useful crutch therefore for the clumsy writer of prose; a poet never consults it.

But Coleridge was right nevertheless in requiring 'unity' in the prosaic literary object. The stylistic devices of prose are less prominent than those in poetry, and they vary from one prose genre to another. In the novel, for instance, a repeated use of dialogue often balances the use of description or *oratio obliqua*.

[1] *Specimens of the Table-Talk* (1835), I, 84.
[2] *Ibid.*, II, 214.

The frequent recurrence of proper names too, both of the actors and of the place where the action takes place, is another standard stylistic device in the novel. Unlike poetry, in which the names normally describe as well as denominating, a proper name in a novel is not expected to point beyond itself. Such names as Allworthy, Squire Western, Thwackum and Square in *Tom Jones* are survivals from Restoration comedy with its self-explanatory type-characters. The recurrent constituents of the strictly realistic novel are implicit, almost unnoticed, but an adherence to them is necessary for the style to be that proper to the novel.

The words in a novel must not call attention to themselves for exactly the same reason that its author must be self-effacing: the genre forbids it. A novel must create the illusion of telling itself. Analysis, however, will detect in its neutral style a process of repetition that is comparable with the synthetic devices of poetry. The main source of a novel's unity is the consistency of its particularity (which includes the proper names); the particularity is a signal of the genre. We are invited to concentrate our attention on a series of concrete objects and differentiated individuals whose authenticity seems to be guaranteed by their apparently recognizable familiarity. But the series, as it progresses in time, which is both reader's time and novel's time, develops an implicit pattern which may, perhaps should, finally conceptualize itself. (The titles sometimes attempt it: *Pride and Prejudice, Crime and Punishment, The Sound and the Fury.*) It must be added that by the time conceptualization occurs the novel has ceased to be a novel, except in retrospect. At this point the critical reader has turned to the third stage described by Coleridge in *Biographia Literaria.* Having separated the distinguished parts, those that are explicitly concrete and those that are implicitly abstract, synthesis restores them 'in our conceptions to the unity, in which they actually co-exist'.[1]

A short story will illustrate the characteristic style of realistic prose fiction better than a full-length novel because nothing

[1] See p. 59 above. David Lodge's *Language of Fiction* (1966) can be recommended to the reader who is interested in this approach. An exposition of modern theories of the novel is followed by discussions of *Mansfield Park, Jane Eyre, Hard Times, Tess, The Ambassadors, Tono-Bungay,* and the novels of Kingsley Amis.

essential need be omitted. Some short stories are, of course, shorter than others, but Katherine Mansfield's 'The Fly', written in February 1922 and included in *The Garden Party and Other Stories* (1922), is probably the shortest *good* short story in English. Although only some 2,000 words long it does not achieve greatness until its second half, which is here given verbatim. The first half, however, has supplied some indispensable information and must therefore be summarized briefly.

The story begins with a call that a retired London businessman called Woodifield pays on a friend of his who is referred to throughout as 'the boss'. Woodifield has had a stroke and his frail condition is contrasted vividly with the hearty geniality of the boss, who is in fact five years his elder. It is the boss's office however, not the boss, which is described in the most significant detail. Over the table a photograph hangs of a boy in uniform, who we learn later had been killed in the 1914–18 War six years before.

Woodifield's daughters have just returned from Belgium where they had seen the boss's son's grave, as well as that of their own brother. For 'various reasons' the boss had not seen his son's grave, and Woodifield's news seems to distress him acutely. The reader's curiosity has been aroused. When Woodifield leaves, the boss orders Macey, the office messenger, not to admit anybody for half an hour. 'He wanted, he intended, he had arranged to weep. . . .' But the tears refuse to come – in spite of the boss reminding himself how popular the boy, his only son, had been in the office and what a natural successor he would have been to himself in the business that he himself had worked so hard to build up. Puzzled, he gets up to look once again at the photograph.

Katherine Mansfield can now be allowed to take over:

> At that moment the boss noticed that a fly had fallen into his broken inkpot, and was trying feebly but desperately to clamber out again. Help! help! said those struggling legs. But the sides of the inkpot were wet and slippery; it fell back again and began to swim. The boss took up a pen, picked the fly out of the ink, and shook it onto a piece of blotting paper. For a fraction of a second it lay still on the dark patch that oozed round it. Then the front legs waved,

took hold, and, pulling its small sodden body up, it began the immense task of cleaning the ink from its wings. Over and under, over and under, went a leg along a wing, as the stone goes over and under the scythe. Then there was a pause, while the fly, seeming to stand on the tips of its toes, tried to expand first one wing and then the other. It succeeded at last, and, sitting down, it began, like a minute cat, to clean its face. Now one could imagine that the little front legs rubbed against each other lightly, joyfully. The horrid danger was over, it had escaped; it was ready for life again.

But just then the boss had an idea. He plunged his pen back into the ink, leaned his thick wrist on the blotting paper, and as the fly tried its wings down came a great heavy blot. What would it make of that? What indeed! The little beggar seemed absolutely cowed, stunned, and afraid to move because of what would happen next. But then, as if painfully, it dragged itself forward. The front legs waved, caught hold, and more slowly this time, the task began from the beginning.

'He's a plucky little devil', thought the boss, and he felt a real admiration for the fly's courage. That was the way to tackle things; that was the right spirit. Never say die; it was only a question of. . . . But the fly had again finished its laborious task, and the boss had just time to refill his pen, to shake fair and square on the new-cleaned body yet another dark drop. What about it this time? A painful moment of suspense followed. But behold, the front legs were again waving; the boss felt a rush of relief. He leaned over the fly and said to it tenderly, 'You artful little b. . . .' And he actually had the brilliant notion of breathing on it to help the drying process. All the same, there was something timid and weak about its efforts now, and the boss decided that this time should be the last, as he dipped the pen into the inkpot.

It was. The last blot fell on the soaked blotting paper, and the draggled fly lay in it and did not stir. The back legs were stuck to the body; the front legs were not to be seen.

'Come on', said the boss. 'Look sharp!' And he stirred it

> with his pen – in vain. Nothing happened or was likely to happen. The fly was dead.
>
> The boss lifted the corpse on the end of the paper knife and flung it into the wastepaper basket, but such a grinding feeling of wretchedness seized him that he felt positively frightened. He started forward and pressed the bell for Macey.
>
> 'Bring me some fresh blotting paper', he said, sternly, 'and look sharp about it.' And while the old dog padded away he fell to wondering what it was he had been thinking about before. What was it? It was . . . He took out his handkerchief and passed it inside his collar. For the life of him he could not remember.

The passage is dense with implications which Katherine Mansfield has rightly refused to make explicit. After her death her husband (the critic Middleton Murry) said, no doubt correctly, that 'the profound and ineradicable impression made upon her by the War . . . found perfect utterance in the last year of her life in the story "The Fly" ',[1] but it would be a critical error to say that the War was what the story was about. The 1914–18 War was no doubt one ingredient in this story; her own fight against the tuberculosis that was about to kill her was another; her dislike of her father, a New Zealand banker, was probably a third. There are two words that recur more often than might be expected in normal prose, 'the boss' (used twenty-five times) and 'the fly' (used ten times, including its use in the title of the story). And the most significant comment on the two unequally matched antagonists comes at the end of the story, when the boss 'took out his handkerchief and passed it inside his collar'. The mighty boss is sweating from exhaustion after the battle with the fly. As he has also forgotten what he had been thinking about before it – the son's death which had once provoked a genuine if selfish emotion in the coarse fibre of his being – we can be allowed to wonder what that 'grinding feeling of wretchedness' was caused by. Was it partly a realization that the boss himself was a mere animal, one inferior morally even to a housefly? If so, the conclusion is one that the reader has reached for himself on the basis of the carefully selected particulars presented to him. It has not been imposed by the

[1] *Journal of Katherine Mansfield* (1954 ed.), p. 107.

author as Thackerary, for example, might have tried to impose it.

Note on stylistics

Stylistics begins with Charles Bally,[1] Saussure's successor in the chair of General Linguistics at the University of Geneva. Because of its origins in structural linguistics it has been limited to what Saussure called the 'synchronic' study of style, although there seems no reason why the 'diachronic' approach (historical linguistics) might not be more useful to the literary student. A study of what has already been accomplished, especially on the Continent, will be found in Graham Hough's short and lucid *Style and Stylistics* (1969), which has a bibliography with short pertinent comments. The much fuller *Critical Bibliography of the New Stylistics* (Chapel Hill, 1953) by H. Hatzfeld, which is, however, confined to work in the Romance Languages, is useful as an indication of what may be hoped from stylistics generally. The most elaborate attempt I know to define the new discipline is that by N. E. Enkvist in *Linguistics and Style* (ed. J. Spencer, 1964), but the unhappy conclusion that seems to emerge from it is that the professional linguist has very little to contribute to style considered as the *best* words in the *best* order. (The exclusion of any 'value' except the number of each linguistic occurrence seems to be a fatal limitation.) Certainly the symposia in which critics and linguists have both joined, such as *Style in Language* (ed. T. A. Sebeok, New York, 1960) and *Essays on Style and Language* (ed. R. Fowler, 1966), have not been encouraging. And the occasional attempts by linguists to attempt the practical criticism of a single lyric or passage of prose have been uniformly disastrous. For the time being it seems that a linguistics-based stylistics can be ignored by the literary student. (Wellek's chapter in *Theory of Literature* on 'Style and Stylistics' does precisely that.)

[1] *Traité de stylistique française* (Heidelberg, 1902); *Précis de stylistique* (Geneva, 1905). Bally's main concern was with the emotive elements in language.

FIVE

INTERPRETATION

The literary cycle

The two preceding chapters have concentrated on the literary object as a datum, and the responses to it to which every serious reader of literature is necessarily committed. In addition, there are certain specialized modes of research to which he may have to resort from time to time. (Some of these are described in later chapters of this book.) But the question to be answered now is: 'What is the central activity in which the scholar-critic is engaged in the process of literary research?' The answer to this question is, I suppose, 'Interpretation'. A successful interpretation requires both scholarship and criticism, each modifying the other, a minute and comprehensive factual accuracy interacting with stringent and distinguished evaluative criticism. In its ideal form, then, the interpretative procedure is necessarily one of considerable delicacy and complexity, the initial difficulty being that, whereas a professional interpreter simply translates (or provides an oral précis) from one language into another, a literary interpretation extends into the pre-linguistic and post-linguistic origins, meanings, implications and consequences of the artifact. Moreover, though the various levels of meaning have their separate conventional pigeon-holes, in practice the differences are only approximately distinguishable and the distinctions vary or overlap from work to work and from author to author. The traditional assumption which as we have seen[1] I. A. Richards must be given the credit for exposing in *Practical Criticism* has been that each reader of a poem – or of any other

[1] See pp. 67–8 above.

literary artifact – is reading the same poem. In fact, only some readers read the same poem.

In a test I once conducted in a small class for seniors and graduate students at one of the best American universities, the word 'Avon', an obvious reference to Shakespeare, was thought to be a magical poison by one third of the students. (The context had apparently misled them.) Three of them actually thought that 'Eve' – a commonplace poeticism for 'even' (evening), but in this case occurring at the beginning of a line and so receiving an initial capital – was Adam's Eve! Such misreadings made it difficult for the students to make coherent sense of the passages where they occurred and provoked the strangest and most intimately subjective interpretation.[1] But such misinterpretations are not always a matter of sheer incompetence, as *Practical Criticism* often seems to imply. An expert linguist may be unaware of the stylistic associations of a particular word or phrase – or of the literary genre or 'movement' that the author is using or is a member of. Equally, of course, as with my American students and in some of the 'protocols' of *Practical Criticism,* a reader with genuine literary sense may mistake the meaning of a rare word or an odd grammatical construction.

Such misreadings are incomplete rather than necessarily careless or stupid. A work of literature is a temporal artifact and at each moment of its assimilation by the competent reader a complex temporal process occurs that can be compared with the increasingly conscious spatial response demanded by a painting or a statue. It follows that, to interpret a work of literature with justice, we must describe a series or sequence of psychological experiences, the sum of which will constitute its full meaning as an aesthetic unit. To begin a play with Act II – or to walk out of the theatre at the start of Act V – is obviously a glaring offence against its temporal unity; but the principle also applies 'vertically', as it were, in a more complete sense. This is what I like to call the literary cycle.

[1] The test-piece was the extract of fifteen lines from Landor's *Gebir* which Richards discusses in *Speculative Instruments* (1955), pp. 181–97. In *Practical Criticism* Richards had prudently not given his own presumably correct interpretations; with the Landor lines he does so but commits his own error of omission in not recognizing the autobiographical as well as the Shakespearean reference in 'Avon'. Landor spent much of his boyhood near Warwick.

What is this literary cycle? A work of literature has a beginning, historically and aesthetically, with its original conception by the author. Until a certain point in time it did not exist, even as an aesthetic embryo. At this pre-natal stage it is no more than a vaguely promising theme, an 'inspiration', a hunch, the working out of which will still be obscure to the author himself. But images and concepts will gradually accumulate in the author's mind around the original theme before any detailed verbalization occurs. The originating conception is implicit in some associated image *without being detached from it* – just as in a popular proverb such as 'Rolling stones gather no moss' we *see* the stones but only later *deduce* the social comment. We may agree to call such image/concepts semi-conscious 'symbols'. The next stage is the elucidation of this inchoate matter with the help of verbal patterns and 'repeats'. Words now enclose the artifact, though not necessarily in any strictly logical or grammatical order. The grammatical arrangements, even in 'inner speech', follow later but with their arrival the creative verbalization is already more or less complete, though later revision, the inclusion of an author's afterthoughts to complete the theme's expression, will still be possible. Under modern conditions the author will then alphabetize his oral artifact, recording it on paper in conventional spellings with punctuation marks inserted. The oral composition has now become a *text*, either in manuscript or at a still later stage in print, which in due course is 'published' by circulation in manuscript or in book form. The author may then himself forget the details of the preceding process, retaining eventually only a sense of satisfaction or dissatisfaction.

But this is only the first or authorial half of the literary cycle. Readers, or some sort of aural audience, are needed to complete it. In this second half of the cycle the reader repeats the writer's progress from the work's vague conception to its ultimate and often equally vague recollection – *but in exactly the reverse order.* Thus the reader *begins* with the black marks on white paper that the author (or his scribe or printer) has *ended* with. This phenomenon of exact reversal has tended too often to be taken for granted in literary theory. Its technical importance, however, as an aid to interpretation cannot be overstressed. As a guiding formula, an Ariadne's thread in the labyrinths of communication theory, it is the principle that the scholar-critic must continually return to. Even at the level of text, for example, one has always to ask if the reader's speed of mental transliteration is equalling or exceeding that of the author's speed of ideal transcription. Most writers tend to *interrupt* the essentially mechanical translation of oral meaning into letters and word, revising the aesthetic intention in the process of its alphabetization. A conscientious reader responds by mentally accepting and then deleting the author's revisions, not mechanically, but because he recognizes that they are superior, or at least add interesting shades of meaning to the artifact. Such perfectionism in the experienced reader presupposes a tabulation of variant readings or (preferably) the availability of facsimiles of the author's early manuscripts. Fortunately such facsimiles, especially in the case of the poets,[1] are now becoming increasingly numerous.

At the oral stage, the author who is known to have composed aloud, as Wordsworth always did,[2] or to have preferred to read or recite his poems to admiring friends as Keats, Tennyson and Swinburne did, calls for a more vocal reading than for those writers who compose in 'inner speech', in which the words on the page have only a semi-oral condition. A characteristic of 'inner speech' compositions is that little attempt is made, or need be made by the reader, to reproduce the exact pronunciation of proper names or of quotations from foreign languages. Even the author's English accent (Keats's Cockney, Tennyson's Lincolnshire growl) is no more than a curiosity. The modern reader of the *Canterbury Tales* will perhaps do his best to reproduce Chaucer's long vowels and final *-e* as Chaucer must be presumed to have pronounced them, because Chaucer wrote his poems for reading aloud to Richard II's Court or to gatherings of his friends. With *The Faerie Queene*, on the other hand, or *Paradise Lost*, such philological conscientiousness is quite unnecessary; these are 'inner speech' poems, to be read to the reader's inner

[1] Photographic facsimiles of the Ellesmere MS. of the *Canterbury Tales*, the Trinity MS. of Milton's earlier poems, Pope's *Windsor Forest* and the *Epistle to Bathurst*, and Blake's *Notebook* have already been published.

[2] See my *Wordsworth: a Re-interpretation* (2nd ed. 1956), pp. 187–91, for Wordsworth's 'bummings and booings' (as his peasant neighbours described them).

ear in Modern English, with only an occasional change of stress, or of the pronunciation of the vowel, to accommodate a Tudor or Stuart rhyme.

The reader's response is in a reverse direction – *from* the text, the sounds of speech, or the half-sounds of 'inner speech', and merging then into the meanings of words, clause and sentence. From the author's 'language' he now proceeds to his 'style', with 'style' bombarding him with its 'repeats' and other devices until his mind surrenders its consciousness of words as words to enter the world of symbolic 'illusion' which is the essential aesthetic condition. Finally, with the conclusion of this temporal reversal by the reader of the author's mental progress, the reader is left with a vague awareness of the artifact's basic 'theme'. It is at this point that interpretation ends and criticism begins.

The diagram on p. 106 may help to clarify the parallel processes of authorial composition and reader's response. Neither is complete without the other, and the scholar-critic's commentary on his chosen artifact will ideally assemble all that is known or can be inferred about its evolution at each level and on each side of the cycle. The 'vertical' analysis summarized above is also complemented, of course, by a 'horizontal' temporal progress, in which line follows line, symbol follows symbol, stylistic device follows stylistic device.

This 'horizontal' extension may at first seem to complicate enormously the commentator's task. In practice, however, it will generally be found that a 'vertical' analysis suggests the relevant questions that a 'horizontal' commentary is required to answer. This applies particularly to Stages 2 and 3 (symbol and style) in the 'Author' column and their correlative Stages 7 and 8 in the 'Reader' column.

The arrows in the diagram indicate the temporal direction (and the beginning and end) of the cycle. The point at which the two psychological streams reverse is at their point of conjunction in the text. Here the author's externalization of meaning is completed and the reader's processes of internalization begin.

The two columns are examples of the analytical process recommended by Coleridge on p. 59 above. They are separate parts intellectually distinguished in the search for an adequate notion, but once distinguished they must be restored to 'the unity in which they actually co-exist'. A caveat must therefore

Diagram of the literary cycle

AUTHOR	READER
1 Theme (author only semi-conscious)	9 Implicit or tentative evaluation of artifact as unit
2 Symbol (fusion of image and concept)	8 Deverbalization ('illusion' is now creating its own aesthetic reality, which a reader can describe)
3 Style (verbalization in 'repeats' of appropriate genre)	7 Style (recognition of genre and appropriate if often unconscious response to 'repeats')
4 Language (conventions of vocabulary and grammar superimposed, often muted in inner speech)	6 Language (standard meanings, usually translated into inner speech)

5 Text (language alphabetized in conventional spelling and punctuation)

be inserted, or two columns may prove to be dangerous models. A reader does not in fact limit himself to the almost passive process represented by Stages 6, 7, 8 and 9. In order to respond properly as reader he must be able to identify himself, at least to some degree, with the author at each of the various stages of composition, just as an author must be able to see himself as in part a reader if successful communication is to be possible between them. (Hence the frequency of textual revision – either by author or, as in folk-songs and ballads, by audience in the process of oral transmission.) The complexity of what a reader/author relationship requires no doubt explains the critical success of the Wimsatt/Beardsley 'Intentional Fallacy'. How much easier interpretation would become if the author could be ignored! But a work of literature, even an anonymous one, must in some sense always have had an author. Wimsatt and Beardsley do not deny it:[1]

[1] *The Verbal Icon* (Lexington, Kentucky), p. 4.

> A poem does not come into existence by accident. The words of a poem, as Professor Stoll has remarked, come out of a head, not out of a hat.

But they add a sinister corollary:

> Yet to insist on the designing intellect as a *cause* of a poem is not to grant the design or intention as a *standard* by which the critic is to judge the worth of the poet's performance.

The objection may seem reasonable, but the hypothesis of a literary cycle provides an immediate answer to it: the author's intention must be *supplemented* by the reader's response. A cause must be presumed; it is certainly not limited to an author's intentions, but those intentions cannot be excluded altogether.

What was intended may or may not be adequately expressed, or buried in its totality in a dead man's skull, but it is always a relevant factor, one which must be guessed as intelligently as possible if it cannot be ascertained by conclusive evidence. Wimsatt and Beardsley substitute for an author's intention the public evidence provided by language and human nature in general:[1]

> The poem belongs to the public. It is embodied in language, the peculiar possession of the public, and it is about the human being, an object of public knowledge.

Language is certainly one element or level in the literary cycle (Stages 4 and 6 in the diagram), but it must be related to style, symbolism and theme for a word's full meaning to be released – and these larger factors will depend on the unit that is involved (sentence, genre, author's complete works, literary 'movement', etc.). Depending on its context, for instance, the first person singular may mean 'the author', 'a representative writer in the lyric genre', 'the poet' (in a particular 'movement'), a particular poetic 'persona', or 'the speaker of a dramatic monologue'. Nor are other senses excluded, sometimes more than one operating simultaneously. (Consider the use of 'I' in an autobiographical novel.)

[1] *Ibid.*, p. 5.

But the Wimsatt/Beardsley emphasis on language as the principal tool of literary interpretation is to be deprecated because it may encourage an undue dependence on either historical or structural linguistics. These are both reputable sciences, but they have little or nothing to contribute to the direct study of literature. Historical linguistics encourages the illusion that a language is continually changing, whereas the truth is that the English language, for example, has remained remarkably uniform, apart from its local or special dialects, since the fifteenth century, and a basic continuity since *c.* 1200, with the same exceptions, can hardly be denied. A student will naturally consult the dictionary from time to time, and a working knowledge of the various changes in pronouns, accidence and grammar is useful; but a familiarity with the history of the changes of style is infinitely more valuable for purposes of literary interpretation. Modern structural linguistics has its own interest too, but the promises it once seemed to provide of a new approach to literary interpretation have not been fulfilled.[1]

The exact reversal of the author's role by the reader raises some difficulties when the stratum of style or symbol is reached. It is style that is the author's principal medium of conscious self-expression. *Le style c'est l'homme même.* And metre, with its allied devices of alliteration, assonance, rhyme and onomatopoeia, is for the poet a matter of intimate conscious craftmanship. But for the reader, reading a poem for the first time, the metre may be almost unnoticed, just as the beats of the clock are almost unnoticed by a hypnotist's subject. What the unsophisticated reader is most aware of is the almost (but not quite) unreal world of 'illusion', which metre and the other stylistic devices have persuaded him to enter. The presence of style, in almost any form, is often not discovered until a second or third reading, unless our scholar-critic is exceptionally sophisticated or the style is offensively unrealistic.

The point can be clarified by a return to Stages 2, 3, 7 and 8 in the diagram, which must now be re-phrased:

[1] I have elaborated this sceptical verdict in an essay in honour of my friend René Wellek in the collection *The Disciplines of Criticism* (ed. P. Demets, T. Green and L. Nelson, New Haven, 1968), pp. 3–16.

AUTHOR	READER
2 Almost unconscious symbolism	8 Illusion of reality
3 Stylistic self-consciousness	7 Unself-conscious absorption of stylistic devices

The author's progress from a condition of semi-conscious symbolic expression to a self-conscious cultivation of style is not matched by any similar development in the naïve common reader – for whom the advance, if achieved at all, from language to style and from style to aesthetic illusion is gradual and almost imperceptible. But a reader must always acquire at least a quasi-identification with his author and to jump Stage 7 makes this impossible; it may also convert the aesthetic reality of Stage 8 into a reality without illusion. Partridge's reactions in *Tom Jones* to the acting of Garrick typify the common reader's dilemma: 'If that little man there upon the stage is not frightened, I never saw any man frightened in my life' (Book XVI, Ch. V). Partridge does not believe in ghosts, but the Ghost in *Hamlet* has so frightened the little man on the stage that it *must* be an authentic spectre. In other words, delusion tends to be the natural condition of the naïve reader (the death of a heroine has still to be avoided in a TV serial); illusion is only available to those for whom Life can be filtered through Art. The filter in literature is style. It is possible to be more precise. One's proper understanding of literature requires as a prerequisite an awareness of all the implications of genre. Interpretation has certain minor functions to perform such as the explanation of non-literary allusions or of obsolete words or grammatical usages, but genre, used in the widest sense, must be a principal preoccupation of the literary scholar-critic. Milton was right therefore in insisting that 'decorum', with its stylistic implications for the particular genre employed, is 'the grand master peece to observe'.[1]

But a genre's causes and functions are not always, or indeed generally, self-evident. Granted that 'repeats' are necessary, why do they vary so remarkably from one group or 'school' of writers to another? A Stage 10 must be presupposed in the diagram for readers, with a parallel Stage 0 for authors. All that it seems possible to say – unless one resorts to a Jungian Collective Unconscious (which might now be allied to a Chomskyan

[1] See p. 91 above.

Universal Generative Grammar) – is that the preconception and the post-evaluation levels must both have their origins in what can be called the Social Order (or Zeitgeist, if you are an individualist). The *OED* defines 'Zeitgeist' as 'The spirit or genius which marks the thought or feeling of a period', giving as its earliest occurrence a quotation from *Literature and Dogma* (1873). The Marxist critics are not much more helpful, but at least, as the discussion of Wellek's norms has already demonstrated,[1] some ultimate social basis must be presupposed. For the moment the scholar-critic will be well advised to handle it gingerly, but it (or something like it) must be presumed to complete the symmetry of the literary cycle, with a human writer and a human reader uniting the two columns inter-subjectively at the top of the diagram as they have been externalized physically in the text.

A specimen interpretation

The author's half of a typical literary cycle must usually be reconstructed from the reader's own experience as a creative or semi-creative writer. Distinguished writers tend to avoid public introspection, or else to exploit it recklessly for use by their own personae. As a consequence there are very few accounts of the way in which a work that is genuinely literature came to be written which are autobiographically trustworthy. One of the few English exceptions is Robert Graves's account of the genesis of his own 'half-comedy', as he has described it, 'The General Elliott'. This is a poem that is certainly literature. Moreover, as I was seeing Graves almost daily at the time of its composition, I can also guarantee the general authenticity of the account he gives of its composition in *On English Poetry* (1922).[2]

The poem originated from an inn-board ('The General Elliott. Morrell's Ales and Stout') that Graves noticed in South Hinksey when walking from Oxford to his cottage on Boar's Hill.[3] '. . . once I asked a man working in the garden who this

[1] See p. 54 above. [2] pp. 55–62.

[3] Though no Arnoldian Graves took the same path as Arnold and Clough in their Oxford days: 'Runs it not here, the track by Childsworth Farm' ('Thyrsis', l. 11). Graves's cottage was half a mile or so above Childsworth (now Chilswell) Farm in John Masefield's garden.

General Elliott was, and he answered that really he didn't know; he reckoned he was a fine soldier and killed somewhere long ago in a big battle.' There was no inn-sign depicting the General, who was really George Augustus Eliott, better known as Lord Heathfield, the defender of Gibraltar 1779–83, though Graves did not discover this until after he had written the poem. An interval of some months then occurred, when Graves passed the inn again 'and suddenly a whole lot of floating material crystallized in my mind'. The following verse ('more or less') came into his head:

> Was it Schellenberg, General Elliott,
>   Or Minden or Waterloo
> Where the bullet struck your shoulderknot,
>   And the sabre shore your arm,
> And the bayonet ran you through?

A whole poem followed up this moment of inspiration, but Graves was dissatisfied with it, even after five drafts. A few days later he rewrote it in a different style, and by the time he showed it to me it had reached its fourteenth version. In this final form it was printed in *The Spectator* and in the collection *Whipperginny* (1923). The poem now describes an imaginary sign-board of a comically heroic English general.

> He fell in victory's fierce pursuit,
>   Holed through and through with shot,
> A sabre sweep had hacked him deep
>   'Twixt neck and shoulderknot . . .
>
> The potman cannot well recall,
>   The ostler never knew,
> Whether his day was Malplaquet,
>   The Boyne or Waterloo.

In the account of the poem in *On English Poetry* Graves proceeds to list what he thought its various sources had been – generals and a colonel he had known, 'My own faith in the excellent qualities of our national beverage', etc. But the only item in the list that carries much conviction is, 'My hope of settling down to a real country life in the sort of surroundings that the two Hinkseys afford, sick of nearly five years soldiering'. Graves settled on Boar's Hill in the summer of 1920, soon after his recovery from shell-shock and his marriage to Nancy Nicholson. The 'floating material' that crystallized in his mind was presumably some unconscious or semi-conscious 'theme' concerned with war and peace, killing and loving (Stage 1 in the diagram on p. 106 above). General Elliott, the eighteenth-century military man surviving unidentified as the name of a country inn, suggested itself spontaneously after some months in his sub-conscious mind as the 'symbol' of Stage 2. A poet's difficulties generally begin with Stage 3 and the discovery of an appropriate 'style' in which to verbalize his symbols. (Compare the facetious opening of 'The Ancient Mariner' with its subsequent 'romantic' evolution.) In Graves's case the spontaneous first draft of the first stanza proved an unworkable nucleus, but after a few days and many drafts the right semi-comic tone was at last achieved and with it a metre suitable to it. As the poem proceeds his General becomes a grotesque English equivalent of some benevolent rural deity *without once leaving his sign-board.* The following are the last two stanzas:

No upstart hero may usurp
  That honoured swinging seat;
His seasons pass with pipe and glass
  Until the tale's complete.

And paint shall keep his buttons bright
  Though all the world's forgot
Whether he died for England's pride
  By battle, or by pot.

It is difficult to be sure if the 'honoured swinging seat' includes a reference either to *swing* in its popular sense of *hang* (on the gallows) or to 'Captain Swing', the folk-hero of the machine-wrecking and rick-burning riots of 1830–1 which have been called by J. L. and Barbara Hammond 'The Last Labourers' Revolt'. Whether intended by Graves or not the sense is certainly appropriate; some of the 'Captain Swing' riots occurred not far from the Hinkseys.

At this point interpretation is passing from author's intention to reader's critical response. Graves's account of the poem's origins in *On English Poetry* provides no justification for attributing a sinister irony to 'honoured swinging seat', but the tone of 'By battle, or by pot' invites us, at least on the second reading, to be on the look-out for such anti-heroic or anti-pastoral sub-intentions. A reader may occasionally be permitted to know more about a poem's meaning than its author.

I hope I may be forgiven a personal anecdote here. When Graves became the Professor of Poetry at Oxford in 1961, I discussed several of his poems at an undergraduate class that I held at Corpus Christi College at the time. One of the poems was 'The General Elliott', which Graves had partly revised in the various editions of his *Collected Poems* since its original publication in *The Spectator* in 1921. While still admiring the poem I was dissatisfied, as I explained in detail to my class, with almost all of his revisions. A lunch given by a mutual friend, who acted as a sort of referee between us, soon enabled me to make my points to Graves himself. I still have my copy of *Whipperginny* in which Graves has restored in the margin the principal changes I complained of.

I need only give one example here. The stanza preceding that beginning 'No upstart hero . . .' originally ran as follows in *On English Poetry* and *Whipperginny*:

> He grips the tankard of brown ale
> That spills a generous foam:
> Oft-times he drinks, they say, and winks
> At drunk men lurching home.

'Why,' I asked Graves, 'did you change "Oft-times" to "Often" in the *Collected Poems*?' With exemplary patience, as of one explaining the obvious to an idiot child, he told me that 'Oft-times' was poetic diction, an artificial archaism inappropriate to a half-comedy. 'Yes,' I agreed, 'but the line [my italics] is

> Oft-times he drinks, *they* say, and winks . . .

Who are the "they" in "they say"?' And then, putting on my best Berkshire accent, I read it as 'Oft-toimes 'e drinks, they say'. I was about to elaborate the inferiority of 'Often' in the mouth of a Hinksey labourer when Graves interrupted me: 'O.K. You win'. And then he added another *stet* in the margin to the changes I had copied in from the later revision.

This episode of 'The General Elliott' may be permitted to illustrate the dialogue between writer and reader that is always theoretically taking place, though the writer is not usually available for our cross-examination. It might indeed be argued that the writer is *never* available. Graves wrote 'The General Elliott' early in 1921; he was inevitably not the same man or poet as the genial sexagenarian I had my argument with in the autumn of 1961. That we could discuss the poem fruitfully at all might, then, be taken to confirm the Intentional Fallacy. On the other hand, just as in 1961 Graves still remembered the poem he had written forty years before, so I too was able to remember what the poem had once been – the style I had responded to – in that remote period. The recollection made it just so much easier for me to detect stylistic defects in the more recent changes. A note that I wrote in 1961 – shortly before the dramatic lunch – may be of interest to anyone who has both versions of the poem available:

> The poem obtains its comic vivacity from the tension between the real (historical) General Elliot (who miraculously survives in the inn-sign) and the physical concomitants of his survival – his picture on the sign, his painted buttons and his pipe. Whatever weakens that tension, e.g. the substitution in the later text of a 'china' pipe for a 'painted' one, is undesirable. Note that the General's continuity, from Malplaquet, etc., onwards, is maintained by the repetition of 'he', 'him', 'his' (13 in all; at least one in each verse). Graves should have resisted the deletion of the 'his' in verse II and the 'he' in verse V. The restriction of each verse to a single sentence should also have been maintained.

I quote this note as a sample of one reader's contribution to critical interpretation. Although 'language' has occasionally to be elucidated (as in 'Oft-times'), it is 'style' that the student or editor will be most concerned with. And for the determination of style it is both the artifact itself and the author and his other writings, or those of his associates, that provide the most instructive evidence.

Whipperginny (1923), the first collection to include 'The General Elliott', contains an important prefatory 'Author's Note' in which Graves describes his evolution from 1918. Here we have the author's point of view once again. The poems in *Country Sentiment* (1920), most of which were written in 1918, reflect, he says, 'the desire to escape from a painful war neurosis into an Arcadia of amatory fancy'. *The Pier Glass* (1921), the next collection, is described as reflecting the same neurosis, but the prevailing mood is 'aggressive and disciplinary . . . rather than escapist'. The later poems in *Whipperginny*, on the other hand, provide evidence of greater detachment in the poet and the appearance of 'a new series of problems in religion, psychology and philosophy, no less exacting than their predecessors, but, it may be said, of less emotional intensity'. Graves's ultimate realization that the poems of religion, psychology and philosophy were comparative failures is implicit in their exclusion from the *Collected Poems*. I regret that he did not instead follow up the success of 'The General Elliott' – which was *not* excluded from the *Collected Poems* – and develop more fully the vein of 'half-comedy', which might be described as a rustic English equivalent of the sardonic absurdity of the more or less contemporary urban 'Sweeny' series by T. S. Eliot.

Aesthetic content

As the diagnostic diagram on p. 106 was intended to demonstrate, though the author must necessarily be allowed the first word (Stages 1–3), the last word is inevitably with the reader. The condition of 'illusion' – in Graves's poem the suspension of disbelief in the living reality of the general on the inn-sign – is one that the reader must enter unaccompanied. The author's 'repeats' have made the suspension of disbelief natural and possible, but once the illusory condition has been reached (Stages 8–9) the reader should be almost unaware of an author controlling the puppets. The poem says itself as a novel tells itself. The scholar-critic must not allow himself to be content – as critics as able as F. R. Leavis have often been – with summaries of Stages 8–9. Inevitably, when summarized the events narrated and the personages involved in them lose their aesthetic identity and become a 'plot' or a 'character' similar to the plots and characters of history. L. C. Knights has parodied this tendency in A. C. Bradley's *Shakespearean Tragedy* by asking *How Many Children had Lady Macbeth?* (Cambridge, 1933). Stages 8–9 in the diagram, being unified and non-verbal, cannot be discussed or described as if they belonged to the world of common experience. During the process of reading – or seeing a good play well acted – we are enthralled, we 'cannot choose but hear'; some such word as 'intensity' or 'sublimity' describes our condition. All we can do to communicate it is to introduce a metaphor or some awkwardly abstract formula. It will be remembered that Aristotle, after he had listed the technical constituents of a tragedy, had to be content with a very homely metaphor to describe the essential tragic experience – 'incidents arousing pity and fear, wherewith to accomplish its *catharsis* of such emotions.'[1] The celebrated *catharsis* is simply a transliteration of a Greek word, which means 'purging' in its gross medical sense.

The reader's metaphors describing his experiences in the immediately post-verbal period of the literary cycle parallel the opposite condition in the author. Stage 1 ('Theme') and Stage 2 ('Symbol') are largely pre-verbal and resist description in the ordinary sense. What may be called the Aesthetic Moment of conception evokes in a competent reader the Aesthetic Moment of imaginative response. The author, feeling his way, as it were, to communication with his contemporaries, uses symbols, as the reader, asked to describe the literary experience he has undergone, will use metaphors. Tennyson, when asked his opinion of Ben Jonson's comedies, answered: 'he appears to move in a wide sea of glue'.[2] This was Tennyson in the role of reader, and it may be fairly objected that the metaphor is more concerned with form than with content. It is only in Stage 9 – which is only reached some time after the Aesthetic Moment or a series of such moments, is passed – that 'language' returns to the cycle.

The difficulty is to find any authorial record, long or short, using either images or words, of the Aesthetic Moment *per se*. Cleanth Brooks has called such attempts 'The Heresy of Paraphrase'. At our hypothetical Stage 8 the aesthetic experience is self-justifying and only describable in terms of itself. The evaluation at Stage 9 only becomes possible by eliminating some elements in the experience itself. Hence all critical judgments are necessarily incomplete. The reader has selected certain aspects of what he remembers his response to have been – and his final considered reaction to those selected parts will

[1] Ch. vi (Bywater translation).

[2] *Tennyson. A Memoir. By his Son* (1897), II, 205.

inevitably be affected by various personal, moral, political and social factors, of some of which he may be totally unaware. All of this makes the evaluation of a particular artifact changeable and unreliable, varying not only from individual to individual and period to period but within the same reader at different ages or in different moods. The appreciation of style, on the other hand, is less likely to vary; the different metrical and rhetorical devices, the particular genre, and the choice of 'topoi' are all inherent in the particular artifact, always available for the careful reader to recognize and respond to. In other words, it is to Stage 7 ('Style') rather than to Stage 8 ('the Aesthetic Moment') or Stage 9 (evaluation) that the scholar-critic must particularly turn his attention. Stage 8 tends to be dominated by the conventions of realism, a genre comparable to that of *trompe l'oeil* in painting and the 'programme music' that attempts to imitate the actual sounds of cannon-fire, railway trains, the songs of various birds, etc. Stage 9, on the other hand, is best considered, in so far as it is a reflection of the objects of knowledge, as part of the History of Taste, or as an aspect of social history. If the sense of fact is to be maintained, 'evaluation' must be qualified by 'interpretation'.

Authorial revision

The most instructive introduction to literary interpretation is probably via a study of authors' revisions – either of detail as in the case of 'The General Elliott' or of more elaborate reconstructions as with *The Rape of the Lock, The Dunciad, The Prelude* or *Lady Chatterley's Lover*. With revisions the scholar-critic finds himself challenged to decide if one reading is preferable to another. Instead of the passive and somnolent exercise that the reading of a literary classic may easily become, an active and quasi-creative role is thrust upon him. In responding properly to the stimuli offered by our author's words we are in effect collaborating with him – and like other professional collaborators we may on occasion improve upon him or at least differ from him instructively.

The assumption that improvement was possible was taken for granted when literature was transmitted orally. Nowadays it is virtually limited to light verse such as the obscene limerick. A non-obscene example is the familiar lines on Jowett in *The Masque of Balliol*. As originally composed by H. C. Beeching the lines were:[1]

> First come I; my name is Jowett.
> There is no knowledge but I know it.
> I am Master of this college;
> What I don't know isn't knowledge.

But by the time I reached Oxford (in 1920) a more concise version had been evolved in undergraduate tradition. It was now in anapaests:

> I am Benjamin Jowett,
>   Master of Balliol College;
> Whatever is known I know it,
>   What I don't know isn't knowledge.

The change of metre – from trochaics to anapaests – is less important than the verbal economy it makes possible. Here there are no superfluous words as in Beeching's version and the addition of Benjamin and Balliol completes the necessary biographical detail with a pleasant alliteration. The changes result in effect in a change of genre. Instead of the quasi-dramatic parade of Balliol dons and personalities presented in *The Masque of Balliol* – which was only a masque in name and was never performed – the Jowett lines have now detached themselves from the framework and survive as an academic squib or a pseudo-epitaph. An eighteenth-century Oxford equivalent would perhaps be Abel Evans's couplet on the very fat Dr Tadlow of St John's:

> When Tadlow walks the streets, the paviours cry,
> 'God bless you, sir!' and lay their rammers by.

But Evans's epigram does not need any amending; the eighteenth century was more conscious of genre and the need for *le mot juste* than its successor.

The emendations of oral tradition – not by any means always for the better – do not apply to the printed word or to an artifact intimately linked to its author. A reader may sometimes be

[1] For other versions see W. G. Hiscock, *The Balliol Rhymes* (Oxford, 1955), p. 1.

able to improve on some detail in the author he is studying, but such improvements if recorded at all must be left to the footnotes of a variorum edition; to foist them into the text is to misquote his author. Nevertheless, simply as a critical exercise, they are often worth attempting. Only a reader who is in intelligent sympathy with the particular artifact he is trying to improve can ever succeed even partially in the venture.

A nice example is provided by William Collins. One of the most popular of his *Odes on Several Descriptive and Allegoric Subjects* (1746, misdated 1747) is that beginning 'How sleep the brave'. Its second stanza's opening lines are:

> By fairy hands their knell is rung,
> By forms unseen their dirge is sung . . .

The emendation consists in substituting 'choirs unseen' for 'forms unseen'. The word 'forms' is not objectionable in itself; it is the conjunction with the singing of a dirge (forms do not sing) and the epithet 'unseen' (a form that is unseen is not a form) that is clumsy. A choir, on the other hand, in the sense of 'The band of singers who perform or lead the musical part of the service in a church or chapel' (*OED*), is surely the appropriate body to sing a dirge and there is no difficulty in conceiving an unseen choir. The offence of 'forms' against the genre Collins was employing – the lesser or Horatian ode – is verbal imprecision. The introduction of 'choirs' for 'forms' would have the additional virtue of a suggestion of 'Il Penseroso':

> Let the pealing organ blow
> To the full voic'd quire below.

(Milton's minor poems are, as is generally acknowledged, a dominant influence on Collins's poetry.)

It is not suggested, of course, that a scholar-critic would delete Collins's 'forms' for my 'choirs'. The emendation is more of the nature of a critical comment illustrating Collins's uncertainty as to the kind of poem he was writing. As Roger Lonsdale, Collins's most recent editor, has pointed out, this 'ode' is a medley of Pope's 'Elegy to the Memory of an Unfortunate Lady' and Collins's own earlier 'Ode to a Lady'. It has nothing of its own to offer except the perfection of its phrasing. But 'forms' is not *le mot juste* in the poem's pre-romantic setting; to suggest the alternative of 'choirs' is primarily to call attention to a failure of detail. To insert the emendation in the text, however, would be to falsify the historical authenticity of the poem. Collins wrote 'forms'; the scholar-critic may deplore it, but he is not entitled to fabricate even a superior reading.

A somewhat similar situation arises when an author attempts to improve a word or phrase of his own that does not seem, on his maturer reflection, to be quite 'good English'. Most modern editions contain lists of such authorial corrections, either in footnotes or tucked away in an appendix, but editors have a bad habit of leaving the variants to speak, as it were, for themselves. The reason why this reading is finally chosen by the author and another reading rejected (or *not* rejected, the author returning to the original or an earlier reading) is often not sufficiently explained. But such deficiences of editors provide a scholar-critic's challenge. Stylistic changes demand the 'explication' that is crucial to interpretation, whether our interest is in the author's intentions or the genre which he is writing in.

Keats made his own position clear in the conversation with Richard Woodhouse which has already been referred to:[1]

> He never corrects, unless perhaps a word here or there should occur to him as preferable to an expression he has already used – . He is impatient of correcting, and says he would rather burn the piece in question and write another or something else –

The conversation took place in 1820 when all Keats's greatest poetry had already been written; the truth that it enunciates had therefore been learnt by experience. A simple example of the process is l. 20 of the 'Ode to a Nightingale':

> And with thee fade away into the forest dim.

This is the last line of the second stanza; it is strictly extra-syllabic, a line of twelve syllables, whereas all the other lines with the exception of the short eighth line in each stanza are decasyllabic. Presumably realizing this Keats omitted the 'away' in the manuscript copies made by Woodhouse as well as in the version printed in *Annals of the Fine Arts*. The only versions to include 'away' are the original draft of the poem and

[1] *The Keats Circle*, p. 128.

Lamia, Isabella, the Eve of St. Agnes, and Other Poems (1820), which may be considered the definitive text. And in spite of the apparent irregularity there can be no doubt that 'away' is needed to give the line sufficient stress-weight.[1]

The case of 'La Belle Dame Sans Merci' is similar. The earliest version – to be found in the long journal-letter of April 1819 to his brother George and George's wife Georgiana – begins

O what can ail thee Knight at arms . . .

and concludes the eighth stanza:

And there I shut her wild wild eyes
With Kisses four.

The version printed in Leigh Hunt's *Indicator* (10 May 1820) is vaguer and also clumsier:

And there I shut her wild sad eyes
So kiss'd to sleep.

Woodhouse's transcripts of the poem, however, which have become via Monckton Milnes's *Life, Letters, and Literary Remains, of John Keats* (2 vols, 1848), the standard text, return to the four kisses, which are certainly *right* aesthetically, though they seem to have bothered Keats. Indeed, even in the journal-letter, immediately after transcribing the poem into it, he has to be facetiously apologetic:[2]

> Why four Kisses – you will say – why four because I wish to restrain the headlong impetuosity of my Muse – she would fain have said 'score' without hurting the rhyme – but we must temper the Imagination as the Critics say with Judgment. I was obliged to choose an even number that both eyes might have fair play: and to speak truly I think two a piece quite sufficient.

And so on with more in the same strain. Though Keats could not be expected to know it, pseudo-specific numbers are a favourite figure of speech in English Romantic poetry. Wordsworth

[1] See p. 57 above.
[2] *Keats's Letters*, ed. Hyder E. Rollins (Cambridge, Mass., 1958), II, 97.

had scandalized the readers of *Lyrical Ballads* (1798) with ll. 32–3 of 'The Thorn':

> I've measured it from side to side,
> 'Tis three feet long, and two feet wide.

In deference to criticism a clumsy substitute was finally provided, and Wordsworth, unlike Keats, did not finally return to the superior earlier reading. But like many other poets – the novelists are more immune, Henry James being the principal exception – Wordsworth suffered from what has been called the *cacoethes corrigendi*. Dramatists have had the same complaint, notably Congreve and Sheridan.

The degree to which Shakespeare revised any of his plays is still uncertain and provides the scholar-critic with perhaps his most formidable challenge. Genre is again likely to be a deciding factor, but we have often to be content with Shakespeare's general stylistic habits as far as they are recognizable.

The dead-end into which textual criticism is driven if it ignores aesthetic considerations may be illustrated by a passage from the trumpet-call against the critics blown by Fredson Bowers of the University of Virginia.[1]

> not much is changed whether Hamlet's father's bones were *interred* as in Q2, or *inurned* as in the Folio (I, iv, 49). Yet I hold it to be an occupation eminently worth while, warranting any number of hours, to determine whether Shakespeare wrote one, or the other, or both. The decision, if clear-cut, might be crucial in the accumulation of evidence whether on the whole the Folio variants from the quarto Hamlet are corruptions, corrections, or revisions. If this is a problem no editor has fairly faced, neither should a literary critic be indifferent to the question. Depending upon what can be proved, some hundreds of readings will be affected if an editor decides that Shakespeare revised the text after its second quarto form; for in that case the Folio variants should be chosen in all but the most obvious cases of sophistication. Or he might decide that in only a few cases, where the second quarto compositors have corrupted the text, should the Folio readings take precedence over the generally authoritative second quarto.

[1] *Textual and Literary Criticism* (1959), pp. 7–8.

It is impossible not to warm to that 'occupation eminently worth while, warranting any number of hours'. This is the heroic spirit of scholarship. But an examination of the problem soon shows that the respective status of *interred* and *inurned* can only be finally determined from the internal evidence of style. The bibliographical evidence is quite indecisive. No doubt Q2 does derive more or less directly from Shakespeare's autograph, but its Act I was set up, as Bowers agrees, either from a copy of the 'reported' Q1 partly corrected by the autograph, or (more probably) from a special transcript of this corrected copy. Now Q1 also reads 'interr'd' here, and the possibility must be faced that the reading is simply a mistake of the reporter's carelessly carried over into Q2. The Folio 'enurn'd' is certainly the *difficilior lectio*: whereas *inter* is a common Elizabethan word, *inurn* has not so far been traced before its occurrence here, and the word is probably a coinage of Shakespeare's. He was fond of words of this type; the following verbs are not found before Shakespeare according to the *OED*: *emball, embound, enclog, endart, enrank, enridge, enschedule, entreasure, illume, immask, impaint, impleach, impress, inclip, incorpse, inhearse, injoint, inscroll, inship, insinew*. In other words, on the merely textual evidence both readings are just about equally plausible. No more and no less.

Well, even the most cursory stylistic analysis can do better than that. It is clear from the preceding and succeeding lines that the elder Hamlet was buried and not cremated. 'Why thy Canoniz'd bones Hearsed in death, / Have burst their cerments, why the Sepulcher / . . . Hath op'd his ponderous and Marble jawes, / To cast thee up again?' (F1 text, but Q1 and Q2 are in substantial agreement with it) can mean nothing else. In the light of these direct references to burial *inurn* can only be defended as a dead metaphor. But to impute to Shakespeare of all people an unconsciousness of the cremation image latent in the word, one that was his own creation too, is indeed a desperate conjecture. When the play was originally written the line must surely have read as in Q2.

Wherein we saw thee quietly interr'd,

Nevertheless *quietly inurned* has a very Shakespearean ring. I suspect it is the product of a later revision. It is a characteristic of authorial revision, especially of poetry, that it improves the immediate meaning at the cost of that of the wider context.[1] The ashes implied by *inurn*, though nonsense in the passage as a whole, do go very nicely with *quietly*. This urn like Keats's is a bride of quietness, whereas a decaying corpse, unembalmed and uncremated, carries with it a faint suggestion of movement – the body disintegrates, the flesh corrupts, the worms enter on their grisly feast – and even such a slight hint of movement is incompatible with posthumous quietness. Another stylistic consideration also points to *inurned* as a later revision by Shakespeare himself. In terms of style the original passage was not in Shakespeare's best manner. Like so much of his blank verse at this period (*Henry V* is the notorious example) it is 'Parnassian' in Hopkins's sense of the word: the words and images have come rather too easily; Shakespeare is relying too much on a rhetoric that resounds a little mechanically. If we can feel this, Shakespeare must certainly have been aware of it too, and it is at least possible that he tried later on, when his blank verse had recovered from its 'Parnassian' phase, to touch the passage up. Word for word, just as pure poetry, *quietly inurned* is an improvement on *quietly interred* as it certainly is on *canonized bones*, and even on *ponderous and marble jaws*. Unfortunately, however, they make dramatic sense and it doesn't. And the fact that *inurned* is a word coined by Shakespeare, and as such stylistically typical of all his best work, seems to me to clinch the matter.

I may be wrong. But even if I am right and *inurned* is a case of revision, that is still no guarantee, of course, as Bowers would like us to believe, that the other Folio variants in *Hamlet*, apart altogether from the 'obvious' corruptions, are also revisions by Shakespeare. They may easily be revisions by somebody else, Burbage, for example, or the printer's reader.[2] Each reading must be considered on its own merits, external and internal, and both kinds of evidence must be used together, one as the corrective or supplement of the other. Our external-internal dialogue

[1] See for another example of this characteristic Goldsmith's change of 'Soft' to 'Sweet' that is discussed in the note, p. 133 below.
[2] The Folio proofs were almost certainly only read by Isaac Jaggard, the most active of the proprietors of the concern. For Charlton Hinman's account of Jaggard as proof-reader, see p. 137 below.

may often be prolonged and sometimes indecisive. That is the nature of most literary problems. They cannot be solved by the methods appropriate to sub-literature. But whether the enquiry is decisive or indecisive the last word in it must always be allowed to 'style'. Inconvenient though it may be for research purposes, the literary artifact remains obstinately in the last resort 'an intellectual thing', which cannot be pinned down on a laboratory bench.

This discussion of revision will provide an introduction to some more general problems of textual criticism.

SIX

TEXTUAL CRITICISM

> The core of practically every problem in textual criticism is a problem of *style*, and the categories of stylistics are still far less settled than those of textual criticism. And there is the further danger that the editor in making his recension may fall into the habit of forgetting his responsibility for being continually alive to the author's style. Here I may be allowed to end by recalling a remark of Richard Bentley's in his note on Horace, *Odes* 3. 27, 15 *nobis et ratio et res ipsa centum codicibus potiores sunt.* This remark has always tempted some scholars to misuse it, and it will always continue to do so; but it is true.
>
> Paul Maas[1]

Maas was a German classical scholar of some distinction, and his *Textual Criticism* is confined almost exclusively to Greek and Latin literature. But it provides a lucid and humane general introduction to this specialized technique. Bentley's note that Maas quotes is a commendation of the sense of fact (*res ipsa*) when proposing an emendation, but the facts that underlie almost every textual crux are, as Maas says, problems of style. A great writer continues to be read because there is a consensus that he is still well worth reading. The assumption, then, is that any local lapses from greatness misrepresent what he must be assumed to have written. And when interpretation has failed to explain or justify the meaningless or trivial word, phrase,

[1] *Textual Criticism* (translated from German by Barbara Flower, 1958), p. 41. By 'stylistics', as is clear from several passages, Maas meant the study of style divorced from content; he was not referring to the structural-linguistic approach of Bally and others.

sentence or passage, textual criticism is called in either to offer an emendation or at least to define the nature of the corruption. (The two processes will usually go hand in hand.)

An example from Shakespeare: technical considerations

Shakespeare is, by general agreement, the greatest of English poets and dramatists. Appropriately, therefore, the condition of his text raises the most difficult English textual problems. It will be useful to approach the general issues raised by textual criticism in English – issues that are similar to rather than identical with those of the classical textual criticism practised by Bentley and his modern representatives such as Maas – by applying to a single passage in Shakespeare all the apparatus of modern scholarship.[1] The more general premises underlying the discipline will follow later in this chapter.

One of the most famous of Shakespearean cruxes occurs in the Hostess's account of Falstaff's death in *Henry V*. Because of the number of interpretations and emendations it has provoked it can be used as a test-case to illustrate the methods that have to be employed in almost every similar crux in English literature. The passage runs as follows in the First Folio (1623):

> *Hostesse.* Nay sure hee's not in Hell: hee's in *Arthurs* Bosome, if ever man went to *Arthur's* Bosome: a made a finer end, and went away and it had beene any Christome Child: a parted ev'n just betweene Twelve and One, ev'n at the turning o' th' Tyde: for after I saw him fumble with the Sheets, and play with Flowers, and smile upon his fingers end, I knew there was but one way: for his Nose was as sharpe as a Pen, and a Table of greene fields. How now Sir *John* (quoth I?) what man? be a good cheare: so a cryed out, God, God, three or foure times: now I, to comfort him, bid him a should not thinke of God; I hop'd there was no neede to trouble himselfe with any such thoughts yet: so a bad me lay more Clothes on his feet: I put my hand into the Bed, and felt them, and they were as cold as any stone: then I felt to his knees, and so up-peer'd, and upward, and all was as cold as any stone.

[1] I assembled most of the material on this passage in *Shakespeare-Jahrbuch*, 98 (1962), 51–63.

To avoid any unnecessary misunderstanding my transcription modernizes the long *s* and the Elizabethan use of *i* and *j*, and *u* and *v*.[1]

Using the account of Falstaff's death as an example, what are the questions – and in what order – that a modern textual critic would normally ask? Let me list them:

1 *Is the passage literature rather than sub-literature, would-be literature or non-literature?* Unless he is dealing with what is unquestionably literature, the textual critic may be wasting his time; the criteria that apply to these lesser verbal artifacts are in general different because they differ in kind from what is agreed to possess literary value. However, the Hostess's speech passes this test with flying colours.

2 *Are there parts of the literary artifact under examination that are unintelligible in their context?* In this case 'a Table of greene fields' seems to qualify for unintelligibility; if it cannot be explained it will have if possible to be emended. (Some far-fetched attempts to explain the phrase will be found on p. 131 below.)

3 *What was the 'copy', in manuscript or in print, from which the text under consideration was transcribed or printed?* Greg has discussed the problems of the text of *Henry V* in the 1623 Folio in detail and reaches the conclusion that it was printed from Shakespeare's 'foul papers' (original manuscript).[2] Ultimately no doubt every writer's text – except those that are transmitted from an oral original, or those dictated by a blind man (*Paradise Lost*, for example) – goes back to an autograph, but the number of intervening copies or reprints may make it difficult to reconstruct if they no longer survive. In English the earliest surviving text of a work of literature is, if not an autograph, at worst only two or three steps from one, whereas a thousand years will often separate the earliest extant text of a Greek or Latin masterpiece from the autograph. Hence the irrelevance of many of the devices of classical scholarship for modern literature.

4 *If the original manuscript does not survive, what use can be*

[1] Until *c.* 1800 the modern *s* was only used at the end of a word. Until early in the seventeenth century *j* was only used in the combination *ij*, *v* was used at the beginning of a word and *u* medially.

[2] W. W. Greg, *The Shakespeare First Folio* (1955), p. 287.

made of available specimens of the author's handwriting? In Shakespeare's case only seven signatures survive and the three pages from the unacted manuscript play *Sir Thomas More* (*c.* 1600), a collaboration in which Hand D's contribution is now generally accepted as Shakespeare's foul papers.[1] *Henry V* was approximately contemporary with *Sir Thomas More*, having been probably produced in 1599, and some of the oddities of Hand D's spelling (such as the preference for an initial capital *C* even in the middle of a sentence) seem to be reproduced in the Folio text of *Henry V*. It is perhaps also significant that Hand D does not use a capital *I* at the beginning of a sentence. The 'Table' (of green fields) may therefore be a compositor's misreading of a word that did not begin with a *t* in the foul papers. The possibility would justify Theobald's emendation 'a babbled' (which assumes an original spelling *babld*). The Hostess is certainly free with 'a' (the unemphatic form of *he*), and D's medial *b* does look rather like a *k*. But D's initial *ba* is always easily legible (e.g. l. 75, 'their babyes at their backes'), nor is it likely to be confused with its initial *ta* (e.g. l. 80, 'taught'). Moreover, though *babble* occurs elsewhere in Shakespeare (nine times altogether, twice in the possibly pseudo-Shakespearean *Titus Andronicus*, six times as *babbling*), the meaning is always 'talk like a baby'. And Falstaff's green fields are not those in which babies play but the sea as it looks to a sailor in the high fever known as a calenture. A more plausible emendation, in terms both of handwriting and meaning, would be that suggested to Theobald by a 'Gentleman sometime deceas'd',[2] viz. 'a 'talked' (which Hand D would have written 'a talkd'). D's *k* could easily be confused with a *b* in the 'English' or 'secretary' hand of the period (which Shakespeare always used when signing his name), and his *e* and *d* are virtually identical. A compositor confronted with what looked like *talbe* (but was really *talkd*) may

[1] Shakespeare's participation in the play was originally suggested by Richard Simpson in 1871, but the present consensus that Hand D was Shakespeare's derives from *Shakespeare's Hand in the play of Sir Thomas More* (ed. A. W. Pollard, 1923), in which the handwriting, the eccentric spellings and 'The expression of ideas – particularly political ideas' are shown in impressive detail to be consistently Shakespearean. No rival claimant has hitherto been produced in spite of the intensive research that has been done in the Elizabethan period since 1923.

[2] *Shakespeare Restored* (1726), p. 138.

well have thought it *table*, to which he prefixed a capital simply because he took it to be a noun.

5 *What is the physical process by which the text has come to be preserved?* A printed book, for example, such as the 1623 Folio, presupposes one or more compositors. By *c.* 1650 the individual vagaries of compositors tended to have been ironed out by a common system of spelling and punctuation, as well as by more efficient 'correctors of the press' in each printing-house, but earlier compositors are usually identifiable by idiosyncrasies of spelling. Although five compositors – known as A, B, C, D and E – were employed by Jaggard in setting up the 1623 Folio most of it was the work of A and B, whose different mental habits are often relevant for a Shakespeare emendation. The page with 'a Table of greene fields' is apparently, to judge by the spellings and some bibliographical clues, the work of Compositor A. The obvious objection to 'a Table of greene fields' is that it does not seem to make sense. But sentences that do not make sense were the characteristic failing of Compositor A. Whereas his fellows tended, even in their most careless moments, to look beyond the word to its immediate context, A (an engagingly simple-minded man) was content if each word made sense by itself. Provided each separate word that he set was a real or possible English word A was generally satisfied. A specimen of his handiwork is to be found at the end of the Hostess's speech:

> then I felt to his knees, and so up-pear'd, and upward, and all was as cold as any stone.

The quartos, the Third Folio and all modern editions correct 'up-pear'd' to 'upward', which is clearly the right reading, as A would have discovered if he had read the next two words of his 'copy'. But for him, proceeding word by word instead of clause by clause, 'up-pear'd' was good enough; it was after all a possible English word. A's methods, primitive though they may seem, have the great virtue of approximate fidelity to his copy. What he has mis-read was really there; he does not insert words of his own to try to make sense of a passage that he has not been able to decipher. We may be certain that something that looked like *a table* was actually in the manuscript from which A was working, and the range of plausible emendations is therefore greatly narrowed. Indeed, *a' babled* and *a' talked* are, I believe, the only emendations so far proposed.

6 *In addition to the authoritative text or texts, is there a pirated or unauthorized text with some degree of semi-independent status?* The 'reported' Quarto of *Henry V* (1600) is an example of just such a text: it was probably assembled from the various actors' parts, or what they remembered of them, perhaps for a performance in the provinces or on some occasion when the Globe prompt-book was not available. The Hostess's speech in it omits the 'Table of greene fields' and is reduced at this point to:

> His nose was as sharpe as a pen: For when I saw him fumble with the sheetes, And talk of flowers, and smile upon his fingers ends I knew there was no way but one.

The fact that, instead of fumbling with the sheets and playing with flowers, the 'reporter' makes Falstaff fumble with the sheets and *talk* of flowers supports the emendation suggested by Theobald's 'Gentleman sometime deceas'd' rather than Theobald's own 'babbled'.

7 *Cannot one suggest an interpretation of the original reading, demonstrating that what was thought meaningless really makes excellent sense?* The crux in *Henry V* has inevitably stimulated much ingenious conjecture of this kind. According to Henry Bradley Falstaff's nose is as sharp as a pen *on a table covered with the green cloth usual in counting-houses*. Percival R. Cole has countered with *and a memorial tablet pointed in Gothic fashion in the green fields of a cemetery*, and Leslie Hotson proposes *in an engraving of Sir Richard Grenville*. Ephim G. Fogel has suggested more plausibly that 'table' here means 'picture', but in all the Shakespeare parallels that he cites the word means the flat surface on which a picture could be drawn or painted, never an actual picture.[1] The pen in these explanations has been the ordinary quill-pen, but the pen too can be reinterpreted as by Hilda M. Hulme (*a device on a coat-of-arms, the field vert*) and by John S. Tuckey (*a mountain peak rising steeply from a tableland consisting of green fields*). The game will no doubt continue.

Two objections immediately suggest themselves to the interpretations offered above. The first is a dramatic one: *they ruin the Hostess's part.* It would be far better to leave the whole

[1] *Shakespeare Quarterly*, 9 (1958), 485–92.

clause out, as the 1600 Quarto does, than to spoil her best speech with such laboured and quite uncharacteristic witticisms as those proposed by Henry Bradley, Leslie Hotson and their competitors. No such objection can be used to either *babbled* or *talked*, both of which were probably within the range of her vocabulary (*talk* is actually used by her in *The Merry Wives of Windsor*, I, iv). If Dogberry can say 'for the Watch to babble and to talke, is not tollerable' (*Much Ado*, III, iii, 36), why shouldn't the Hostess, who might well be his sister, use one or the other word in their ordinary sense?

The second objection is more literary than dramatic. To the scholar-critic the Hostess (Mrs Quickly in 2 *Henry IV* and *The Merry Wives*) is a masterpiece of comic characterization, but a masterpiece in virtue of what she says rather than what she does. It is her mode of speech – brilliantly breathless, touchingly domestic, ambitiously malapropist – that enchants him. She has an idiom of her own that is maintained with extraordinary consistency throughout the three plays. It is the almost Dickensian peculiarity of this idiom that is fatal to the various attempts that have been made to retain the Folio's 'and a Table' either unemended, or with 'on' substituted for 'and'. The phrase is apparently either part of a simile ('his nose was as sharp as a pen') or an extension of a description immediately following the simile. It is relevant then to list the Hostess's few other similes to see which of the stylistic alternatives is more probable. Is this an extension of a simile or an extension of a description?

That the phrase is an extension of the *pen* simile is to all intents and purposes ruled out by listing the other similes used by the Hostess either in *Henry V* or 2 *Henry IV* or in *The Merry Wives of Windsor*. 2 *Henry IV* has *red as any rose, rheumatic as two dry toasts* and *an 'twere an aspen leaf*; *Henry V* has *honey-sweet, an it had been any christom child* and *as cold as any stone* (as well as *as sharp as a pen*). In *The Merry Wives,* Mrs Quickly contributes only one simile: *a great round beard like a glover's paringknife.*

We may take it, then, on the balance of all the evidence extant, that whatever the clause was that is inbedded in 'a Table of greene fields' it is not an extended or sophisticated simile of the type proposed in the interpretations or emendations of Henry Bradley, Leslie Hotson and the others. In her numerous appearances in three plays the Hostess only uses eight similes altogether and they are all short, simple, familiar, the most sophisticated being that in *The Merry Wives* which is probably the latest of the plays. The *technical* evidence supports *a' talked of green fields* (written *a talkd*, etc.). The literary evidence, dramatic and stylistic, is perhaps less conclusive, supporting either *a' talked* or *a' babbled*, with a slight preference for the former. The problem of an 'indifferent' reading is one that frequently recurs in textual criticism, though its theoretical implications both for *le mot juste* and for 'the best text' have not always been realized. The indifference is often in the sensibility of the scholar rather than in the quality of the reading *per se.*[1]

The 'biblio-textual' approach

The preceding analysis of the interpretations and emendations proposed for 'a Table of greene fields' would not have been possible until the twentieth century. It is true that 'stemmatics' (the application of the genealogical principle to literary texts) was employed in Karl Lachmann's remarkable edition of Lucretius (1850), but its application to English literature in the determination of what McKerrow called the 'copy-text' was delayed by a fundamental difference in the problems of textual criticism in classical and modern literatures. The special problems of classical textual criticism have been summarized by Maas:[2]

[1] Arthur Friedman's 'The Problem of Indifferent Readings in the Eighteenth Century, with a Solution from Goldsmith' (*Studies in Bibliography*, 5 (1960), 143–7) is typical. The 'solution' depends upon parts of the 4th edition of *The Deserted Village* being in standing type carried over from the 2nd or 3rd edition. Of the four new indifferent readings in the 4th edition two occur in the standing type sections and are presumably authorial. But are they indifferent? Thus l. 113 instead of beginning 'Soft was the sound' becomes 'Sweet was the sound' – a distinct improvement, especially as l. 116 runs

The mingling notes came soften'd from below; . . .

Unfortunately Goldsmith had already used *sweet* five times in the preceding lines. The problem is therefore not to decide between indifferent readings here but between two readings that are both genuine but with separate and different merits.

[2] *Textual Criticism*, p. 1.

> We have no autograph manuscripts of the Greek and Roman classical writers and no copies which have been collated with the originals; the manuscripts we possess derive from the originals through an unknown number of intermediate copies, and are consequently of questionable trustworthiness.

None of these limitations apply to the Elizabethan classics and their successors, and there is even a manuscript of Chaucer that may well be autograph.[1]

McKerrow's meticulous edition of *The Works of Thomas Nashe* (5 vols, 1904–10) has had much the same seminal importance in English textual criticism that Lachmann's Lucretius had in Latin studies. A preliminary 'Note on the Treatment of the Text adopted in this Edition' defines (1) the system of spelling adopted ('The spelling of the copy-text, by which, here and throughout the book, I mean the text used in each particular case as the basis of mine, has been followed exactly except as regards evident misprints. These are corrected, the reading of the original being given at the foot of the page'); (2) the typography (long *s* modernized, black-letter texts in roman, except for short passages in a roman context, running titles in roman and their mistakes ignored, one size of type throughout); (3) the punctuation ('hopelessly inconsistent, but with the Elizabethan superfluity of commas reduced, and otherwise the original punctuation kept except if actually misleading'); (4) collations ('I have not followed any particular theory of what may be called a complete description – would there were such a theory to follow!').

The final *cri de coeur* may have stimulated A. W. Pollard and W. W. Greg to compile the important 'Some Points in Bibliographical Description', a paper read to the Bibliographical Society in 1906 and published with an appendix by Falconer Madan (which introduces the crucial 'degressive principle . . . of varying a description according to the difference of the period treated or of the importance of the work to be described') in the Society's *Transactions* for 1909. McKerrow himself assembled some 'Notes on Bibliographical Evidence for Literary Students and Editors of English Works of the Sixteenth and Seventeenth

[1] *The Equatorie of the Planetis* (ed. D. Price, 1955).

Centuries' which will be found in Volume XII of the same Society's *Transactions*. (McKerrow's notes were to be the basis of his *Introduction to Bibliography for Literary Students* (1927), a text-book that has dominated Elizabethan research for the last half-century.)[1]

But what is 'bibliography'? And why should a literary student bother his head with it? The questions – which are evaded in McKerrow's *Introduction* – were the persistent concern of Greg, McKerrow's friend and colleague from their Cambridge days, though history is likely to recognize Greg's far greater intellectual distinction. Greg's *Collected Papers* (ed. J. C. Maxwell, 1968) might indeed be described as a continuous series of attempts to define 'bibliography', a term for which he would have preferred 'bibliology', and which he illustrated in the masterly *Bibliography of the English Printed Drama to the Restoration* (4 vols, 1939–59).

For Greg, bibliography's ultimate justification was its contribution to textual criticism, one which he believed to be wholly disinterested because it confined itself to the *physical* description of the printed book in its various complexities.[2] The

[1] A revision bringing the *Introduction* up to date is now being prepared by Philip Gaskell.

[2] Greg's definition in 'Principles of Emendation in Shakespeare' (British Academy Shakespeare Lecture, 1928; reprinted in *Aspects of Shakespeare*, 1933, but not included in Greg's *Collected Papers*) of what constitutes 'an acceptable emendation' is one 'that strikes a trained intelligence as supplying exactly the sense required by the context, and which at the same time reveals to the critic the manner in which the corruption arose' (p. 81 of *World's Classics Shakespeare Criticism 1919–35*, ed. Anne Bradby, 1936). In fact, of course, the dissatisfaction of the trained intelligence with the traditional reading *precedes* any enquiry into the possible source of corruption. The words 'at the same time' are misleading. And, as the range of possible corruptions is almost infinite – perhaps the compositor was drunk or in a day-dream? – an emendation that supplies 'the sense required by the context' is likely to carry more weight than any merely physical explanation. Bibliography certainly has a contribution to make to textual criticism, but the mysteries it can unveil have been greatly exaggerated by Greg and and his disciples. As Maas has pointed out (*Textual Criticism*, p. 40), the discovery of new classical MSS. is continually justifying the 'bolder' emendations, i.e. those dependent entirely on the literary sense of the editor.

fallacy latent in the dependence on merely physical evidence to distinguish between two different readings or meanings was dramatically illustrated in a challenge issued by Fredson Bowers, Greg's most enthusiastic American disciple, who told a meeting of the English Institute in New York that he could prove 'on physical evidence not subject to opinion' that Shakespeare wrote *sallied flesh* and not *solid flesh* in *Hamlet*, I, ii, 129. Bowers has since argued out his case at length in the 1956 *Shakespeare Survey*, the 'physical evidence' being that the second quarto of *Hamlet* was set by two compositors, one responsible for

O that this too sallied flesh would melt . . .

and the other for Polonius's line to Reynaldo (II, i, 39),

You laying these slight sallies on my sonne . . .

Could two different compositors, each working independently on his own separate forme, have made exactly the same misprint? To Bowers it is inconceivable, and so he reaches his conclusion 'not subject to opinion' that Shakespeare must have used a verb and a noun derived from the French *sale*, though neither are hitherto unrecorded. (*Sully* comes from the French *souiller*.) The philological improbability of all this has been demonstrated by Helge Kökeritz in a devastating article.[1] Bowers also conveniently forgot that in the 'English' hand used by Shakespeare the loop at the top of a small *a* is often left unclosed, *a/u* or *u/a* misprints being therefore frequent. Moreover, the folio of 1623, which has *solid flesh*, has *slight sulleyes*, a variant perhaps reproducing Shakespeare's own spelling that complicates the issue; again two compositors were involved.[2] Moreover Q1, a 'reported' text that was apparently occasionally used by the Q2 printers (at least in Act I), also has *sallied flesh* – in which *sallied* may be what Burbage's 'Essex' pronunciation of *solid* sounded like to a 'traitor actor' or reporter.

In brief, the bibliographical case for *sallied* is far from decisive. But it is Bowers's initial premise that two compositors will not misprint the same word in the same way that is really fatal to his argument. The possibility is at best a psychological

[1] *Studia Neophilologica*, 30 (1958), 3–10.

[2] I have discussed some of the finer implications of *sullyes* in *English Studies Today* (Berne, 1961), II, 69.

probability; it can never be a typographical law. Bowers did not in fact claim that his two compositors always made the same misprints, but unless such an *a priori* criterion can be produced, or at least one which will enable an editor to distinguish between the Bowers rule and its exception, the rule is clearly not worth having.

Kökeritz concluded his article by deciding that 'the problem of *solid-sallied* will never be solved'. It will certainly never be solved by using either philological or bibliographical tools alone. These disciplines provide us with some subsidiary assistance from time to time, but their principal function in textual criticism is negative – to exclude the irrelevant or to correct what is historically impossible. Charlton Hinman's elaborate *Printing and Proof-reading of the First Folio of Shakespeare* (2 vols, 1963) – based on the findings of a special Collating Machine applied to fifty-five of the eighty copies of the 1623 Folio in the Folger Library at Washington – has made little or no difference to the actual text of the plays. The fact, for instance, that only 134 of the nearly 900 pages containing Shakespearean text were proof-corrected, and of the 510 variants that manifestly reflect proof-reading only a few dozen correct real substantive errors – with 'only about ten variant readings in the entire Folio which even *suggest* correction of the text by reference to copy; there are but two about which we can be certain . . . and three others about which we can be fairly sure'[1] – is certainly *negatively* important. And Fredson Bowers's conscientious edition of Thomas Dekker's plays (4 vols, 1953–60) has performed a somewhat similar negative function. The first editions of Dekker have not attracted the interest of an acquisitive millionaire, and Bowers's bold ambition to collate the text of every extant copy of the early editions of Dekker's play has taken him far afield. Unfortunately, as Hinman found with Shakespeare, the textual differences between corrected and uncorrected copies of the same edition are hardly ever attributable with any certainty to Dekker. Moreover Bowers's preoccupation with such differences has meant that misprints or corruptions common to both corrected and uncorrected copies have too often been reproduced in his own text without comment or emendation.

The real contribution of modern or analytical bibliography

[1] Hinman, I, 331–2.

has been to call attention – by the analysis of typographical features, paper, cancels, retention of standing type, compositors' spelling, press figures, catch-words, etc. – to differences within what had before been considered single textually identical editions, and so to make it possible to identify unauthorized or misdated editions that had been trying to pass themselves off as the genuine article. The total effect of the bibliographical revolution has therefore been to multiply enormously the *number* of editions or quasi-editions known to literary scholarship; the *texts* of our standard authors have remained comparatively unaffected.

Old spelling or new?

The first object of a critical edition is to establish a text. This is a proposition that will no doubt be generally accepted. But what does it mean? As usual it is to Greg that the modern scholar-critic turns for guidance in such matters. Greg had delivered the Clark Lectures at Cambridge in 1939 on *The Editorial Problem in Shakespeare. A Survey of the Foundations of the Text.* But the lectures were not immediately ready for publication, and in the meantime McKerrow, who had been asked to edit an Oxford Shakespeare to compete with Dover Wilson's brilliant New Cambridge Shakespeare, had brought out his *Prolegomena for the Oxford Shakespeare* (1939). Under the stimulus of McKerrow's *Prolegomena* Greg was able to prefix to the original lectures seven rules for the guidance of future editors of Shakespeare and other Elizabethan authors.

Much the most important of Greg's seven rules is the first, which is partly derived from McKerrow. As he formulated it in the revised second edition of *The Editorial Problem in Shakespeare* (1951), it runs as follows (p. x):

> The aim of a critical edition should be to present the text, so far as the available evidence permits, in the form in which we may suppose that it would have stood in a fair copy, made by the author himself, of the work as he finally intended it.

Greg's reputation has given his 'rule' an authority it may not altogether deserve. As he states it, it combines the Intentional

Fallacy (if it is a fallacy) with a fallacy from which the textual criticism of the Greek and Roman classics has been free, viz. that the ability to compose great literature necessarily carries with it the ability to spell and punctuate it correctly. Blake's manuscript poems have no punctuation at all; in their engraved state they depend upon a generous and often quite irrational use of colons and exclamation marks. Wordsworth was a competent speller, but he had to leave the punctuation of the second edition of *Lyrical Ballads* to Humphry Davy, a scientist whom he hardly knew; Yeats has confessed a similar inadequacy in a letter to Robert Bridges. Milton, on the other hand, was a spelling crank, at any rate in *Paradise Lost*, as was Bernard Shaw. The most remarkable case of all is that of Shakespeare. Not only does his spelling of his own name vary in his signature, but his spelling in his three pages of the manuscript of *Sir Thomas More* is exceptionally erratic, as is also the punctuation and the use of capital letters, even by Elizabethan standards. Thus, to take a single example, the word *sheriff* actually appears in five different spellings (*sheriff, shreef, shreere, shreive, shreve*) in five lines.[1]

Greg's rule seems peculiarly perverse in view of the fact that he had edited the whole of *Sir Thomas More* from the original manuscript in 1911 and Hand D's one scene in further detail in A. W. Pollard's symposium on it (1923). According to Greg himself the number of minims in sequences like *in* or *un* is incorrect seven times in D's 147 lines, and there are also 'slips', 'errors', malformed letters, a word the writer 'forgot to cross out' and another in which 'the writer's intention is quite obscure'.[2] No doubt a fair copy will eliminate such imperfections, but the question they force on us is whether a great creative writer like Shakespeare could, or even should, be expected to achieve a fair copy in Greg's sense. Is there not an almost necessary contradiction between the writing of 'good English' and 'correct English'? The question becomes more urgent when we pass from readings Greg called *substantive* (those directly affecting the meaning) to his *accidentals* (punctuation, spelling, use of italics and initial capitals and so on). An author's fair copy is surely a mirage. Few authors have ever succeeded in producing one in the ideal sense required by Greg,

[1] ll. 41–5.

[2] *Shakespeare's Hand in the Play of Sir Thomas More*, pp. 23–43.

and those who have are generally of little literary interest. It is a characteristic of the creative writer that, whenever he makes a copy of what he has already written, major or minor changes either in what is 'substantive' or in what is 'accidental' insert themselves almost spontaneously. Fair copies are the work of professional scribes and with the invention of printing the correction of spellings and the normalization of punctuation and capitalization have increasingly passed to the scribe's successor – the printer. No doubt it is desirable for the author to read and pass the printer's proofs, but a critical edition – far from reproducing with complete fidelity an author's mis-spelled and mis-punctuated text – is normally the product of a collaboration between author and printer. The printer's role is essentially a part or an extension of that collaboration between the individual author and his society that all literary communication presupposes, and nowadays the 'fair copy' is likely to be the responsibility of the printer rather than the author.

Greg's variant of the Intentional Fallacy is vitiated by an Edwardian individualist bias. The spelling and punctuation of the first edition are to be retained, because (although most of them are certainly the work of the compositors) *some* of the author's idiosycrasies *may*, he believes, have been inadvertently retained. Similarly (according to Greg), the author's final revision of the substantive readings must always be preferred to those in any earlier text because, although he was possibly senile at the time and was at any rate a different person from the younger self who had actually composed the particular literary artifact, it was still *his* work on which he must be allowed the last word. (The analogy seems to be with the law of property, on which the owner's last will and testament is legally decisive after his death.)

In the last resort, in textual criticism as in other aspects of literature, a compromise has in fact to be reached between what T. S. Eliot called 'Tradition' on the one hand and 'the Individual Talent' on the other. What the author finally intended must be weighed against what the passage really means – what it *must* mean if it is to be 'good English' in its particular context with all that implies in genre and subject-matter.[1] But 'good English' is

[1] James Reeves's agreeable poem 'Lines for the Duchess' (*Collected Poems 1929–1959*, 1960, p. 158) begins its second section: [*cont'd. opp.*

a singular noun – as English literature and the English language are also singular nouns. In some sense then (English) 'Tradition' stands for a continuum in which all the (English) 'Individual Talents' are involved. The implications of this grammatical necessity for literary history are discussed in the next chapter.

A related fact, one with important textual implications, is our habit, when reading Shakespeare's plays aloud, or seeing and hearing them acted, of pronouncing them, or hearing them pronounced, as though they were written in modern English. Phonetically, each generation actually speaks a slightly different English, but we do not change the *meaning* of Shakespeare's words to accommodate them to the most recent pronunciation. The words remain virtually the same semantically, though not phonetically. It would be a pretentious affectation to act or read Shakespeare in the pronunciation Shakespeare himself used when he read his latest play to the Chamberlain's Men (who became the King's Company of Players on James I's accession), or to speak one of Richard Burbage's great parts – Richard III, for example, or Hamlet or Macbeth – as Burbage himself spoke it, even if the philologists could answer either question with any precision.[1] What Shakespeare meant, on the other hand, has

---

Beggars and choosers throng the roads
With ho! what smoke of horse and wheel,
But you must stare away your hour
And nightly circle to the famished tower.

The last line puzzled me when I first met it and I consulted Reeves about it. Presumably it must mean that in her morbid imaginings the Duchess returns in memory to the fatal tower, wheeling round it like a bird, before actually visualizing herself as in it. But Reeves's actual intention, as he explained to me soon after the poem's composition, was to suggest a tower with a spiral staircase which the Duchess literally ascended. 'Surely she could circle up a spiral stair in a castle *to* a tower which didn't actually contain the stair.' This is ingenious, but it is not what the poem says. What the poem says is that the Duchess *circles* (not a spiral ascent) *to* a tower (with apparently no castle attached to it). The English language does not permit any alternative interpretation. And memories of 'Childe Roland to the Dark Tower Came' clinch the genre that is being used. In reply Reeves could only grumble, 'You exegetists are a bit literal-minded!'

[1] The standard work is *Shakespeare's Pronunciation* by Helge Kokeritz (New Haven, 1953), but its findings have been challenged by E. J. Dobson in a long review in *RES*, 6 (1955), 404–14.

scarcely changed at all in the last three or four centuries. The difference is once again between a temporarily 'correct English' (the current habits of pronunciation, vocabulary and grammar whose finer shades do undergo a process of continual change) and 'good English' (what is aesthetically effective in the literary artifact), which has scarcely changed at all since the culture of this country dissociated itself from its Germanic origins and achieved the blend of French (including Latin) with Anglo-Saxon that was virtually complete by *c.* 1200. The criteria of 'good English' that apply to Chaucer apply equally to Shakespeare, to Swift, to Dickens and to our own contemporaries. If there are some changes, reflecting changes in our class-structure or technology, the continuum is at most a gradual slope.

There are two textual implications in this general concept of English literature as a single semantic continuum, which can be stated as editorial rules:

1 Though substantive readings that are clearly authorial must be retained, either in the text or as variants in the footnotes or a special appendix, their spelling, punctuation and similar 'accidentals' should always be modernized, unless (a) such a process affects the meaning, or (*b*) dialect forms have been deliberately used (though even such forms should presumably be normalized if possible);

2 If two or more substantive readings survive, all of which seem to be certainly authorial, the preference should be given in a critical text to those that can be shown to be superior *as literature* in the particular literary context.[1]

[1] The *sallied/solid* crux illustrates this rule. To begin with, the near-identity of verbal form – whether *sallied* is retained or emended, as is usual, to *sullied* – excludes the possibility of revision by Shakespeare. It seems as though he must have intended either *sullied*, a word he uses occasionally elsewhere, or *solid* (which occurs in a similar context in 2 *Henry IV*). Which is the better word? Flesh, however sullied, does not melt (if dirty it should be cleaned). But the metaphor initiated in *solid*, i.e. ice-like, is appropriately continued in 'melt', 'thaw', and 'resolve itself into a dew'. Hamlet is depressed, disgusted at his mother's hurried marriage, and conscious that he can do nothing. At this point he has not seen the Ghost and is unaware that his uncle has murdered his father. He has not been 'sullied'; he is merely distressed by the inactivity in which he finds himself and from which he cannot escape. He has become an *icicle*.

The first of these rules has been the normal and natural practice of scribes and printers until the beginning of this century whenever an older manuscript or book was copied or reprinted. Even today 'Old Spelling' editions of Shakespeare are rare; in Chaucer's case, though the spelling (which is really that of the best fifteenth-century manuscripts) is generally retained, the punctuation is invariably modernized. The logical alternatives are *either* (for specialists) an exact photographic facsimile *or* (for all other purposes) a critical text that has been more or less completely modernized. The hodge-podge of some first-edition spellings (hardly ever including the long *s*, for example), some authorial spellings, and some compositors' or printing-house spellings and punctuation – but with no serious attempt to distinguish between what is authorial, what is compositorial or a particular printing-house 'style' – is comparable with 'Ye Olde Tea-Shoppe' and similar monstrosities.[1]

The scholar-critic who is told that such editions convey the flavour of a distant epoch will reply that he does not read literature for its flavour but for its meaning. *The Complete Angler* is 'quaint', not because the early editions spell it *Compleat* but because Izaac Walton was quaint.

The 'biblio-textual' school has spent much time discussing editorial principles. The initial assumption has been that the second of the two rules formulated above (generally labelled 'eclecticism') is mischievous because it involves the danger of editorial subjectivity. In his edition of Nashe, McKerrow's procedure was therefore ruthlessly 'objective'. Greg finally refuted McKerrow's assumption (which McKerrow had repeated in his *Prolegomena for the Oxford Shakespeare*) that if a later edition

[1] An extraordinary example of editorial obtuseness is Fredson Bowers's treatment of final *-e* in the text of Dekker's plays. The scene by Dekker in *Sir Thomas More* is in Dekker's autograph and it shows him consistently using the spellings *mee*, *bee* (for *be*), *hee*. Moreover the first edition of *The Shoemakers' Holiday* (1600), which Bowers believes to have been printed from Dekker's 'foul papers', has in Act I alone *hee* (6 examples), *wee* (3), *shee* (1), *mee* (1). If an editor is told *à la* Greg to print the 'accidentals' of the first edition in the pious hope that some of the author's habits will have escaped a normalizing compositor's attention, Dekker's fondness for the extra final *-e* surely deserves editorial insertion when absent in a first edition – though what Dekker 'intended' by it is another matter (its use is not as in *Paradise Lost* to indicate stress).

taken as a whole contains variants attributable to the author we must accept all the alterations in it (except obvious misprints or blunders) in an appendix to the 1958 re-issue of the Nashe. Since it represents Greg's final conclusion on a matter to which he had devoted continuous thought for some sixty years it deserves to be quoted in full:

> This will have struck many as doubtful, and it seems to me definitely perverse. It admittedly belongs to what is commonly called the 'conservative reaction' against the unprincipled eclecticism of most editors of the eighteenth and nineteenth centuries, and it forms, indeed, but an element in the concerted attempt of a later generation to substitute objective or mechanical rules in place of personal judgement. It seems to me, however, that any such attempt is in its nature mistaken and bound to lead to uncritical results. Judgement must inevitably be exercised alike to detect the presence of authorial alterations and to eliminate 'obvious blunder and misprints', and there can be no logical reason for refusing to exercise it likewise to discriminate between alterations for which the author must be considered responsible and those due to some other agency. . . . The truth is that no critical principle can be devised that will relieve an editor of ultimate responsibility, and the risk of overlooking some authorial corrections is no excuse for an editor's including in his text readings that he himself believes to be of no authority at all. Essential as it is to eschew the excesses of eclecticism, any attempt to evade the responsibility of individual judgement is an abdication of the editorial function. See also W. W. Greg, *RES* 1941, xvii, 140–4; *The Editorial Problem in Shakespeare*, 1942, pp. xxxvii, xlviii, lv.

But Greg did not quite reach the logical conclusion to his argument. If 'the excesses of eclecticism' are to be avoided, in what does a non-excessive eclecticism consist? Greg was a superb scholar, but he was not a literary critic. (The account of *Comus* in his *Pastoral Poetry and Pastoral Drama*, published in 1906 when he was only thirty, is ludicrously inadequate.) And it is, of course, to criticism that the scholar must turn when he is required to exercise 'the responsibility of individual judgement'. The procedure already illustrated in the case of *too too sallied / solid flesh* is an example of the discipline inescapable by any editor, however objective his ambitions may be. As Greg points out, the elimination of a misprint or an 'obvious blunder' is in itself a degree of eclecticism. What must be demanded of the textual critic is a responsible eclecticism.

To be eclectic is 'to borrow freely from various sources, to be not exclusive in opinion, taste, etc.' (*Concise Oxford Dictionary*). An irresponsibly eclectic reader will turn with equal enthusiasm to any one of the thirty-six plays in the Shakespeare Folio; a more responsible eclecticism will prefer 1 *Henry IV* to 1 *Henry VI*. And the same principle applies to the parts of a literary artifact: some scenes are better than others, some speeches are more memorable than others, and so are some sentences, some clauses, some single words. The art of textual criticism consists in the ability to make such distinctions and to use them to demonstrate the superiority of one reading or version to another. Bentley's criterion is still the only valid one: *ratio et res ipsa centum codicibus potiores sunt*. The best reading is the one that makes the best sense – with the one limitation that it is, as Greg put it in 'The Rationale of Copy Text', 'one that can reasonably be attributed to the author . . .'[1]

One of the illusions of the 'biblio-textualists' has recently been exposed in an able article by D. F. McKenzie – 'Printers of the Mind', *Studies in Bibliography*, 22 (1969), 1–75. The illusion was that whenever two compositors can be shown to have been engaged in a single work or gathering they must have been setting simultaneously. It was admitted that an elaborate preliminary 'casting-off' would have been required to determine the exact point in the copy where the second compositor began, but the early printers were apparently able to do this. No evidence was provided, and with Q2 of *Hamlet*, according to Bowers, Compositor Y was able to begin sheet E in the middle of a sentence! McKenzie has now shown that 'casting off' was simply a device for determining the amount of paper required, which could then be costed. Absolute accuracy was not necessary; and simultaneous printing by two compositors only

[1] *Studies in Bibliography*, 3 (1950–1), 32. Reprinted in Greg's *Collected Papers* (ed. J. C. Maxwell, 1966, p. 387).

occurred in page-by-page reprints. What normally happened was that one took over where the other left off.

It is something to learn what 'casting off' really means. But the moral of the episode is the indifference of bibliographers to textual considerations. If 'casting off' had really meant what Bowers and Hinman and the others thought it meant, the first thing two compositors would have had to do after determining the place where one took over from the other would be to cut up their copy (McKerrow's 'copy-text') accordingly. Who will believe that Jaggard, the printer of Fl, cut up the copy of Q6 of *Richard III* that the players had had collated 'with a full and authoritative manuscript' (Greg, *The Shakespeare First Folio*, 1955, p. 192)? An obvious objection is that cutting up a corrected quarto will deprive the other compositor of his copy on the verso of a page. Would the players obligingly provide Jaggard with two copies of Q6 of *Richard III*? Since they would both need to be collated with the full and authoritative manuscript, it seems unlikely.

SEVEN

LITERARY HISTORY

> Any satisfactory study of the works of Shakespeare, or indeed probably of any other author, must take full account of the order in which they were written, and . . . it is advisable actually to study them, so far as possible, in that order.
>
> R. B. McKerrow[1]

> We cannot consider fiction by periods, we must not contemplate the stream of time. Another image better suits our powers: that of all the novelists writing their novels at once . . . All through history writers while writing have felt more or less the same. They have entered a common state which it is convenient to call inspiration, and having regard to that state, we may say that History develops, Art stands still.
>
> E. M. Forster[2]

The implications of a continuum

McKerrow was one of the best Elizabethan scholars of our time. The dictum quoted here is of special interest because it represents, as he informs us, the most important methodological conclusion he had reached after the many years he had devoted to the Oxford Shakespeare (he died before the edition was made ready for publication). Forster, on the other hand, at any rate in *Aspects of the Novel,* may be taken to represent

[1] *Prolegomena for the Oxford Shakespeare* (1939), p. vi.
[2] *Aspects of the Novel* (1927), pp. 14, 21.

English criticism of the same period. In the passages quoted above the scholar and the critic are apparently in flat contradiction in their approach to literature. For McKerrow an author's works must be read chronologically; for Forster the works exist outside time. It is true that the examples Forster gives of novelists of different dates 'seated together in a room, a circular room, a sort of British Museum reading-room – all writing their novels simultaneously' do not carry complete conviction.[1] Richardson sits next to Henry James ('two novelists who are looking at life from much the same angle'), Dickens is next to H. G. Wells ('the same point of view and even using the same tricks of style'), and Sterne sits by Virginia Woolf ('There is even the same tone in their voices'). Do they? Is there? But even if Forster is rather forcing the evidence here there is certainly something in his general proposition. For the scholar it is the differences between one author and another, one artifact and another, even one edition and another, that really matter; the critic on the other hand is less concerned with differences than with that general quality I have called 'good English', the creative quality which makes certain works of our literature still so eminently worth reading – whatever their dates may be and however imperfect the edition he is using.

The logical contradiction is resolved in the concept of a continuum. The term is useful in literary theory because it provides an approach to the history of literature that parallels or duplicates the balance of opposites that is the characteristic differentia of literature itself. To comprehend and appreciate literary meanings the reader must be something of a scholar as well as something of a critic; the ideal scholar-critic combines both aptitudes in equal proportions, though one or the other quality may sometimes appear to be merely incidental. Greg, for example, though professionally a scholar and without literary interests, was a master of English prose. No one in our time has written more vigorous, masculine, consistently lucid and economical English. The stylistic parallels that suggest themselves are the prose of Bernard Shaw or of George Orwell. E. K. Chambers, who was Greg's colleague in Elizabethan studies (though less limited in his range), wrote almost as well

[1] *Aspects of the Novel* (1927), p. 9 *et seq.*

and with a faint flavour of elegance that is curiously reassuring in the thickets of brute fact. R. W. Chapman was another pure scholar of the same generation who fascinates by a personal tone of dry, intermittent irony. Among the older American scholars George Lyman Kittredge and George Sherburn were outstanding in different ways for the excellence of their prose style. And the catalogue could be continued among the younger scholars.

Our concern here, however, is with the more abstract implications of the concept of a continuum. If English literature is to be thought of as at once continuous and in process of change, with periods of continuity or even apparent stability perhaps following or preceding periods principally of change, time must be central to the process. The point has already come up. But how are we to define the role of time – not only in the English continuum that begins *c.* 1200 and in which we still live as producers and consumers of literature, but also in the shorter continuities of a single 'movement', or an author's complete works, or even one artifact?

We can perhaps begin by saying that literature abstracts the dimension of time from the spatio-temporal totality of normal human experience, the world we know and live in, just as the visual arts abstract the dimension of space. The distinction between temporal literature and spatial sculpture or painting was made with great acumen by Lessing for his own polemical purposes in the *Laokoön,* but it has a wider relevance than Lessing or his modern followers have realized. The three central parts played by time in the creation and appreciation of literature might be summarized as follows:

1 In literature as in common speech a period of time must inevitably separate the beginning of a sentence from its end. The larger the literary unit the longer the time-gap will be. And whatever pattern of events fills such a verbal interval can only be enacted, described or responded to in temporal terms. Beginnings, middles and ends – with such Aristotelean complexities as the *anagnorisis* (recognition of what is present in what was past), and the *peripeteia* (reversal of fortune, as when those who were prosperous end miserably) – are therefore naturally a prime concern of the scholar-critic.

2 The technical necessity of temporal extension makes literature

an 'imitation' of the universal human process of birth, adolescence, maturity, old age and death. By its abstraction of these elements from their ordinary physical or spatial backgrounds the literary artifact is always tending towards tragedy. Thus the most 'serious' of the genres is, as it were, built into literature as a simple technical necessity.

3 Whereas time is irreversible in the spatio-temporal reality of common human experience, a book once read can be read again. More generally, in the process of reading, we are almost *compelled* to compare what is now being read with what preceded it in the same artifact – often indeed in the preceding sentence or line.

In practice, in the actual reading of specific works of literature, what do these generalizations mean?

Three temporal artifacts

In this section specimens are offered of the various ways in which the temporal criterion works. A single question is being asked in each case: 'How will a fuller understanding of the aesthetic meaning be obtained by the use of a temporal check or the extraction of a temporal scheme?'

1 *Blake's 'London'*

How, for example, does Blake use time in his 'London'? As a revolutionary torch? As the sombre human present extended into a vindictive future? Or what?

What may well be the first draft of the poem appears on p. 109 of the *Notebook* (also known as the Rossetti MS. because it was once owned by Dante Gabriel Rossetti who allowed it to be used in Alexander Gilchrist's *Life of William Blake*, 2 vols, 1880). The draft (which is on the same page as 'The Tiger' but preceding it) has been corrected and expanded in the process of composition. The title was squeezed in and is clearly an afterthought. If it and minor deleted words or phrases are ignored the poem reads as follows (major deletions in square brackets and italics):

I wander thro each dirty street
Near where the dirty Thames does flow

And [*see*] mark in every face I meet
Marks of weakness marks of woe

In every cry of every man
In every [*voice of every child*] infants cry of fear
In every voice in every ban
The [*german forged links*] mind forged manacles
   I hear

[*But most*] How the chimney sweepers cry
[*Blackens oer the churches walls*] Every blackening
   church appalls
And the hapless soldiers sigh
Runs in blood down palace walls

[*But most the midnight harlots curse*] But most thro
   midnight streets I hear
How the youthful harlots curse
Blasts the new born infants tear
And [*hangs*] smites with plagues the marriage
   hearse

The poem in its original form was written in 1790 or perhaps 1791. As engraved three or four years later in *Songs of Experience* only two changes of any interest have to be recorded: in ll, 1, 2, 'dirty' has become 'charter'd', and in l. 16 'smites' has become 'blights'. (No doubt 'blights' is better than 'smites', but Blake might have done better to return to 'hangs'; 'charter'd' is a more difficult case, but the explicit 'dirty' seems better to me than the more pretentious and obscure 'charter'd'.) The eccentric punctuation added in the *Songs of Experience* version gives the impression of evading the grammatical difficulties. Why should 'every voice' (l. 7) be followed by a colon, 'every ban' by a comma and 'I hear' (l. 8) by no stop at all? Similarly with the use of initial capitals. The draft has only 'Thames' (apart from those at the beginning of each line); *Songs of Experience* has 'Thames', 'Man', 'Infants', 'Chimney', 'Soldiers', 'Palace', 'Harlot' and 'Marriage' – but not those of any of the other nouns. It is clear that whatever pictorial significance the poem may have had to Blake,[1] its essential

[1] The engraving in *Songs of Experience* is of a bent old man with an enormous beard being addressed by a boy.

importance to him was as direct social comment. An editor will therefore modernize its spelling, punctuation and use of capitals, so that the meaning can become generally and immediately available, and not remain, as in so much of Blake's later work, private or outside the traditions of English culture.

In most modern editions and anthologies l. 8 ends with a full stop:

The mind-forged manacles I hear.

Such a punctuation is only grammatically possible if the next stanza ('How the chimney sweepers cry/Blackens . . .') is read as a prolonged exclamation, but the fourth stanza makes this impossible with its '. . . I hear/How . . .'. Clearly what Blake intends is that 'I hear' in l. 8 governs the preceding clauses (ll. 5–8) and *also* the succeeding clauses (ll. 9–12). Such an elliptical construction requires a finesse in punctuation that he did not possess, but a modern editor will presumably use a dash:

In every cry of every man . . .
The mind-forged manacles I hear –

How the chimney sweepers' cry
Every blackening church appals . . .

Grammatically, the 'I hear' of l. 8 is the pivot on which the poem balances. It is also the moment of *peripeteia* in the drama enacted in London's internal temporal continuum. The Londoners who are seen or heard in the poem's first two stanzas are the passive victims of an industrial or financial tyranny, the hand-cuffed prisoners of a system imposed on their minds by the minds of their oppressors. But in the last two stanzas the situation has completely changed. The forty City churches built after the Great Fire of 1666, having suddenly lost the original whiteness of their Portland stone, are now blackened, Blake asserts, by the cries of the boy chimney-sweeps. And a similar phantasmagoria is occurring at Buckingham Palace, where the tears of press-ganged soldiers are staining the elegant stucco. The climax to this 'reversal of fortune' is left to the last stanza, in which a single harlot's unspecified curse apocalyptically converts the wedding carriages of London's rich into a hearse for their dead offspring.

The poem's pattern, if this interpretation is correct, is achieved by a balance of the first two stanzas with the last two stanzas which is also a contrast between them. It is surprising and unexpected – and yet satisfying to one's sense of the ultimate justice of things. And the *material* in which the tragic progress is effected is the dimension of time. Thus 'every ban' (curse) in l. 7 is *followed* by 'harlot's curse' (l. 14) not only in the literal sense of coming seven lines later but also in the dramatic sense that the futile complaints of the miserable multitude are about to be revenged by the single midnight harlot. The *post quod* is a *propter quod*.

There is a similar general temporal relationship between *Songs of Innocence* and *Songs of Experience* as aesthetic wholes. The *Innocence* poems were written before the *Experience* poems, as the condition of being a child precedes the condition of maturity. Blake's general concern in *Experience* is with the tragic consequences of the temporal process which deposits the immature among the mature, as the innocent, miserable poor of 'London' are deposited among and exploited by their rich and cruel oppressors. Blake was a political and social revolutionary at the time these poems were written. If only by implication they reflect and express two temporal historical stages, each the product of the other: (1) the contemporary moral justification for an English Revolution similar to the American and French Revolutions, (2) its sequel in a future elimination of the contemporary ruling class. But the coherent ideal continuum of literature mitigates the separate day-by-day horrors of such actualities as the guillotine.

A still wider literary continuum would include *Songs of Innocence* in the English quasi-pastoral tradition represented by such things as folk-song, nursery rhymes and Isaac Watts's *Divine Songs for Children*; *Songs of Experience* (which Blake would never sell separately from *Songs of Innocence*) is a part of the *consequent* literary tradition in which *Paradise Lost* is the dominant influence – though for the scholar-critic it is perhaps the *consequences* of Blake, for Yeats, for example, that naturally attract most attention.

An interesting example of the continuity of this pastoral/

tragic English literary tradition, at least from *c*, 1200. is the short medieval lyric which fuses into its four lines both the innocence of Blake's 'Blossom' and the experience of his 'Sick Rose':

> All night by the rose, rose,
> All night by the rose I lay;
> Darf [need] I naught the rose to steal,
> And yet I bore the flower away.

The general title-page to Blake's two collections claims in its sub-title to be 'Shewing the Two Contrary States of the Human Soul'. In the best of the *Songs*, however, the contrariety merges into a continuity. Blake did not need to steal his rose, but yet – as is the nature of the triumphs of the literary process – he stole the flower away from all his contemporaries.

2 *'A Mister Wilkinson, a Clergyman'*

The three temporal characteristics of the literary artifact summarized on pp. 149–50 above may seem closer to criticism than to scholarship. But the scholar-critic, as McKerrow's dictum indicates, is necessarily, if only primarily, concerned with the exact place in the temporal continuum that the work being investigated can be demonstrated to occupy. To study Shakespeare, 'or indeed probably . . . any other author', some account must be taken of the order in which the works were written. If that order is already known the scholar can and should study them in it; if it is not known the scholar's first duty is to establish the chronological order of their composition.

Speaking strictly as a scholar, then, McKerrow was certainly right. If you think, as Coleridge did at one time,[1] that *The Tempest* followed *As You Like It* and preceded *Twelfth Night*, it will be difficult to discuss it with any plausibility either as a scholar or a critic. The two orders of enquiry are intimately interrelated. The object of the remaining sections in this chapter is to illustrate this interrelationship by showing how an apparently trivial or dry-as-dust problem of literary

[1] This was in 1810. See *Coleridge's Shakespearean Criticism*, ed. T. M. Raysor (1930), I, 239, and p. 161 below.

chronology may contribute to the most sophisticated literary criticism if the analysis is carried far enough.

The case of 'A Mister Wilkinson, a Clergyman' has the advantage of factual limitation. Who was the author of the line? At what date and under what circumstances was it composed? Was this Mr Wilkinson a historical or a fabulous clergyman? The answers to these questions are all discoverable without much labour or uncertainty.

The work of reference that might be expected to provide immediately reliable replies to such questions is *The Oxford Dictionary of Quotations*. And sure enough the line does appear there. In the first edition of the *Dictionary* (1941), the line is assigned to Edward FitzGerald (1809–83), with the following note: 'Benson's *Life of FitzGerald*, p. 62 and Hallam Tennyson's *Tennyson*, i, 153. An imitation of Wordsworth's worst style.'

A scholar is entitled to complain that this entry is seriously misleading. Tennyson has as much right to be considered the author of the line as FitzGerald; and the note is incomplete as well as committing several errors of scholarly presentation. A. C. Benson's initials should certainly have been given, as should the date of his book on FitzGerald (1905); and its title is not, as the italics imply, *Life of FitzGerald* but *Edward FitzGerald.* In any case Benson's account of the origination of the line has no authority and is simply a conflation of two passages in Hallam Tennyson's *Alfred Lord Tennyson. A Memoir* (2 vols, 1897).[1]

However, accounts of the line are provided on five separate occasions by three first-hand or second-hand witnesses. Since they are all quite short they can be quoted here in full in the chronological order of their publication:

1 *Letters of Edward FitzGerald to Fanny Kemble,* ed. W. Aldis Wright (1895), p. 123. Note by Wright: 'Why Fritz,' said Tennyson, 'that's a verse, and a very bad one too.' And they would afterwards humorously contend for the authorship of 'the worst line in the English language'.

[1] The second edition of *The Oxford Dictionary of Quotations* (1953) eliminates A. C. Benson and gives the Hallam Tennyson reference as II, 276 – both steps in the right direction. But it misses the crucial 1862 letter from FitzGerald to Tennyson. And the erroneous comment on 'Wordsworth's worst style' is retained.

2 Hallam, Baron Tennyson, *Alfred Lord Tennyson. A Memoir. By his Son*, 2 vols, (1897). Under 1835, (I, 153): 'My father and Fitzgerald [*sic*] then had a contest as to who could invent the weakest Wordworthian line imaginable. Although Fitzgerald claimed this line my father declared that he had composed it . . .' This was at Ambleside and is said to be the first meeting of FitzGerald and Tennyson.

3 *Ibid.* Under 1883 (II, 276): FitzGerald complains in a letter to Hallam Tennyson, 19 April 1883, that 'Wright had heard from someone that he, the Laureate, had added to his wreath one of the grandest lines in all blank verse . . . of which I was the author, while speaking of my brother-in-law'.

4 *More Letters of Edward FitzGerald*, ed. W. Aldis Wright (1901), p. 284, FitzGerald to Wright 1883: 'A. T. yields to *me* – unwillingly – the glory of A Mister Wilkinson, etc.'

5 *Tennyson and his Friends*, ed. Hallam, Baron Tennyson, (1911), Includes 'Tennyson, FitzGerald, Carlyle and Other Friends' by Sir Herbert Warren, which prints on p. 130 an undated letter of *c.* July 1862 from FitzGerald to Tennyson: 'I have just lost a brother-in-law – one of the best of Men. If you ask "Who?", I reply in what you once called the weakest line ever enunciated:

A Mister Wilkinson, a Clergyman.

You can't remember this: in Old Charlotte Street, ages ago.'

Of the witnesses paraded here FitzGerald is the only one who can be described as first-hand. Hallam Tennyson's account in (2) may represent a garbled recollection of what he had been told by his father, just as (1) may be based on what Aldis Wright had been told by FitzGerald. But the three first-hand accounts – (3) (4) and (5), all by FitzGerald – tell a plausible and consistent story, (5) the last to be published being the earliest and the most detailed.

The one external fact needed to reconstruct the occasion of the line's composition is the date of the Rev. John Brewster Wilkinson's marriage to FitzGerald's sister Isabella. However, this is easily obtainable from the *Gentleman's Magazine*, *Crockford* or Venn's *Alumni Cantabrigienses*, who agree that the wedding was on 29 May 1832. From the casual tone of FitzGerald's allusion to Wilkinson both A. C. Benson and

Hallam assumed incorrectly that the marriage was still in the future. Certainly, when he mentioned this clerical Wilkinson FitzGerald can hardly have thought of him as 'one of the best of Men', and no doubt he scarcely knew him ('A Mister' implies non-acquaintance).

This inference enables us to advance the date of Tennyson's friendship with FitzGerald. They had not met at Cambridge, though they were contemporaries at Trinity, but on going down they both had occasional periods in London. 'Old Charlotte Street' is now Bloomsbury Street, which runs into Great Russell Street, where J. M. Kemble, another Trinity contemporary, was to be found. (This future editor of *Beowulf* was the son of Charles Kemble, the actor-manager, and the brother of Fanny Kemble.) It is clear too from Tennyson's joking dismissal of FitzGerald's family news as 'the weakest line ever enunciated' that they must already have been intimate before the death of Arthur Hallam in September 1833. The impression Hallam Tennyson gives that his father and FitzGerald only got to know each other at all well in 1835 is certainly incorrect. 1832 or 1833 is more probable – and London rather than Ambleside.[1]

There are critical implications in this reconstruction of the biographical background to 'A Mister Wilkinson a Clergyman'. Briefly summarized they are these:

1 FitzGerald was Tennyson's most perceptive and most outspoken critic. If 1832–3 (until October 1833 when the news of Hallam's death reached him) was Tennyson's *annus mirabilis*, as the evidence of the manuscripts suggests, even though most of the poems were not published until much later, some of the credit may well be due to FitzGerald.

2 Tennyson's immediate iambic reaction to FitzGerald's innocent information suggests an excessive metrical consciousness, a 'poetic' rather than a human response to reality.

3 The introduction of Wordsworth into the episode is not authenticated by any first-hand evidence. Tennyson and his Cambridge friends were in fact all passionate Wordsworthians.

[1] Tennyson specified London in 'To E. FitzGerald' (1885):

When, in our younger London days,
You found some merit in my rhymes,
And I more pleasure in your praise.

In any case Miltonic apposition in an inappropriate or indecorous context is more characteristic of Cowper or of Crabbe. 'And at the Hoop alighted, famous inn' (*The Prelude*, iii, 17), almost the only Wordsworth parallel, was not published until 1850. Hallam Tennyson had perhaps confused John Brewster Wilkinson with Thomas Wilkinson, whose spade Wordsworth had honoured in *Poems in Two Volumes* ('Spade! with which Wilkinson hath tilled his lands'). In the Preface to his selection from Wordsworth (1879) Matthew Arnold had given the latter poem a certain comic celebrity[1]

> I am a Wordsworthian myself. I can read with pleasure and edification *Peter Bell*, and the whole series of *Ecclesiastical Sonnets*, and the address to Mr. Wilkinson's spade, and even the *Thanksgiving* Ode; – everything of Wordsworth, I think, except *Vaudracour and Julia*.

By 1879 Tennyson and FitzGerald had both developed critical reservations towards Wordsworth and his poetry, but at Cambridge around 1830 he was incomparably the greatest living poet. 'Tithonus' (written 1833) and the *Rubáiyát* are manifestations of a later development of English Romanticism, but they could not have been the poems they are if it had not been for their temporal relationship to *Lyrical Ballads*, though Coleridge was clearly a more dominant influence than Wordsworth.

3 *Spenser or Marlowe?*

In any problem concerned with the history of English literature the first move, I have suggested, must be with the scholar and the last with the critic. McKerrow's dictum on the full account to be taken by a scholar of the order in which a particular author's works were written applies equally to two contemporaries. Here, for example, is *The Faerie Queene*, I, vii, 32, ll. 5–9:

> Like to an Almond tree ymounted hye
> On top of greene *Selinis* all alone,
> With blossomes brave bedecked daintily;
> Her tender locks do tremble every one
> At every little breath, that under heaven is blowne.

[1] pp. xxv–xxvi.

Spenser is at this point comparing Prince Arthur's helmet's plumes to the almond blossoms. And here, almost word for word, is Marlowe (2 *Tamburlaine*, IV, iii, 119–24):

Like to an almond tree ymounted high,
Upon the lofty and celestiall mount,
Of every [*sic*] greene Selinus queintly dect,
With bloomes more white than Hericinas browes,
Whose tender blossoms tremble every one,
At every little breath that thorow heaven is blowen:

The two passages are certainly connected, but which is copying which? Until the order of priority has been established, any critical comment is not worth attempting. The traditional assumption has been that Marlowe was copying Spenser, but an American scholar has recently challenged this assumption, and it must be admitted that the external evidence is far from conclusive.[1] The first three Books of *The Faerie Queene* were published in 1590. And so were the two Parts of *Tamburlaine*. It is true that this instalment of *The Faerie Queene* was entered in the Stationers' Company's Register on 1 December 1589, whereas the two Parts of *Tamburlaine* had to wait until 14 August 1590. But 2 *Tamburlaine* was almost certainly being acted by 1588, and *The Fairie Queene* I and II, or parts of them at any rate, were being circulated in manuscript about the same time. (Two stanzas from Book II are quoted in full in Abraham Fraunce's *The Arcadian Rhetoric*, which was entered in the Stationers' Register on 11 June 1588.)

But if the external evidence does not amount to much in this case, the internal evidence is decisive. Fortunately there are concordances of both Spenser and Marlowe, and they reveal such facts as the following:

1 Spenser has 126 different past participles, some of them used many times, with the *y*-prefix; Marlowe, on the other hand, has only one (*ysprung* in *1 Tamburlaine*) apart from *ymounted* in this passage.

[1] T. W. Baldwin, 'The Genesis of Some Passages which Spenser borrowed from Marlowe', *ELH*, 9 (1942). A reply by W. B. C. Watkins appeared in *ELH*, 11 (1944).

2 This is the only example of *blossoms* in Marlowe; Spenser uses the word forty-five times.
3 Marlowe uses *tender* five times as against Spenser's ninety-five (including *tenderly*).
The alexandrine at the end of the Marlowe passage also looks like a careless repetition of Spenser's alexandrine; it is true there are in all thirty alexandrines in 1, 2 *Tamburlaine*, but none of the other examples occur in the climax of a passage; indeed, in the whole of Marlowe's work there is only one other climactic alexandrine (in the 1616 version of *Faustus*). Moreover, the fact that Arthur's plume is a single one, whereas Tamburlaine's is triple (l. 116), seems suggestive. The one addition made in the Marlowe passage,

> With bloomes more white than Hericinas browes,

is, on the other hand, the only example in it of Marlowe's 'mighty line' (note the hyperbolic use of the comparative and the sensual use of colour). Finally, the fact that virtually every phrase in the passage with the exception of this line is found elsewhere in Spenser's poetry seems to decide the issue. It is only necessary to cite *The Faerie Queene*, I, iv, 5:

> it mounted was full hie,
> That every breath of heaven shaked it:

Spenser was born in or about 1552 and Marlowe in 1564. It would be more natural for the younger man, still in his early twenties when *Tamburlaine* was written, to imitate an already famous contemporary than *vice versa*, and Marlowe's debt to Spenser – or improvement upon Spenser – in this passage is now generally accepted. The true temporal relationship is reflected in most of the differences already cited. A helmet with one plume, for example, is the natural precursor of one with three plumes. More generally, the details of style that distinguish Spenser in the passage represent an earlier phase of English Renaissance poetry than Marlowe's characteristic manner. Spenser's poetic diction is still that of a writer feeling his way; Marlowe's has the assurance of a writer confident of what it is possible to say in the idiom he is employing – and confident too of an intelligent and sympathetic audience.

Chronological gaps and the literary detective

The temporal continuum is easiest to trace when the study is of a single work or of a single author. Coleridge's criticism of Shakespeare was seriously impeded by his ignorance of the order in which the plays were composed. His three attempts to classify the plays in their chronological order – one made in 1802, one in 1810 and one in 1819[1] – make it clear that he was concerned with the temporal nature of the complex literary artifact that constitutes 'Shakespeare', and they become more accurate at each attempt. But even in 1819 the first two plays are *Love's Labour Lost* and *Pericles* and the last two *Antony and Cleopatra* and *Troilus and Cressida*. And the 'Fourth Epoch' of the five that he hypothesizes begins with *The Tempest* which is followed by *As You Like It*. Coleridge was not unaware of some of the external evidence assembled by Malone in *Attempts to Ascertain the Order in which the Plays of Shakespeare were Written* (1778), a masterpiece in its way of literary detection, but he relied principally upon the very subjective 'internal evidence furnished by the writings themselves'.

The century of intensive professional specialization that followed Coleridge's amateurism was summed up in E. K. Chambers's 'The Problem of Chronology' (Chapter viii of *William Shakespeare: a Study of Facts and Problems*, 2 vols. 1930), which is still the definitive discussion of the plays' chronological order and provides a model for similar investigations into the order of other authors' works. Chambers begins with the order that can be inferred from the external evidence, listing for each play a *terminus a quo* and a *terminus ad quem*. This scaffold is then filled in with a scrutiny of the topical allusions and such internal evidence as parallels between two or more of the plays and the statistical order provided by a battery of metrical tests (percentage of rhyme, enjambment, stress, feminine endings, 'light' and 'weak' monosyllables at the end of the line, etc.). Chapter ix ('Plays of the First Folio') arranges the F1 plays in the order that an application of such evidence suggests. And to a remarkable extent Chambers's order still stands today, though the probability of some revision

[1] *Coleridge's Shakespearean Criticism*, ed. T. M. Raysor (Cambridge, Mass., 1930), I, 235–42.

in several plays is now generally agreed to complicate things to a greater degree than he realized.

The combination of external and internal evidence that has made it possible to read the whole of Shakespeare's extant output as a single temporal artifact has been applied, more or less thoroughly, to most of the earlier English poets and dramatists. But there are still far too many gaps. We know the order in which Chaucer's poems were written, but we do not know with scholarly precision if, for example, the *Book of the Duchess* and the *Parliament of Fowls* are or are not two fragments of perhaps different periods that have been cunningly amalgamated into a single poem. (There is *some* evidence that they are amalgams, though it is far from conclusive.) The *Canterbury Tales* is certainly not a continuous temporal whole, but much work has still to be done on the dates of composition of the separate Tales and the degree of revision they have each undergone. In Chaucer's case the extant external evidence has probably all been assembled, but only a beginning has been made with the analysis of the internal evidence. Here is an area where the literary critic and the literary detective can profitably join hands.

A few later examples will, however, be worth giving in greater detail. I shall begin with Malory's *Morte D'Arthur*, which consists of eight separate 'Tales' in the Winchester MS., now brilliantly edited by Eugène Vinaver (1947). The scholar-critic will naturally wish to know what the order of composition of the eight books was. Unfortunately he gets little assistance from Vinaver in the section 'The Sequence of Malory's "Volumes"' – even in Vinaver's second edition (1967). On the basis of a single parallel passage the second book, which is based on the English alliterative *Morte Arthur*, is said to precede the first.[1] But it is a general rule of all source-hunting that the parallels must accumulate to be acceptable as more than coincidences.[2] One parallel proves nothing. And there is a

[1] Even if the similarity is conceded the order of imitation must be established. Which is the original passage and which the imitation? Malory may have read the alliterative *Morte* and been struck by Vinaver's passage *before* writing his Book II.

[2] See the perceptive article by Hardin Craig, 'Some Problems of Scholarship in the Literature of the Renaissance', *PQ*, I (1922).

clue of far greater significance lying unused in Malory's text in the form of words in which Malory acknowledges his debt to his source. (The device is also employed to conceal a departure from the source – much as Chaucer used the non-existent Lollius as a screen for his deviations from Boccaccio in *Troilus and Criseyde.*)

In Malory's last two books the formula is 'as the Freynshe booke seyth' (or 'maketh mencyon'). Altogether there seem to be seventeen occurrences of the 'French book' in Books VII and VIII. The 'French book' also appears, though less frequently, in Books III, IV and V. It is naturally absent altogether from II, whose source is not French but the English 'romaynes'. But much the most significant fact that emerges from the enquiry is the discrepancy between the standard formulas and those used in VI (the Grail episode), where the formula is 'as the tale tellith', 'Now turnyth the tale' and variations on this form of words. The only reference to a French original is in the colophon ('drawn out of Freynshe') which may not be Malory's. Book I also has 'the Freynshe Booke' in its colophon, and 'as the booke rehersyth in Freynsch [the books of French]' twice in the text; its standard formula, however, is 'as hit tellith' or 'as hit rehersith'. Apart from the anomalous II, then, the various formulas point to VI as the earliest of the separate books with I following it. The exact order of composition of III, IV and V must remain conjectural, though they will certainly have preceded VII and VIII. Vinaver describes VI (the *Tale of the Sankgreall*) as 'the least original' of Malory's works, being 'to all intents and purposes a translation of the French *Queste del Saint Graal*'.[1] Most of us find it the dullest and the worst written. Vinaver's ingenious theory that Malory acquired his excellent prose style in the process of reducing the alliterative redundancies of the English *Morte Arthur* into narrative prose need not be rejected altogether, but the absence of any echoes of the *Morte Arthur* in it suggests that VI may be earlier than II – in fact, the earliest extant work that we have by Malory. And in that case the whole problem of the evolution of his

[1] *The Works of Sir Thomas Malory*, ed. E. Vinaver (2nd. ed. 1967), III, 1534. The two references to 'the SANKGREALL' or its 'BOOKE' in Book I also suggest that VI had already been completed when I was in process of composition.

prose style and structural method will have to be reconsidered.

A later example of the help that chronological order can provide for the determination of meaning on internal evidence alone is raised by Marvell's lyrics. With the exception of the contributions to the Lovelace and Hastings memorial volumes, 'A Dialogue between Thyrsis and Dorinda', and the anonymous 'Elegy upon the Death of my Lord Francis Villiers', none of Marvell's early poems in English were published until the posthumous *Miscellaneous Poems* (1681). As the poems in this collection include Marvell's masterpieces – such as 'To his Coy Mistress', 'A Dialogue between the Soul and Body', 'The Mower against Gardens' and 'The Garden' – and the poems are all undated, the critic naturally clings to whatever straws the allusions in them provide. These are reasonably specific in 'An Horatian Ode upon Cromwell's Return from Ireland' (early summer 1650), but in general the order of composition is far from clear. A clue provided by the confusion of *you* and *thou* is therefore of considerable interest. The poems which use the two forms of the second person indiscriminately include 'A Dialogue between the Resolved Soul and Created Pleasure', 'Young Love', 'The Gallery', 'Daphnis and Chloe', 'The Picture and Little T. C. in a Prospect of Flowers' and 'Ametas the Thestylis making Hay-Ropes'. Perhaps the clearest case of all is 'To his Coy Mistress' in which both *thou* (*thine, thy*) and *you* (*your*) occur indiscriminately six times. As there is no *thou/you* confusion in the long 'Upon Appleton House' (1651–3) it seems likely that poems in which the confusion occurs are relatively early. Another characteristic of these poems is the preference – already general in Yorkshire – of *-s* to *-eth* in the third person singular. 'To his Coy Mistress' has no *-eth* forms. But euphony has clearly determined the preference of *-eth* in some of the poems (to avoid a sequence of sibilants) and the test cannot be considered a decisive one. Nevertheless 'The Nymph Complaining for the Death of her Faun' – with no *thou/you* confusion and more *-eth* than *-s* for the third person present indicative – does now look like a comparatively late poem. These are intersubjective facts that would impress a jury in a court of law and they cannot be ignored in any future discussion of Marvell. No doubt there are others awaiting the astute literary detective.

Two general technical morals may be drawn from the preceding examples of the operation of the time-check. One is that external evidence, because of its greater degree of intersubjectivity, provides the proper point of departure in literary research. The student's first duty is to assemble *all* the relevant first-hand external evidence. Second-hand evidence must be treated with more caution, and third-hand evidence can usually be ignored completely. (Consider the case of 'Mr. Wilkinson'.) But before it is accepted as valid the external evidence is best submitted to the internal temporal checks latent in every literary artifact. Though one *begins* with external evidence one has always to *end* with internal evidence, the evidence, that is, that what we are reading makes good sense. Literature is by definition meaningful, fuller of meaning than sub-literature or would-be literature, and if when all the external clues to its comprehension have been assembled it is still necessary to guess, that is a risk that has to be taken. To guess intelligently, as scholar and critic, is better than to surrender to meaninglessness – which excludes the artifact from the right to be considered literature at all. (But the guesses *must* be intelligent – and *must* also be recognized to be provisional.)

The second moral that any use of the temporal check suggests is that order of composition is more important than actual historical dates. Should one, in obedience to McKerrow's advice, read the 'Ode to a Nightingale' before or after the 'Ode on a Grecian Urn'? Both seem to have been written in May 1819, though the exact dates of composition are unknown and there is no external evidence extant to determine what the order was. No one will doubt, however, that the order in which they were written is more important than the precise days of the month or hours of the day of composition. And in this case, as in most, internal evidence solves the problem to which external evidence has nothing decisive to contribute. It is virtually certain that the order in which the two odes were printed in the 1820 *Poems* is the order of their composition. The 'Nightingale' ends with a repeated question; the 'Grecian Urn' ends with an emphatic answer. For Keats, at least in May 1819, the poetic imagination was not a mere 'waking dream' like 'Kubla Khan' but a Wordsworthian 'vision'. The logical aesthetic order may reasonably be presumed to reproduce the historical order of composition.

EIGHT

PRESENTATION

It is difficult – it is perhaps the supreme difficulty of criticism – to make the facts generalize themselves.

T. S. Eliot[1]

Eliot's dictum will be found at the beginning of his essay on Massinger, this part of which had originally been a review of A. H. Cruickshank's pedestrian study of that dramatist in *The Times Literary Supplement.* Having premised that 'English criticism is inclined to argue or persuade . . . instead of forcing the subject to expose itself', Eliot goes on to pay Cruickshank a half-compliment. 'Mr Cruickshank,' he concedes, 'at least presents us with facts which are capable of generalization.' And, as the essay proceeds, Eliot uses the facts assembled by Cruickshank to generalize themselves through a series of juxtaposed quotations that do have the effect of 'forcing the subject' (the nature of Massinger's dramatic talent) to expose itself.

The passage provides a useful definition and illustration of the principle that governs a scholar-critic's presentation of his material. Avoiding argument and persuasion he will try to force his subject to expose itself, or generalize itself, by an irresistible parade of the relevant authenticable evidence. Eliot did not go on to distinguish between, on the one hand, the single 'hard fact' of verifiable evidence which is the principal concern of the pure scholar and, on the other hand, the concatenation of such facts by which they generalize themselves. But the two processes, though allied, are essentially different and they demand their separate modes of presentation. A single fact

[1] *The Sacred Wood*, p. 112.

validates itself by the accumulation of miscellaneous information – indeed, the more miscellaneous the witnesses the better. But the miscellaneous nature of the evidence, because it is not intellectually *in pari materia*, justifies a sort of short-hand in its presentation. The test is brevity and immediate intelligibility, and if the abbreviations are conventionally standard nobody will object if the English language appears to have been maltreated in the process. It follows that the generalization of single facts represented by Eliot's essay on Massinger – or by any essay or treatise that combines scholarship with criticism – calls for two separate levels of presentation: (1) the process by which bare facts 'factualize' themselves; (2) the commentary accompanying the evidence. In (1) much of the evidence can be relegated to footnotes, but for (2) a critical long-hand in correct or even 'good' English is required to elaborate the short-hand of the crude facts – without the same degree of abbreviation, though as far as possible with a comparable pithiness.

Quotations and titles

Quotation, effective and precise quotation, is the principal device of literary research. It is important therefore not to confuse its rules and conventions with those that an editor employs when presenting a text. The essential distinction is simple. An editor, in the proper sense of that word, *establishes a text* (by a judicious selection both of his 'copy-text' and of the particular variant readings and emendations with which he corrects it); the function of a quotation, on the other hand, is to *reproduce the relevant verbal evidence* (or illustration) as accurately and concisely as possible. In a scholarly article or treatise a quotation is expected to be virtually identical *verbatim et literatum* with its original. Any deviation even in the 'accidentals' (spelling, punctuation, the use of capital letters, italics, etc.) will constitute a minor tampering with the evidence. Misprints, however obvious, are therefore retained, though a *sic* in square brackets is usual after each such misprint as a sort of reassurance to the reader that the error is not your doing.

The rigour of precise reproduction of the original passage quoted is conventionally mitigated in the following respects:

1 the long *s* general in printed books, except at the end of a word, up to *c.* 1800 is now almost always modernized;[1]
2 the Elizabethan *i*, *j*, *u* and *v* are generally normalized;
3 the early printers' gothic type is almost always modernized, as is (more rarely) the later habit of italicizing each proper name;
4 a quotation that is itself a complete sentence may drop its initial capital when embodied in a sentence of modern commentary (older scholars resist this trend).

The most important devices for reducing the length of a quotation without falsifying the original text are:

1 three dots to indicate short omissions of irrelevant material within the quotation. They should be used terminally when what is quoted ends before the completion of the sentence in which it occurs. The dots are never strictly necessary at the beginning of a separate quotation (one not embodied in your text) that is not a complete sentence, as the use of lower case indicates that some word or words must have preceded it. For long omissions in the course of a quotation a line of dots should be inserted.
2 square brackets should be used for all editorial insertions within a quotation. If through omitting intervening matter a pronoun has become ambiguous there is no objection to substituting a noun or proper name for the original pronoun providing that the substituted word is in square brackets.

The choice of the text or edition to be quoted from in your article, etc., will naturally depend upon the nature of the material presented and the audience envisaged. In general, a first or original edition (or a photographic facsimile of such an edition) is to be preferred whenever textual minutiae are being

[1] First discarded in Joseph Ames's *Typographical Antiquities* (1749), according to McKerrow (*Introduction to Bibliography*, p. 309) who credits the effective introduction of the modern *s* to John Bell who used it all through his *British Theatre* (1791). The long *s* survived erratically even in print until the mid-nineteenth century, H. N. Coleridge, for example, using it in his edition of *The Friend* (3 vols, 1837, 1844).

discussed. (The test is the degree of responsible authority ascribable to the edition selected.)[1]

As an editor (to return to the distinction between establishing a text and reproducing a quotation), Helen Darbishire was certainly justified, if perhaps mistaken, in emending every emphatic *me* to *mee* and each unemphatic *their* to *thir* in her edition of Milton.[2] But if a critic or commentator wishes to quote a passage from *Paradise Lost* he will use the spelling of the first (1667) or the revised second (1674) edition, even if it includes an emphatic first person spelt *me* or an unemphatic third person spelt *their* – unless of course Helen Darbishire's own edition is for some reason the subject of discussion.

In any similar case the reader is entitled to assume that the text quoted is that of either the first or the last edition authorized by the author (or printed from his final manuscript) – unless he is warned that a later edition or a manuscript is being used. The choice of edition will depend upon the particular case. Thus a quotation from Congreve will normally be from the *Works* (1710), which Congreve intended to be the definitive edition of his plays and poems, or of some reliable reprint from it.[3]

[1] Quotations from Shakespeare are generally from a modern edition. Since the Bartlett concordance is from the Clark/Aldis Wright 'Cambridge' edition (reprinted in the 'Globe' series with negligible differences), this is usually the edition selected, although it is now out of date. Even so it is a far more responsible text than that of the 1623 Folio. Charlton Honman's Norton edition of the Folio (New York, 1969) may soon supersede it.

[2] It is instructive and not unentertaining to read the two principal critiques of the Darbishire edition – B. A. Wright's 'Textual Introduction' to his own Everyman edition of *Milton's Poems* (1956) and R. M. Adams's *Ikon: John Milton and the Modern Critics* (1955).

[3] Bonamy Dobrée's reprint in the World's Classics series (2 vols, (1925–8) is an entertaining case. In general this is an extremely accurate reproduction of the 1710 edition, but the text of one of the lyrics ('On Mrs. Arabella Hunt Singing') includes a line from the text in the two miscellanies where it first appeared. An earlier owner of the copy from which Dobrée's edition was set had entered the earlier reading in the margin for his own edification, but the innocent compositor at the Clarendon Press mistook the marginal note for a correction, and the error was not detected.

For most non-textual purposes the standard modern edition suffices. A reader who wishes to check or follow up a quotation will then be able to do so without difficulty. Modern editions are usually reliable, especially those emanating from university presses, and the objection to modern spelling, etc., is often mere intellectual snobbery. But a crucial document should always be quoted, if possible, in its original form. If it is in manuscript the abbreviations or slips of the pen are best reproduced, square brackets being used for elucidating obscurities or indecipherable words.

A special case is a book's title. A title-page as distinct from a title should be reproduced, preferably photographically; a title is best modernized. The case for modernizing titles was made by Greg with his usual lucidity:[1]

> The first essential, in my opinion, is that titles should be given in modern spelling. This is the universal custom so far as Shakespeare's plays are concerned, but in the case of other writers there has sprung up a habit of giving titles in some form of 'old spelling'.[2] Although the habit has the sanction of some scholars for whom I have the highest regard, it none the less seems to me an inconvenient

[1] *A Bibliography of the English Printed Drama to the Restoration*, IV (1959), cviii.

[2] It has in some instances no doubt been due to understandable diffidence, when faced by the admitted difficulties of modernization, and to a fear lest in the process some subtlety of meaning or association should be lost, though the problem has perhaps been more often shirked out of pure laziness. Most powerful, however, and pernicious has been the superstition of the half-baked thesis writer that there is some inherent virtue, something 'scientific', in preserving an archaic orthography. There are, I agree, reasons why, in a critical edition of an old text, it is desirable that the spelling and other peculiarities of the original should be preserved, but these reasons apply less to quotation, and do not apply at all to the labels we use to designate the works in question, labels that belong essentially to our own speech. (Greg's note.) Photography has recently proved a more specious crutch for laziness to rely on, though some of the photo-facsimiles – such as those issued by the Scolar Press (Menston, Yorkshire) which are both scholarly and inexpensive – certainly have their uses.

> and even ridiculous practice.[1] To demand that a writer, every time he wishes to mention an Elizabethan work, should remember or ascertain how its name is spelt in some particular page of some particular edition is a monstrous and pedantic imposition, a mere waste of time and energy, and no authority, however august, can make it anything else.

Greg adds a final note to the effect that his comments must be taken as only applying to the sixteenth and seventeenth centuries, though he gives examples of anomalies in the titles ascribed to medieval works by modern scholars. Thus *The Legend of Good Women* is a purely fictitious title – as incidentally is *Comus*. But similar principles clearly apply to more recent titles, though there is now no question of modernizing the spelling. For almost all literary purposes, for example, *The Personal History, Adventures, Experiences, and Observations of David Copperfield the Younger, of Blunderstone Rectory (which he never meant to be Published on any Account)* – the title of the wrapper of the issue in parts which was reduced to *The Personal History of David Copperfield* on the title-page when published in volume form – is now simply *David Copperfield.*

A convention only recently introduced is to reserve italics for the title of a *book*, however short, provided that it was originally published separately. Works within works, such as the 'Ode to a Nightingale' (which Keats included in his 1820 *Poems*), are now generally referred to in quotation marks, either single or double, though any work that is being frequently cited in the course of a critical discussion is better italicized. A refinement adopted by some journals is to reserve capitals for the more important words when a title that repeats the first line (or part of it), e.g. of a lyric, is that actually used by the author, merely editorial titles being kept in lower case: thus 'A slumber did my spirit seal' (editorial), but 'She Walks in Beauty' (authorial). The title of a work in French, whether authorial or not, always requires lower case; in English it is

[1] The height of absurdity is reached by those who insist on calling the play of *Sir Thomas More* by the title of *The Booke of Sir Thomas Moore* because that is how the manuscript happens to be inscribed, ignoring the fact that 'The Booke' can be no part of the title since it means no more than the prompt copy. (Greg's note.)

usual, though not universal, to use an initial capital for nouns, adjectives and most verbs, whether the capitalization conforms to the original title-page or not, except in the most formal bibliographies. The great *Short-Title Catalogue* reduced all initial capitals (except those of proper names) to lower case and the convention has now been adopted by the *New CBEL*. The objection to it is the risk of confusing a title with the continuous prose with which it may be surrounded; a title should stick out, as it were, so as to be immediately recognizable as non-prose.

References

Whereas the accurate reproduction of whatever is *quoted* (a title is not a quotation) must be considered a rule of scholarship with only minimal deviations permissible from it, the system of references to be adopted in a particular work of literary research is essentially a matter of balancing a reader's conveniences. Brevity is desirable, provided it is not sacrificed to obscurity; over-elaborate references are simply a nuisance, the degree of precision required, from the relevant part of the column on a two-column page to the bare number of a chapter or a scene, depending upon the nature of the evidence being presented. The conscientious reader's convenience must always be a consideration, one second only to accuracy. (It will be easier for a scholar-critic to skim through the *chapter* in a Victorian novel on his own book-shelves than to inspect a first edition in a university library in order to identify a particular *page*.) Unless the readings of the first edition are crucial to the argument all that is usually needed in the case of a novel is the number of the chapter (or chapter within a 'Part' or 'Book') quoted or referred to. If a standard edition does exist, such as the Tillotsons' *Vanity Fair* (1963), the reference should still include the number of the relevant chapter, so that the reader who does not possess their edition can still to some degree check the critical validity of the argument being used. The common notion that eighteenth – and nineteenth – century texts are grossly corrupt is a delusion.

Other things being equal, however, the ideal reference combines both precision and concision. The dual necessity is the excuse for the short-hand employed in footnotes. As with the treatment of quotations the most elaborate tabulation of current conventions is *The MLA Style Sheet*, which was prepared by William Riley Parker, then the secretary of the Modern Language Association of America; a second edition with important modifications was begun by Parker and has been completed by his successor John H. Fisher. The advice provided in the *Style Sheet* is largely technical, e.g. on the proper transliteration of titles and authors' names from foreign languages, and is intended in the first place for contributions to American journals or the thesis of Ph.D. candidates. Nevertheless, even the mature English scholar-critic will benefit from the perusal of its austere pages.[1] Its English equivalent *Notes on the Presentation of Theses on Literary Subjects* (1952: anonymous but in fact compiled by Humphry House with the assistance of Helen Gardner) was primarily intended for those preparing a thesis for the Oxford B.Litt. and is much less detailed.

Three degrees of abbreviation have become customary in footnotes.

1 *The short title. David Copperfield* (London, 1850) exemplifies the short title of a primary work. The year of original publication in book form follows the first mention – in round brackets if a date provided is in the original edition, in square brackets if it has to be supplied on external evidence. Degrees of probability in the latter can be indicated by using a query after the date or a *circa* preceding it, both being enclosed in the square brackets. (The query is just a little more definite than the *circa* or *c.*) The place of publication should precede the date, though London is often omitted, as in this work and *CBEL*, in an English reference. The publishers' names and a publisher's series are not usually necessary; the latter must always be distinguished from an academic series, such as the Early English Text Society, which may be expected to guarantee a scholarly treatment and should therefore be specified.

2 *The cue-title* (the often grotesque but obvious short-hand

[1] The *Style Sheet* is not infallible. I cannot accept its distinction between the possessive of a one-syllable author ending with 's' ('Keats's') and one for a longer name ('Hopkins''). As the possessive is pronounced in each case both should be spelt out ('Keats's', 'Hopkins's'). Alternatively neither should be spelt out.

which takes its name from the cues in an actor's part). Cue-titles are justifiable whenever there are frequent references to a single work; they will normally begin with the second reference, the first having been comparatively full and concluding with some such formula as 'Henceforward referred to as,' e.g. de Selincourt or *G. Expectations.* The one condition a cue-title must satisfy is immediate to partial intelligibility. It is not usually necessary to prefix to a book or article a list of the cue-titles employed, though such lists have their uses in theses as a sop to suspicious examiners.

3 *The siglon* (the technical term for apparently meaningless collections of initial letters, such as *DNB* or *TLS*). Sigla are always in italics. The old habit of inserting a full stop after each letter, though correct grammatically, seems to be dying out. These strange symbols should be limited to familiar works of reference and titles, authors and editors referred to so frequently in a particular discussion as to justify themselves as technical terms combining the essential virtues of concision and precision. It is probably best to reserve them for footnotes and appendixes; a preliminary list of all but a few standard works of reference (with which the reader can be assumed to be familiar) is helpful when prefixed to a book or edition, though it is not always needed in articles, even in the professional journals.

In an article intended for a 'learned journal', or in a thesis, a certain wariness should be observed with the traditional abbreviations of Latin formulae. With the disappearance of universally compulsory Latin even from the universities the distinction between 'v.' and 'cf.', for example, has become blurred, and it is better to use the English equivalents 'see' and 'cp.' (seeing is not the same as comparing). As for 'op. cit.' and 'ibid.' they are hardier perennials, but unless the work referred to has occurred within a page or two they should be avoided and in any case the page must always be given, if not identical with that in the preceding reference.

Some alternative modes of reference to volume and page are exemplified below. The one rule in these matters is to adhere to the same system throughout with complete consistency.

The first reference will naturally be the longest. In a footnote the following are recommended:

A. C. Bradley, 'The Rejection of Falstaff', *Oxford Lectures on Poetry*, 1909, pp. 247–75. (This is the formula suggested in *Notes on the Presentation of Theses on Literary Subjects*.)

A[ndrew] C. Bradley, 'The Rejection of Falstaff', *Oxford Lectures on Poetry* (London, 1909), pp. 247–75. (This is *The MLA Style Sheet* formula.)

Henry Bradley, 'English Place Names', *Essays and Studies*, i. (1910), 7–41. (*Notes on the Presentation of Theses formula;* also that of 'Guidance to Contributors' issued by the *Review of English Studies*.)

Henry Bradley, 'English Place Names', *Essays and Studies*, 1 (1910), 7–41. (This follows *The MLA Style Sheet* recommendation in the 1970 revision. Note that the volume number is now arabic and not roman figures, as in the 1951 edition.)

American references to books usually include both the place of publication and the name of the publisher in the first reference, whereas in England the place of publication – if London this is often omitted altogether (as I have done) – and the date and page numbers are considered sufficient.

If the author's name has been mentioned in the text it need not be repeated in the footnote, but at some point the first name and/or initials must appear. Within the text of a book or article English usage prefixes Miss or Mrs to the names of living feminine authors and the Christian name alone to those no longer alive. (Thus 'Jane Austen', never 'Austen' as in the U.S.A.) Knighthoods conferred towards the end of a scholar's life may usually be ignored, e.g. E. K. Chambers rather than Sir Edmund Chambers, W. W. Greg and not Sir Walter Greg. English scholars tend to ignore the 'Jr' that often follows a contemporary American writer's name on rather the same principle. In a non-technical bibliography the author's name should generally appear as on his title page, though '[Enoch] Arnold Bennett', etc., is permissible if fussy. Such lists are sometimes alphabetical. In those that are chronological it is usual to bunch books or articles by the same author together irrespective of the strict date-order with other authors. Alphabetical lists (including indexes) are without this embarrassment, but it may be difficult to decide the point at which a hyphened or dual surname begins. (And even scholars sometimes change their names.) One convention that is almost a rule is to treat the *de*, *De*, *von*,

Von, etc. preceding the surname as a necessary prefix (De Quincey, de Selincourt, etc., coming under *d*), when the bearer of the name is a native Englishman; with a French author, on the other hand, the process is reversed (thus Remy de Gourmont would be listed under *g*, though there are a few exceptions like De Gaulle).

For second or later references both in footnotes and the text the same principles apply as in the abbreviation of titles (see p. 173). The more often an author, organization, publisher, place of publication, etc. is referred to, the greater the justification for more and more abbreviation, especially in footnotes. Journals, in particular those in general use, especially if their full title is unnecessarily elaborate, almost demand abbreviation. A consciousness of such a decorum no doubt explains why *The Publications of the Modern Language Association of America* has now adopted *PMLA* as its official title. But *The Times* is still *The Times* even in the most rigorous footnote.

Organization

The coherent whole into which, under ideal conditions, the separate facts assembled by the competent scholar-critic generalize themselves, will depend for its structure on the nature of the facts. Occasional attempts have, however, been made to formulate general advice. An article that is particularly worth the attention of every aspiring student is R. B. McKerrow's pithy 'Form and Matter in the Publication of Research',[1] even if some of its recommendations may seem self-contradictory.

McKerrow's name has appeared more than once in the preceding pages, but in addition to being a scholar of great if limited distinction he was the founder in 1925 of the *Review of English Studies* (*RES*), which immediately established itself as the English rival of such American professional quarterlies as *PMLA*, *Modern Philology* (*MP*), *Studies in Philology* (*SP*) and the *Philological Quarterly* (*PQ*). McKerrow edited *RES* until he died (in 1940), and in that capacity he had to read, accept or reject a great many learned or would-be learned articles. Many of them naturally were unsatisfactory in one respect or another, and his accumulated irritation at last found expression in this

[1] *RES*, 16 (1940), 116–21.

lively sketch of the ideal *RES* article. According to McKerrow a workman-like article – and by implication a comparable treatise or even review – falls into five consecutive parts:

1 The *introduction,* in which the author briefly states the present position of research on his subject and the views currently held on it.
2 The *proposal,* in which he describes in outline what he hopes to prove.
3 The *boost,* in which he proceeds to magnify the importance of his discovery or argument. (This is, as it were, a taste of sauce to stimulate the reader's appetite.)
4 The *demonstration,* in which he sets forth his discovery or argument in an orderly fashion.
5 The *conclusion,* or *crow,* in which he summarizes what he claims to have shown, and points out how complete and unshakable is his proof.

The five subdivisions are the weakest part of McKerrow's programme. In a good article, one worthy of publication in *RES*, it is the *demonstration* that will take up most of the words. The *introduction* is best left to a footnote either to the first sentence or the title, and the *proposal* can often be incorporated in the title or the subtitle. As for the *boost* and the *crow* they should surely be implicit rather than explicit; the facts, as Eliot put it, must generalize themselves.

But McKerrow's article improves as it proceeds. Here are some of his eminently sensible recommendations:

> The subject of a research article should always be a unity.
>
> Adjust what you say to the knowledge you may reasonably expect your readers to have.
>
> As far as possible state your facts in chronological order.
>
> Give plenty of real dates (not 'the following spring', 'next year', 'the following decade', etc.).
>
> Don't be (1) cryptic or literary, (2) humorous, (3) ambiguous (avoid 'doubtless', etc.).
>
> Be precise in your quotations.
>
> Avoid back-slapping heartiness ('Tom' Nashe, 'Jack' versus 'John' Donne – even though Donne himself initiated the contrast).

McKerrow's final recommendation – 'Do not allow any doubts as to the importance of your thesis to creep in' – perhaps savours more of journalism than of either scholarship or criticism. On the contrary, in research as in more mundane matters, honesty is decidedly the best policy. It is a simple matter of ordinary intellectual honesty not to conceal objections to your thesis of which you are yourself aware. (This applies too to external evidence for which you have searched laboriously but in vain.)

More elaborate textbooks have been appearing recently: *The Aims and Methods of Scholarship in Modern Languages and Literature* (a Modern Language Association symposium edited by James Thorpe, New York, 1963, which has a masterly section on 'Textual Criticism' by Fredson Bowers); Richard D. Altick's entertaining *The Art of Literary Research* (New York, 1963); James Thorpe's short *Literary Scholarship* (Boston, 1964); George Watson's intelligent *The Study of Literature* (1969). And no doubt there are others. But on the principles as opposed to the mechanics of presentation I have not found them as useful as McKerrow's five succinct pages.

Ronald S. Crane of Chicago, who was perhaps the best scholar-critic of our time in the field of English literature, used to tell his Ph.D. candidates that a literary thesis must be capable of being reduced to a single proposition. The concept of a logical proposition demanding demonstration is certainly etymologically implicit in the term *thesis*, and Crane's formula guarantees the unity that McKerrow rightly demanded in an article. But there is an alternative to logical unity in the organization of a work of criticism or scholarship. This is *narrative* unity. A history or a biography cannot easily aspire to more than a narrative unity, though if it is to be more than a 'chronicle' the narrative sequences must not be 'And then . . . and then . . . and then', but the tracing of effects to their causes. Crane would no doubt have insisted that any such narrative unity presupposes a propositional unity. Agreed, but there are differences in the different degrees of explicitness in argument (logical exposition) and narrative (intelligible chronological exposition). Some of us prefer one method to the other and *vice versa*.

For most scholars it is a matter of finding the right model –

right, that is, for the individual scholar. And the final piece of advice I have to offer the young scholar-critic is to take out a subscription to one of the professional journals. There he will find a variety of models from which he can select one or two that happen to be temperamentally sympathetic to him. A mere skimming of the journals in a university or city library is no alternative. The fact of possession – preferably paid out of one's own pocket – guarantees a much closer attention to all the separate articles and reviews, whether they are of one's own special period or not. As a young man I subscribed to *RES* for several years. The material was not, with rare exceptions, particularly fascinating, but by associating with scholars in their particular area of interest I believe I became infected by the instinct of scholarship. Before long, indeed, I found myself contributing articles of my own on such abstruse problems as 'The *Errata* in *The Tatler*'. I had undergone a 'conversion' comparable in its way with that which T. S. Eliot experienced as a boy of fourteen when he picked up that copy of FitzGerald's Omar Khayyám 'which was lying about'. From the lectures that I attended as a graduate student at Oxford and Harvard I regret to say I learnt almost nothing. (Perhaps they are better today.)

CONCLUSION

I end as I began with the Sense of Fact. Literature is an object of knowledge. But, though the scholar-critic's concern is primarily with what is historically verifiable in literature (its 'meaning'), such verification does not exclude the criterion of intersubjective relevance (its 'significance'). The two senses are interlinked, the one merging into and dependent on the other, and both imply a consensus of mature and responsible individual minds in effective verbal communication in a single society. Some such concept as civilization therefore underlies and authenticates the competent reader's response. We read in order to become more civilized, more humane, more useful because more perceptive citizens. And the refusal to separate meaning from significance is at the heart of the special 'esemplastic' contribution that literature makes to life.

But if literary meaning and literary significance are ultimately indivisible (a recognition of the indivisibility is required to save the scholar-critic from degenerating into a mere specialist), the two terms can be provisionally distinguished. 'Meaning' is the linguistic stage in the literary cycle, whether considered from the point of view of the author or of his audience. Our immediate responsibility is to what has been called Then-Meaning; in other words, the meaning a word, phrase or sentence has for the author himself and his inner audience of intimate acquaintances. What is essential in Then-Meaning, however, is not language but style or genre. A linguistic basis in common speech or non-literature must no doubt be presumed, but in literature language has been modified to a greater or less degree by style. (Consider, for example, the effect of irony or metaphor.) And style depends upon genre.

Thus 'tragic irony' operates in one way (the author and audience share a meaning from which a *dramatis persona* has been excluded), comic or satiric irony in another (the butts are too stupid to comprehend the inverted meanings that the context has made evident to us).

As a Then-Meaning is conditioned by the artifact's genre, the scholar-critic confronted by an unfamiliar work will be well advised to begin by asking himself what is the style appropriate to the literary kind to which this work belongs. The preliminary identification will necessarily be tentative and approximate, one probably to be modified before the temporal progress through the work has been completed. Genres and styles are the most delicate aspects of Then-Meaning and vary, if only marginally, not only between the separate works of a single author but from one part of such a work and another. In Chapter One I gave some short examples of the failures of critics as sensitive as Matthew Arnold and T. S. Eliot, and in each case the critical error derived from a misidentification of the genre being employed. The writer himself may also be mistaken. Arnold's letter to Clough is well known:[1]

> *Homer animates* – Shakespeare *animates* – in its poor way I think Sohrab and Rustum *animates* – the Gipsy Scholar at best awakens a pleasing melancholy.

Few critics of Arnold have been found to agree with him. 'Sohrab and Rustum' is most successful when it abandons its epic models; 'The Scholar-Gipsy' is one of the most memorable of English pastorals – not because of the occasional melancholy but because of the fascinated descriptions of the Berkshire countryside – as Arnold himself later realized:[2]

> Do you remember a poem of mine called 'The Scholar Gipsy'? It was meant to fix the remembrance of those delightful wanderings of ours in the Cumnor Hills . . . .

The 'merry Grecian coaster' of the final simile is if anything just a little too merry.

If the reader has recognized the genre correctly, the Now-

[1] *The Letters of Matthew Arnold to Arthur Hugh Clough*, ed. H. F. Lowry (1932), p. 146. Letter dated 30 November 1853.

[2] Mrs Humphry Ward, *A Writer's Recollections* (1918), p. 54. Letter to Tom Arnold, dated 15 May 1857.

Meaning may be expected to coincide with the Then-Meaning. The errors of critics in comments on their contemporaries, on the other hand – those of Sainte-Beuve, for example, on Stendhal, Flaubert and Baudelaire, or those of F. R. Leavis on Auden and Empson (whose poems he regarded as inferior to Ronald Bottrall's Pound-and-water rubbish) – are more often errors of significance than of meaning.

What is the difference? In a final analysis, literary meaning is a matter of style – and style, I have argued, is finally a matter of effective verbal repetition. The possibilities and variations of such repetition are endless (far more and more sophisticated than the neo-classic rhetoricians realized), and they vary from author to author as well as from genre to genre. But they have one common characteristic when they are successful: the creation of illusion. Words seem momentarily to become things. I regard the moment of illusion – more strictly, the temporal succession in a period of illusion – as the specifically aesthetic phase of the literary cycle. As the phase reaches its temporal conclusion the artifact begins to acquire significance for the reader. The scholar-critic wakes up, rubs his eyes, and eventually translates the aesthetic experience that he has gone through back into words. A value-judgment is recorded.

Meaning and significance are both intersubjective phenomena, but whereas meanings are small mental units and subject to some extent to the external controls in the conventions of language and literary tradition, significances are more internal and up to a point the reflections of political and economic pressures, even if these are unconscious. Significances are consequently less stable than meanings. One generation's judgments will often be contradicted by those of its successor, as E. E. Kellett has demonstrated effectively in *The Whirligig of Taste* (1929). But such contradictions are often exaggerated. The continuum that constitutes the history of any national literature is certainly not a plain, but neither is it broken up into a series of mountain ranges, as the textbooks tend to assert. One of the functions of the scholar-critic is to demonstrate that the history of a literature is a gradual and continuous slope. And so the sense of fact serves to maintain a perpetuation of the literary tradition without which a civilized society cannot persist as such.

An early review by Lytton Strachey of Birkbeck Hill's edition of *The Lives of the Poets* exemplifies the perils that literary integrity runs from the intrusions of even the highest journalism. The review, which was originally printed in July, 1906, includes this epigram:[1]

> Johnson's aesthetic judgments are almost invariably subtle, or solid, or bold; they have always some good quality to recommend them – except one: they are never right.

One knows what Strachey meant, of course. And the hierarchy of literary significances *was* different in 1906 from what it is today, or even what it was in 1878 when Arnold reprinted *The Six Chief Lives from Johnson's Lives of the Poets* with a sympathetic short preface of his own. But a scholar-critic would never at any time have written as Strachey did. Not only are the facts wrong, the contradiction between what is praised and what is censured is just clever journalism; implicit too in the censure is the vulgar assumption that literature progresses by revolutions. (Because Johnson was once admired it was justifiable to call in question all his judgments.) In reality, as a scholar-critic soon discovers, a gradual, almost imperceptible evolution is occurring all the time. That is literary history. The rest is propaganda – or self-advertisement.

[1] *Books and Characters* (1922), p. 68. Strachey was twenty-six when he wrote this review.

SELECT BIBLIOGRAPHY

Some of the principal works of reference for English literature have been described in Chapter Two (pp. 30–50 above). A good short selection of more general studies will be found appended to George Watson's *The Study of Literature* (1969), pp. 221–9. The notes and bibliographies in *Theory of Literature* (New York, 1949, rev. 1956, and 1964) by René Wellek and Austin Warren are much fuller, though they lack the critical comments supplied by Watson. The following selection is largely based on Chapter XI (mainly by Harrison T. Messerole) of my own *Guide to English Literature* (1965, rev. 1967, 1970), the main part of the *Guide* being devoted to modern editions and commentaries on particular English authors, periods, 'schools' and genres (with brief assessments of each work). The useful *Selective Bibliography for the Study of English Literature* by R. D. Altick and Andrew Wright (New York, 1960, rev. 1963) and D. F. Bond's *Reference Guide to English Studies* (Chicago 1962; a revision of T. P. Cross's 1919 *List of Books and Articles*) are both confined to general works on literature and omit particular works and authors.

Identifying and locating the texts

General bibliographies

General bibliographies of English literature are virtually restricted to *CBEL* (see p. 30 above), Robert Watt's *Bibliotheca Britannica* (4 vols, Edinburgh, 1824, reissued 1965), which has a subject division useful for tracking down authors of anonymous works, and W. T. Lowndes's *Bibliographer's Manual of English Literature* (rev. H. G. Bohn, 6 vols, 1857–64), which has occasional useful notes.

Of the period bibliographies two are outstanding: *A Short Title Catalogue of Books Printed in England, Scotland, and Ireland, and of English Books Printed Abroad, 1475–1640* (1926) by A. W. Pollard and G. R. Redgrave, which is usually abbreviated to *STC*, and its successor Donald Wing's *Short-Title Catalogue of Books Printed in England* [etc.], *1641–1700* (3 vols, 1945-51). *Wing* (the usual abbreviation) omits periodicals. With this exception the two works aim at completeness within their respective periods. Second editions are in preparation which will fill the inevitable gaps and extend the enumeration of copies in public libraries. Microfilms of all the works listed in *STC* and of a selection of *Wing* items are in progress at Ann Arbor, Michigan. The Bibliographical Society (London) is preparing a continuation of *Wing* up to 1800.

Comparable compilations for the Old English period are N. R. Ker's *Catalogue of Manuscripts containing Anglo-Saxon* (1957), and for the Middle English period to 1400 J. E. Wells's *Manual of the Writings in Middle English* (New Haven, 1916, with nine Supplements, 1919–52). Wells confined himself to works of literary interest, summarizing their contents and providing elaborate lists of modern editions and commentaries. A. H. Heusinkveld and E. J. Bashe have provided a similar *Bibliographical Guide* for Old English literature (Iowa City, 1931).

For eighteenth-, nineteenth- and twentieth-century literature resort must be made to such trade lists as *The London Catalogue of Books . . . Published in London, 1700–1855* (8 vols, 1773–1855) and the *English Catalogue of Books* (published annually from 1801). There are useful indexes of both by Sampson Low up to 1889. From 1950 the *British National Bibliography* (issued weekly) has superseded its rivals as a record of current publications.

Genre bibliographies

For *poetry* W. Carew Hazlitt's *Hand-book to the Popular, Poetical and Dramatic Literature of Great Britain* (1867; supplements 1876, 1882, 1889–92, 1903, with index to 1889 by G. J. Gray, 1893) still has its uses, especially for the Tudor and Stuart periods. Russell Hope Robbins's *Index of Middle English Verse* (1943) largely supersedes Carleton Brown's *Register of Middle English Religious and Didactic Verse* (2 vols, 1916–20). The *Bibliography of English Poetical Miscellanies* by Arthur E. Case (1935; from 1521 to 1750) is similarly superseded by Norman Ault's list in *CBEL*, II, 173–256, for 1660 to 1750; Ault continues to 1800. A recent research tool of great value is Margaret Crum's *First-line Index of English poetry, 1500–1800, in Manuscripts in the Bodleian Library* (1969).

For *drama* S. Schoenbaum's revision of A. B. Harbage's *Annuals of English Drama* (Philadelphia, 1964) is complete to 1700, though less detailed bibliographically than W. W. Greg's list of the whole printed drama to the Restoration (4 vols, 1939–59). Allardyce Nicoll's *History of English Drama 1660–1900* (6 vols, 1952–9) is particularly useful for its Vol. VI – a virtually complete *Short-Title Catalogue of Plays Produced or Printed in England from 1660* to *1900*. C. J. Stratman's *Bibliography of English Printed Tragedy, 1565–1900* (Carbondale, 1966) supplements Nicoll. The theatrical history of London from 1660 to 1800 has been covered in great detail by W. Van Lennep, E. L. Avery, A. H. Scouten and G. W. Stone in *The London Stage* (8 vols, Carbondale, 1960–5).

For *prose fiction* the chronological lists by Sterg O'Dell (Cambridge, Mass, 1954; for 1475–1600), Charles C. Mish (3 vols, Charlottesville, 1952; for 1600–1700), William H. McBurney (Urbana, 1960; for 1700–39) are complete. For more recent periods R. D. Mayo's *English Novel in the Magazines*, 1740–1815 (Evanston, 1962), Andrew Block's occasionally erratic *The English Novel, 1740–1850* (1939, rev. 1961), and Michael Sadleir's incomplete *Nineteenth Century Fiction* (2 vols, 1951) are the best lists so far available. William Freeman's *Dictionary of Fictional Characters* (1963; includes plays in English) is useful at a lower level.

For *periodicals* the standard finding list is the *British Union-Catalogue of Periodicals* (4 vols and Supplements 1955–8, 1962); *CBEL*'s lists are complete to 1900.

Separate bibliographies, more or less complete, exist of most of the principal English authors, some of which include elaborate lists of reviews and similar secondary matter. For the more important writers before 1900 one or more bibliographies will be found at the head of each list of an author's works in *CBEL*.

Library catalogues

In addition to the British Museum's *Catalogue of Printed Books* (see p. 46 above), the following libraries have published catalogues of their contents, all of which will prove occasionally useful to the literary student:

The Advocates' Library (now National Library of Scotland): 7 vols, Edinburgh, 1867–78.

William Andrews Clark (now University of California): 19 vols, Los Angeles, 1920–31.

S. Christie-Miller: *The Britwell Handlist* (2 vols, 1933).

Carl H. Pforzheimer: *English Literature, 1475–1700* (3 vols, New York, 1940).

Lord Rothschild: 2 vols, 1954.

E. Gordon Duff: *Catalogue of the John Rylands Library* (3 vols, Manchester, 1899).

R. F. Metzdorf: *The Tinker Library* (now Yale University), (New Haven, 1959).

Thomas J. Wise: *The Ashley Library* (now British Museum), (11 vols, 1922–36).

H. B. Wrenn and T. J. Wise: *A Catalogue of the Library of John Henry Wrenn* (now University of Texas), (5 vols, Austin, 1920).

Catalogues of book sales

American Book Prices Current (New York 1895–), *Book Prices Current* (1886–), and *Book Auction Records* (1902) provide annual summaries of interest to bibliographers as well as to financial speculators. George L. McKay's *American Book Auction Catalogues, 1713–1934* (New York, 1937) and the British Museum's *List of Catalogues of English Book Sales, 1676–1900* (1915) include the earlier sales.

Assembling the secondary material

Most of the relevant modern books and articles are listed in *CBEL* (2nd ed. of Vol. III, 1969). For extra-literary sources the standard compilations are Constance M. Winchell's *Guide to Reference Books* (8th ed., Chicago, 1968) and A. J. Walford's *Guide to Reference Material* (1959, rev. 1966).

Subject indexes (books)

The London Library's *Subject Index* (by C. T. Hagberg Wright and C. J. Purnell, 4 vols, 1909–55) is reliable and intelligently selective. R. A. Peddie's *Subject Index of Books Published before 1880* (4 vols, 1933–48), the British Museum's lists from 1881, and the Library of Congress's *Catalog: Books: Subjects* from 1950 (20 vols, Ann Arbor, 1955) can be terribly time-consuming. For the literary student the *Essay and General Literature Index* (Ann Arbor, 1941–) by Minnie E. Sears and Marian Shaw is often more rewarding, if only because it provides an annotated author, subject and title index to modern composite volumes. An essential research tool is the *ASLIB Directory: a Guide to Sources of Specialized Information in Great Britain* (edited by Miriam Alman, 2 vols, 1957, Supplement 1962).

Indexes to periodicals

Poole's Index to Periodical Literature, 1807–1907 (5 vols, including Supplements, 1887–1908), indexes by subject some 470 English and American periodicals and includes book reviews. The most useful index to twentieth-century periodicals for the student of literature is the *Subject Index to Periodicals 1915–61* and its successor the *British Humanities Index* (1962–). For 1824–1900 the *Wellesley Index to Victorian Periodicals* (ed. W. E. Houghton, Toronto, 1966–) identifies most of the anonymous reviews. *Notes and Queries* (founded 1849) has cumulative indexes for each series of 13 vols. Of the extinct journals *The Gentleman's Magazine* (1731–1907) was almost unique in providing cumulative indexes. For newspapers the most useful index is *Palmer's Index to the Times 1790–1941* (1886–1943). *The Times Official Index 1906–* (1907) is still produced annually.

Lists and summaries of current research

PMLA's 'Annual Bibliography' lists books and articles (from 1150 journals) published during the preceding year in the modern language field, but it was confined until 1956 to the work of American scholars. *The Year's Work in English Studies* (from 1920) has been international in scope in its surveys of the different periods but is less comprehensive. The Modern Humanities Research Association's *Annual Bibliography* is similar to the *PMLA* lists, though less comprehensive (but it lists the principal reviews of each book). The period bibliographies – Renaissance studies in *Studies in Philology* (from 1917); 1660–1800 in *Philological Quarterly* (from 1926; 1925–60 lists reissued with general indexes, 4 vols, 1950–62); 1800–37 in *ELH* (1937–49), then transferred to *Philological Quarterly* and in 1964 to *English Language Notes*; 1837–1900, in *Modern Philology* (1933–52), thereafter in *Victorian Studies* (lists for 1932–54 reissued with general indexes) – are outstandingly useful because of their completeness and the critical comments and reviews that they occasionally include.

Work in progress is not so easily located. *Work in Progress in the Modern Humanities, 1938–42* (1939–43), compiled by James M. Osborn, was continued by 'Research in Progress in the Modern Languages and Literatures' in *PMLA* (1950–60) but has now been discontinued. *Studies in English Literature* (founded 1961), however provides recurrent surveys of 'Recent Studies', each issue being devoted in turn to non-dramatic Renaissance literature, the Elizabethan/Jacobean drama, the Restoration and eighteenth century, and the nineteenth century.

L. F. McNamee's *Dissertations in English and American Literature: Theses Accepted by American, British and German Universities, 1864–1964* (New York, 1968) is unfortunately incomplete.

There is an ASLIB *Index to Theses Accepted for Higher Degrees in the Universities of Great Britain and Ireland 1950/51* – (1950–), arranged by author and subject, as well as *A Survey of Theses; Literature in British Libraries* by P. D. Record (1950) for earlier work. The American counterpart to Record is T. R. Palfrey and H. E. Coleman, *Guide to Bibliographies of Theses* (2nd ed. Chicago, 1940). Richard D. Altick and W. R. Matthews's *Guide to Doctoral Dissertations in Victorian Literature, 1837–1900* (Urbana, 1960) is another useful tool. *An Index to Book Reviews in the Humanities* (Detroit, 1960–) is not confined to literature.

Critical surveys of modern literary scholarship

J. E. Wells's *Manual of Writings in Middle English* (New Haven, 1916, with nine supplements, 1916–51) terminates at 1945. *Contemporary Literary Scholarship: a Critical Review* (ed. Lewis Leary, New York, 1958) covers the whole of English and American literature rather breathlessly under 'Periods' and 'Genres'. A more detailed series organized by the MLA has four excellent guides to research in nineteenth-century English literature: Romantic poets and essayists (ed. T. M. Raysor, rev. ed. New York, 1956; ed. C. W. and L. H. Houtchens, New York, 1957); Victorian poets (ed. F. E. Faverty Cambridge, Mass., 1956); Victorian fiction (ed. L. Stevenson Cambridge, Mass., 1964).

The learned journals

Some eighty journals in the fields of Bibliography, Comparative Literature, English Literature, Modern Languages and Literatures (including English), Journals and Newsletters for Individual Literary Figures, and Literary Journals (semi-scholarly) are listed in my *Guide to English Literature.* A more complete list – with the standard abbreviations for each journal – will be found in *PMLA*'s annual 'Bibliography'. Of the extinct English journals those most likely to interest the scholar-critic are *The Gentleman's Magazine* (1731–1907), *The London Magazine* (1732–85), *The Monthly Review* (1749–1845), *The Critical Review* (1756–1817), *The Edinburgh Review* (1802–1929),

The Quarterly Review (1809–1965), *The Westminster Review* (1824–1914), *The Athenaeum* (1828–1921), *The Criterion* (1922–39, reissued 1967 with index by E. A. Baber), *Scrutiny* (1932–53, reissued in 20 vols, 1963, with elaborate index by M. Hussey).

Composite miscellanies (Festschriften)

Scholars who have been memorably honoured in collections of special essays include the tributes to F. J. Furnivall (1901), G. L. Kittredge (Boston, 1913), H. J. C. Grierson (1938), D. Nichol Smith (1945), G. Sherburn (1949), C. B. Tinker (1949), F. P. Wilson (1959), Marjorie Nicholson (New York, 1962), Hardin Craig (1963), F. D. McKillop (Chicago, 1963), B. Willey (1964) and F. A. Pottle (New York, 1965).

There have been similar tributes to poets – notably to T. S. Eliot and W. B. Yeats. Earlier examples are the tributes in verse to Donne (in *Poems*, 1633), Ben Jonson (ed. B. Duppa, 1638) and Beaumont and Fletcher (in *Comedies and Tragedies*, 1647).

The book trade

F. A. Mumby's *Publishing and Bookselling: a History from the Earliest Times to the Present Day* (3rd ed. 1954) is the standard account and has a comprehensive bibliography.

Biographical dictionaries

In addition to the *Dictionary of National Biography* (*DNB*; for which see pp. 42–6 above), there is *Who's Who* (annually since 1849 for contemporary notables, each entry contributed by the figure concerned) and its companion *Who Was Who* (5 vols, 1897–   ; final entries from *Who's Who* for preceding decade or so, with death date).

Oxford and Cambridge, the nobility, baronets, the landed gentry and the clergy are recorded respectively in: A. B. Emden, *A Biographical Register of the University of Oxford to A.D. 1500* (3 vols, 1957–9), and Joseph Foster, *Alumni Oxonienses 1500–1886* (8 vols, 1887–92); John and J. A. Venn, *Alumni Cantabrigienses* to 1900 (10 vols, 1922–54); G. E. Cokayne, *The Complete Peerage* (rev. ed. 14 vols, 1910–59), and *The Complete Baronetage 1611–1800* (5 vols, plus index, 1900–9); *Burke's Landed Gentry* (ed. L. G. Pine 17th ed., 1952); *Crockford's Clerical Directory* (latest ed. 1968).

Two useful sources for minor figures are William Musgrave, *Obituary Prior to 1800* (ed. Sir. G. T. Armytage, 6 vols, 1899–1901) and Frederick Boase, *Modern English Biography* (6 vols, 1892–1921), which continues Musgrave. More recently the obituaries in *The Times* are usually those most worth consulting.

For autobiographies and diaries William Matthews's *British Autobiographies* before 1951 (Berkeley, 1955) and *British Diaries 1442–1942* (Berkeley, 1950) are indispensable because of the summaries they provide. Matthews is now preparing a complete and fully annotated edition of Pepys's diary, which is likely to provide much miscellaneous seventeenth-century biographical information. L. F. Powell's splendid edition of G. Birkbeck Hill's edition of Boswell's *Johnson* has already proved the best mine for eighteenth-century biographical ore not in the *DNB*.

Techniques of literary research

Palaeography

H. G. T. Christopherson's *Palaeography and Archives* (1938) is a good general introduction. The literary relevance of Shakespeare's hand is effectively demonstrated in C. J. Sisson's *New Readings in Shakespeare* (2 vols, 1956).

Analytical bibliography

The standard full-length introduction is still R. B. McKerrow's *An Introduction to Bibliography for Literary Students* (1927), of which a revision by Philip Gaskell is now in preparation. Articles on various other aspects will be found in *The Library, Papers of the Bibliographical Society of America*, and *Studies in Bibliography*. A standard work is Fredson Bowers's *Principles of Bibliographical Description* (Princeton, 1949). At a lower level John Carter's *ABC for Book-Collectors* (1952, rev. 1961), is indispensable for its lucid exposition of technical terms.

Textual criticism

Outside Shakespeare (see p. 135 above), the most ambitious recent investigation has been V. A. Dearing's quasi-mathematical *A Manual of Textual Criticism* (1960). Dearing is the textual editor of the California edition of Dryden and is using a computer to establish the text.

Attribution and authenticity

The most sensational of recent investigations has been John Carter and Graham Pollard's *Enquiry into the Nature of Certain Nineteenth*

Century Pamphlets (1934), which demonstrated the extensiveness of Thomas J. Wise's forgeries. This has been supplemented by D. F. Foxon's *Thomas J. Wise and the Pre-Restoration Drama* (1959). A masterly survey of the whole problem of internal and external evidence will be found in S. Schoenbaum's *Internal Evidence and Elizabethan Dramatic Authorship* (Chicago, 1966), which is not entirely confined to the special case of the Elizabethan drama. *Shakespeare's Hand in the Play of Sir Thomas More* (1923), in which A. W. Pollard, E. M. Thompson, J. D. Wilson and R. W. Chambers investigated the authorship of Hand D's three pages from different points of view, remains a model of collaborative research, as for a later period does R. S. Crane's single-handed *New Essays by Oliver Goldsmith* (Chicago, 1927). Of the statistical attribution-studies perhaps the best is Alvar Ellegård's of 'Junius' (Stockholm, 1962).

Sources and influences

The best general introduction is still Chapters V and X in André Morize, *Problems and Methods of Literary History: a Guide for Graduate Students* (Boston, 1922); unfortunately most of his examples were drawn from modern French literature. Some classic examples of source/influence scholarship are R. D. Havens, *Milton's Influence on English Poetry* (Cambridge, Mass., 1922); J. L. Lowes, *The Road to Xanadu* (Boston, 1927, rev. 1930); Janet Scott, *Les Sonnets élisabethains: les sources et l'apport personnel* (Paris, 1929); Huntington Brown, *Rabelais in English Literature* (Cambridge, Mass., 1930); Grover Smith, *T. S. Eliot, Poetry and Plays; a study in Sources and Meaning* (Chicago, 1956); and R. W. Dent, *John Webster's Borrowing* (Berkeley, 1960).

An author's after-fame has been recorded in painful detail by Caroline Spurgeon, *Five Hundred Years of Chaucer Criticism and Allusion* (3 vols, 1925), and in John Munro's completion of *The Shakespeare Allusion-Book* (rev. E. K. Chambers, 1932). A masterpiece in a more selective treatment is G. H. Ford, *Keats and the Victorians, 1821–95* (New Haven, 1944).

The process of composition

Authors have not provided much information on the writing of their own works. Apart from such classics as Coleridge's account of his dream-poem 'Kubla Khan' (published with 'Christabel', 1816) and Edgar Allan Poe's of the opposite method he used with 'The Raven'

('The Philosophy of Composition', *Graham's Magazine*, 1846), the poets have been curiously reticent until recently, but in *On English Poetry* (1922) Robert Graves has explained how several of his early poems were written. C. Day Lewis has also described in some detail the composition of one of his poems in *Poetry for You* (Oxford, 1944), as has I. A. Richards in 'Poetic Process and Literary Analysis' contributed to *Style in Language* (ed. T. A. Sebeok, Cambridge, Mass., 1960). Henry James's prefaces to the New York edition of his novels and short stories (1907–9) and Conrad's similar if less explicit prefaces to the Uniform Edition of 1923–8 are the equivalents in the field of prose fiction.

Among the more important works of literary research on this topic are: E. de Selincourt, *The Prelude, by William Wordsworth, Edited from the Manuscripts* (1926, rev. Helen Darbishire, 1960).

J. L. Lowes, *The Road to Xanadu* (Boston, 1927, rev. 1930). On 'The Ancient Mariner' and 'Kubla Khan'.

Josephine W. Bennett: *The Evolution of 'The Faerie Queene'* (Chicago, 1942).

C. D. Abbott: *Poets at Work* (New York, 1948). Account of MSS of modern poets at the Lockwood Memorial Library, Buffalo.

Neville Rogers: *Shelley at Work* (1956).

John Butt and Kathleen Tillotson: *Dickens at Work* (1957).

Jerome Beaty: *'Middlemarch' from Notebook to Novel* (Urbana, 1960).

Jon Stallworthy: *Between the Lines: Yeats's Poetry in the Making* (1963).

The literary profession and audience

The specifically Marxist studies include: 'Christopher Caudwell' [C. St. J. Sprigge], *Illusion and Reality* (1937); George Thomson, *Aeschylus and Athens, a Study in the Social Origins of Drama* (1941); Arnold Kettle, *Introduction to the English Novel* (2 vols, 1952–3). A helpful survey of the less committed studies is provided in Lennox Grey's 'Literary Audience' in *Contemporary Literary Scholarship* (ed. Lewis Leary, New York, 1958).

Alexandre Beljame: *Le Publique et les hommes de lettres en Angleterre, 1660–1774* (Paris, 1881; English translation, with new notes by Bonamy Dobrée, 1948).

Leslie Stephen: *English Literature and Society in the Eighteenth Century* (1904).

Phoebe Sheavyn: *The Literary Profession in the Elizabethan Age* (Manchester, 1909, rev. J. W. Saunders 1967).

Q. D. Leavis: *Fiction and the Reading Public* (1932). Primarily nineteenth-century.

Alfred Harbage: *Shakespeare's Audience* (New York, 1941).

G. H. Ford: *Dickens and his Readers* (Princeton, 1955).

R. D. Altick: *The English Common Reader* (Chicago, 1957). Mainly nineteenth-century.

John Loftis: *Comedy and Society from Congreve to Fielding* (Stanford, 1959) and *The Politics of Drama in Augustan England* (1963).

J. W. Saunders: *The Profession of English Letters* (1964). The best general survey.

Key terms and concepts

Of the dictionaries of literary terms the most ambitious are the *Dictionary of World Literature* (ed. J. T. Shipley, 1943, rev. 1955 as *Dictionary of World Literary Terms*) and *The Encyclopaedia of Poetry and Poetics* (ed. A. Preminger, F. J. Warnke and O. B. Hardison, Princeton, 1965). In both (especially Shipley) the length and quality of the entries vary enormously, but no student of Augustan poetry can afford to miss, to take one example, R. S. Crane's 'Neo-classical Criticism' in Shipley. The best of the short-entry dictionaries is M. H. Abrams's *Glossary of Literary Terms* (New York, 1957), though Abrams provides fewer illustrative quotations than A. F. Scott's *Current Literary Terms* (1965).

Three general surveys are of exceptional value: E. R. Curtius, *European Literature and the Latin Middle Ages* (New York, 1952; originally in German, 1948: especially valuable for its 'topoi', i.e. conventions of subject-matter, such as the May morning); W. K. Wimsatt and Cleanth Brooks, *Literary Criticism: a Short History* (New York, 1957: indispensable for the Renaissance and English neo-classicism); M. H. Abrams, *The Mirror and the Lamp* (New York, 1953: Romantic theory in all its English ramifications).

In addition to specialist articles in the *Journal of the History of Ideas* there are the following collected studies:

Logan P. Smith: *Four Words: Romantic, Originality, Creative, Genius* (1924). Reprinted in *Words and Idioms* (1925).

A. O. Lovejoy: *Essays in the History of Ideas* (Baltimore, 1948). Nature, classicism, Romanticism, Gothic, etc.

W. J. Hipple: *The Beautiful, the Sublime and the Picturesque in Eighteenth-Century British Aesthetic Theory* (Carbondale, 1957).

C. S. Lewis: *Studies in Words* (1960). Nature, wit, sense, simple, conscious, etc.

George Williamson: *Seventeenth Century Contexts* (1960). Mutability, 'strong lines', enthusiasm, wit.

J. B. Leishman: *Themes and Variations in Shakespeare's Sonnets* (1961). Poetry as immortalization (from Pindar to Shakespeare), devouring time and fading beauty (from Greek Anthology to Shakespeare).

René Wellek: *Concepts of Criticism* (New Haven, 1963). Literary criticism, baroque, Romanticism, realism, etc. Also *Discriminations* (New Haven, 1970). Comparative literature, classicism, symbolism.

R. S. Crane: *The Idea of the Humanities and Other Essays Critical and Historical* (2 vols, Chicago, 1967). Ancients and Moderns, 'Man of Feeling', progress, etc.

The terms most elaborately discussed recently have been:

CLASSICISM: Henri Peyre, 'Le Mot "Classicisme"' (in *Le Classicisme français*, 1942); René Wellek: 'The Concept of Classicism in Literary History' (in *Aspects of the Eighteenth Century*, ed. Earl Wasserman, 1965); also Wellek and Lovejoy (above).

COURTESY: Ruth Kelso, *The Institute of the Gentleman in English Literature of the Sixteenth Century* (1929), and *Doctrine for the Lady of the Renaissance* (Urbana, 1956).

CULTURE: Raymond Williams, *Culture and Society, 1780–1950* (1958).

DISSOCIATION OF SENSIBILITY: F. W. Bateson, *Essays in Criticism*, I (1951), 302–12. Also Frank Kermode in *Romantic Image* (1957).

GOTHIC: Samuel Kliger, *The Goths in England* (1952). Also Lovejoy (above) and Paul Frankl, *The Gothic* (1960).

IMAGE: P. N. Furbank, *Reflections on the Word 'Image'* (1970).

IMAGINATION: M. W. Bundy, '"Invention" and "Imagination" in the Renaissance', *JEGP*, XXIX (1930), 535–45; A. S. P. Woodhouse, 'Collins and Creative Imagination' (in *Studies in English by Members of University College, Toronto*, ed. M. W. Wallace, 1931).

IRONY: Norman Knox, *The Word Irony and Its Context, 1500–1755* (1961).

NATURE: J. W. Beach, *The Concept of Nature in Nineteenth-Century English Poetry* (1936). Also Lovejoy, and Lewis (above).

NOVELTY: C. D. Thorpe, 'Addison and Some of His Predecessors on "Novelty"', *PMLA*, LII (1937), 1114–29.

PICTURESQUE: Elizabeth W. Manwaring, *Italian Landscape in Eighteenth Century England* (1925); J. H. Hagstrum, *The Sister Arts* (Chicago, 1958).

PLENITUDE: A. O. Lovejoy, *The Great Chain of Being* (Cambridge, Mass., 1936); Maynard Mack, Introduction to edition of Pope's *Essay on Man* (1950). Lovejoy's book demonstrates brilliantly

his approach to the history of thought via single 'unit-ideas'.
PRIMITIVISM: H. N. Fairchild, *The Noble Savage* (1928); Lois Whitney, *Primitivism and the Idea of Progress in English Popular Literature of the Eighteenth Century* (1934); Margaret M. Fitzgerald, *First Follow Nature: Primitivism in English Poetry, 1725–50* (1947).
REALISM: Harry Levin, 'What Is Realism?' (in *Contexts of Criticism*, 1957, pp. 67–75). Also Wellek (above).
ROMANTICISM: Fernand Baldensperger, '"Romantique", ses analogues et ses equivalents: tableau synoptique de 1650 à 1810', *Harvard Studies and Notes in Philology and Literature*, XIX (1937), 13–105 (examples from French, English and German in parallel columns); Northrop Frye, M. H. Abrams, Lionel Trilling, and René Wellek, *Romanticism Reconsidered* (New York, 1963). Also Lovejoy, Wellek, and Kermode (above).
SENTIMENTAL: E. Erametsä, *A Study of the Word 'Sentimental'* (Helsinki, 1951).
SIMPLICITY: R. D. Havens, 'Simplicity, a Changing Concept', *Journal of the History of Ideas*, XIV (1953), 3–32. From 1700 to *c.* 1815.
SINCERITY: Patricia M. Ball, 'Sincerity: the Rise and Fall of a Critical Term', *Modern Language Review*, LIX (1964), 1–11.
SUBLIME: S. H. Monk, *The Sublime: a Study of Critical Theories in 18th Century England* (1935); J. T. Boulton, Introduction to edition of Burke's *Sublime and Beautiful* (1958).
SYMBOLISM: see Wellek (above).
WIT: George Williamson, *The Proper Wit of Poetry* (1961).

INDEX

INDEX

INDEX

For Product Safety Concerns and Information please contact our EU representative GPSR@taylorandfrancis.com
Taylor & Francis Verlag GmbH, Kaufingerstraße 24, 80331 München, Germany

www.ingramcontent.com/pod-product-compliance
Lightning Source LLC
Chambersburg PA
CBHW070534100726
47907CB00004B/1107

* 9 7 8 1 0 3 2 6 4 2 7 3 4 *